UPGRADING
AND
REPAIRING PCs
TECHNICIAN'S PORTABLE

REFERENCE

Upgrading and Reparing PCs Technician's Portable Reference

International Standard Book Number: 0-7897-2096-5

Library of Congress Catalog Card Number: 99-63283

Printed in the United States of America

First Printing: September 1999

01   00   99   4   3   2   1

Trademarks

Warning and Disclaimer

Executive Editor
Jill Byus

Senior Development Editor
Rick Kughen

Managing Editor
Lisa Wilson

Project Editor
Natalie Harris

Copy Editor
Pamela Woolf

Technical Editor
Bruce Roberts

Interior Design
Kevin Spear

Cover Design
Karen Ruggles

Layout Technicians
Brandon Allen
Liz Johnston
Brad Lenser

Contents at a Glance

Introduction   xx

1   General Technical Reference   1

2   System Components and Configuration   11

3   BIOS Configurations and Upgrades   55

4   Hard Drives and Interfaces   75

5   Floppy, Removable, Optical, and Tape Storage   113

6   Serial, USB, and IEEE-1394 Ports   135

7   Parallel Ports, Printers, and Scanners   157

8   Keyboards and Input Devices   169

9   Video and Audio   187

10   Networking   213

11   Technician's Survival Kit   229

12   Vendor Listing and Useful Web Sites   239

Index   269

Table of Contents

1 General Technical Reference   1

ASCII Control Codes   1
    Extended ASCII Line-Drawing Characters   2
    Hexadecimal/ASCII Conversions   2

Understanding Bits and Bytes   9

Standard Capacity Abbreviations and Meanings   10

2 System Components and Configuration   11

Processors and Their Data Bus Widths   11

Differences Between PC/XT and AT Systems   12

Intel and Compatible Processor Specifications   13

Troubleshooting Processor Problems   19

Motherboard Form Factors   21
    Baby-AT Motherboard   21
    LPX Motherboard   21
    ATX Motherboard   23
    NLX Motherboard   23

Which Motherboard Is Which?   24

Power Supplies   24
    LPX Versus ATX Power Supplies   25
    Power Connectors for the Drive(s)   26
    Quick-Reference Chart for Troubleshooting
        Power Supplies   28

Memory Types   28
    30-Pin SIMM   29
    72-Pin SIMM   29
    DIMMs   30
    RDRAM   30
    Parity Versus Non-Parity Memory   31
    "Divide by 3" Rule   32
    Expanding Memory on a System   33
    Memory Troubleshooting   34
    Memory Usage Within the System   34
    Hardware and Firmware Devices that Use
        Memory Addresses   35

Using Memory Addresses Beyond
1MB (0FFFFF)   37

Determining Memory Address Ranges
in Use   37

Other Add-On Card Configuration Issues   37

IRQs   38

DMA   39

Determining Actual IRQ and DMA Usage   40

I/O Port Addresses   41

Determining Actual I/O Address Ranges
in Use   44

Troubleshooting Add-on Card Resource
Conflicts   44

Expansion Slots   48

ISA   49

EISA—A 32-bit Version of ISA   50

VL-Bus—A Faster 32-bit Version of ISA   52

PCI   53

AGP   53

3 BIOS Configurations and Upgrades   55

What the BIOS Is and What It Does   55

When a BIOS Update Is Necessary   55

Specific Tests to Determine if Your
BIOS Needs an Update   56

Y2K BIOS Tests   56

Power-On BIOS Date Rollover Test   57

Power-Off BIOS Date Rollover Test   57

Power-On DOS Date Rollover Test   57

Power-Off DOS Date Rollover Test   57

Fixing BIOS Limitations—BIOS Fixes
and Alternatives   58

How BIOS Updates Are Performed   59

Where BIOS Updates Come From   59

Precautions to Take Before Updating a BIOS   60

How to Recover from a Failed BIOS
Update Procedure   61

Plug-and-Play BIOS   62

PnP BIOS Configuration Options   62

When to Use the PnP BIOS
Configuration Options   64

Other BIOS Troubleshooting Tips   65

Determining What BIOS You Have   65

Determining the Motherboard Manufacturer
    for BIOS Upgrades   66
        Identifying Motherboards with
            AMI BIOS   66
        Identifying Motherboards with Award
            BIOS   67
        Identifying Motherboards with Phoenix
            or Microid Research BIOS   68

Accessing the BIOS Setup Programs   68

How the BIOS Reports Errors   69
        BIOS Beep Codes and Their Purposes   69
        AMI BIOS Beep Codes   70
        Award BIOS Beep Codes   71
        Phoenix BIOS Beep Codes   71
        IBM BIOS Beep and Alphanumeric
            Error Codes   71

Microid Research Beep Codes   72

Reading BIOS Error Codes   74
        Onscreen Error Messages   74
        Interpreting Error Codes and Messages   74

4 Hard Drives and Interfaces 75

Understanding Hard Disk Terminology   75
        Heads, Sectors per Track, and Cylinders   75
        Hard Drive Heads   75
        Sectors per Track   75
        Cylinders   76

IDE Hard Drive Identification   76

Master and Slave Drives   77

Breaking the 504MB (528 Million Byte) Drive
    Barrier   79

Using LBA Mode   80
        When LBA Mode Is Needed—and When
            Not to Use It   81
        Problems with LBA Support in the BIOS   81
        Dangers of Altering Translation Settings   81
        Detecting Lack of LBA Mode Support
            in Your System   82
        Using FDISK to Determine Compatibility
            Problems Between Hard Disk and BIOS   83
        Getting LBA and Extended Int13h Support
            for Your System   84

Sources for BIOS Upgrades and Alternatives for Large
   IDE Hard Disk Support   86

Standard and Alternative Jumper Settings   87

Improving Hard Disk Speed   88

Ultra DMA   88
      UDMA/66 Issues   89

Benefits of Manual Drive Typing   89

Troubleshooting IDE Installation   90

SCSI   91
      SCSI Types and Data Transfer Rates   91

Single-Ended Versus Differential SCSI   92
      LVD (Low-Voltage Differential) Devices   92

Recognizing SCSI Interface Cables and
   Connectors   93
      8-Bit SCSI Centronics 50-pin Connector   93
      SCSI-2 High-Density Connector   93
      SCSI-3 68-pin P Cable   93
      RAID Array, Hot Swappable 80-pin
         Connector   94

SCSI Drive and Device Configuration   95
      SCSI Device ID   95
      SCSI Termination   97

SCSI Configuration Troubleshooting   97

Hard Disk Preparation   100

Using FDISK   101
      Drive-Letter Size Limits   101
      Large Hard Disk Support   102

Benefits of Hard-Disk Partitioning   102
      FAT-32 Versus FAT-16 Cluster Sizes   103
      Converting FAT-16 Partition to FAT-32   103

How FDISK and the Operating System Create and
   Allocate Drive Letters   104
      Assigning Drive Letters with FDISK   104

High-Level (DOS) Format   106

Replacing an Existing Drive   108
      Drive Migration for MS-DOS Users   108
      Drive Migration for Windows 9x Users   109
      XCOPY32 for Windows 9x Data Transfer   109

Hard Disk Drive Troubleshooting and Repair   110

5 Floppy, Removable, Optical, and Tape Storage 113

Floppy Drives 113
  Where Floppy Drives Fail—and
    Simple Fixes 114
  The Drive Cover 114
  The Stepper Motor 114
  Interface Circuit Boards 115
  Read/Write Heads 115
  Floppy Drive Hardware Resources 115
  Don't Use a Floppy Drive While Running
    a Tape Backup 116
  Disk Drive Power and Data Connectors 116
  Floppy Drive Troubleshooting 118
  Common Floppy Drive Error Messages—Causes
    and Solutions 120

Removable Storage Drives 121
  Emergency Access to Iomega Zip Drive Files in
    Case of Disaster 122
  Troubleshooting Removable Media Drives 123

MS-DOS Command-Line Access to CD-ROM Drives
  for Reloading Windows 124

Bus-Mastering Chipsets for IDE 125

Troubleshooting Optical Drives 127
  Failure Reading a CD 127
  Failure Reading CD-R, CD-RW Disks in
    CD-ROM or DVD Drive 127
  IDE/ATAPI CD-ROM Drive Runs Slowly 127
  Trouble Reading CD-RW Disks on
    CD-ROM 128
  Trouble Reading CD-R Disks on
    DVD Drive 128
  Trouble Using Bootable CDs 128

Tape Backup Drives and Media 129
  QIC-Wide Tape Formats 129
  Travan and QIC Compatibility 130
  Successful Tape Backup and Restore
    Procedures 130
  Getting Extra Capacity with Verbatim QIC-EX
    Tape Media 132

6 Serial, USB, and IEEE-1394 Ports and Devices   135

Understanding Serial Ports   135
    Pinouts for Serial Ports   136

UARTs   138
    UART Types   139
    Determining What UART Chips Your System
        Has   140

High-Speed Serial Ports (ESP and Super ESP)   141

Upgrading the UART Chip   141

Serial Port Configuration   141
    Avoiding Conflicts with Serial Ports   142
    Troubleshooting I/O Ports in Windows   142
    Advanced Diagnostics Using Loopback
        Testing   143
    Loopback Plug Pinouts—Serial Ports   144

Modems   145
    Modems and Serial Ports   145
    Modem Modulation Standards   145
    56Kbps Standards   146
    Upgrading from x2 or K56flex to V.90 with
        Flash Upgrades   147
    External Versus Internal Modems   149
    Modem Troubleshooting   149
    Pinouts for External Modem Cable
        (9-pin at PC)   151

Universal Serial Bus (USB)   152
    USB Port Identification   152
    Pinout for the USB Connector   153
    Prerequisites for Using USB Ports and
        Peripherals   153

IEEE-1394   154
    Comparing USB and IEEE-1394   154

7 Parallel Ports, Printers, and Scanners   157

Parallel Port Connectors   157

Parallel Port Performance   157

EPP Versus ECP Modes   158

Parallel Port Configurations   159

Testing Parallel Ports   159

    Building a Parallel Loopback Plug   159

Troubleshooting Parallel Ports   160

Printers   160

    Hewlett-Packard PCL Versions   161

    Comparing Host-based to PDL-based
        Printers   161

    Printer Hardware Problems   162

    Printer Connection Problems   164

    Printer Driver and Application Problems   165

Troubleshooting Scanners   166

8 Keyboards and Input Devices   169

Keyboard Designs   169

    The 101-Key Enhanced Keyboard   169

    101- Versus 102-key Keyboards   169

    The 104-key Windows Keyboard   169

Using Windows Keys   170

    Keyboard-Only Commands for Windows 9x
        with Any Keyboard   170

Standard Versus Portable Keyboards   173

Keyswitch Types   173

Cleaning a Foam-Element Keyswitch   174

Adjusting Keyboard Parameters in Windows   175

Keyboard Layouts and Scan Codes   175

Keyboard Connectors   179

    Keyboard Connector Signals   180

USB Keyboard Requirements   181

Keyboard Troubleshooting and Repair   181

Keyboard Connector Voltage and Signal
    Specifications   182

Keyboard Error Codes   183

Mice and Pointing Devices   183

    Pointing Device Interface Types   184

    Software Drivers for the Mouse   184

    Notebook Computer Pointing Devices   185

Mouse Troubleshooting   185

9 Video and Audio   187

Selecting a Monitor Size   187

Monitor Resolution   188

LCD Versus CRT Display Size   189

Monitor Power Management Modes   190

VGA Video Connector Pinout   191

VGA Video Display Modes   191

Video RAM   193

Memory, Resolution, and Color Depth   194

Determining the Amount of RAM on Your
Display Card   195

Local-Bus Video Standards   196

RAMDAC   197

Refresh Rates   198
Adjusting the Refresh Rate of the Video Card
198
Comparing Video Cards with the Same
Chipset   199

Setting Up Multiple Monitor Support in
Windows 98   200

Video Card and Chipset Makers Model
Reference   201
3D Chipsets   201

Multimedia Devices   201

Troubleshooting Video Capture Devices   202
Testing a Monitor with Common
Applications   203

Audio I/O Connectors   205

Sound Quality Standards   207

Configuring Sound Cards   207
PCI Versus ISA Sound Cards   208

Troubleshooting Audio Hardware   208
Hardware (Resource) Conflicts   208
Detecting Resource Conflicts   209
Most Common Causes of Hardware Conflicts
with Sound Card   210
Freeing Up IRQ 5 for Sound Card Use
and Still Print   210
Other Sound Card Problems   210

10 Networking   213

Client Server Versus Peer-to-Peer Networking   213

RAID Levels Summary   214

Selecting a Network Protocol   216

Network Cable Connectors   217

Wire Pairing for Twisted-Pair Cabling   217

Network Cabling Distance Limitations   218

Cabling Standards for Fast Ethernet   219

Peer-to-Peer Networking Hardware   219
  Peer-to-Peer Networking with Windows 9x   220

TCP/IP Network Protocol Settings   220
  TCP/IP Protocol Worksheet   221

Troubleshooting Networks   223
  Troubleshooting Network Software Setup   223
  Troubleshooting Networks in Use   224
  Troubleshooting TCP/IP   225

Direct Cable Connections   225
  Null Modem and Parallel Data-Transfer
    Cables   225
  Direct Connect Software   226
  Troubleshooting Direct Cable
    Connections   227

11 Technician's Survival Kit   229

General Information   229

Hardware Tools and Their Uses   229
  Tools of the Trade—Drive Installation   230
  Tools of the Trade—Motherboard and
    Expansion Card Installation   231
  Tools of the Trade—External Device and
    Networking Installation   232
  Tools of the Trade—Data Transfer   233
  Tools of the Trade—Cleaning and
    Maintenance   234

Software Toolkit   235

12 Vendor Listing and Useful Web Sites   239

Index   269

About the Authors

Scott Mueller is president of Mueller Technical Research, an international research and corporate training firm. Since 1982, MTR has specialized in the industry's longest running, most in-depth, accurate and effective corporate PC hardware and technical training seminars, maintaining a client list that includes Fortune 500 companies, the U.S. and foreign governments, major software and hardware corporations, as well as PC enthusiasts and entrepreneurs. His seminars have been presented to thousands of PC support professionals throughout the world.

Scott Mueller has developed and presented training courses in all areas of PC hardware and software. He is an expert in PC hardware, operating systems, and data-recovery techniques. For more information about a custom PC hardware or data recovery training seminar for your organization, contact Lynn at

Mueller Technical Research
21 Spring Lane
Barrington Hills, IL 60010-9009
Phone: (847) 854-6794
Fax: (847) 854-6795
Internet: scottmueller@compuserve.com
Web: http://www.m-tr.com

Scott has many popular books, articles, and course materials to his credit, including *Upgrading and Repairing PCs*, which has sold more than 2 million copies, making it by far the most popular PC hardware book on the market today. His two hour video titled *Your PC— The Inside Story* is available through LearnKey, Inc. For ordering information, contact

LearnKey, Inc.
1845 West Sunset Boulevard
St. George, UT 84770
Phone: (800) 865-0165 or (801) 674-9733
Fax: (801) 674-9734

If you have questions about PC hardware, suggestions for the next edition of the book, or any comments in general, send them to Scott via email at scottmueller@compuserve.com.

When he is not working on PC-related books or teaching seminars, Scott can usually be found in the garage working on vehicle performance projects. This year a Harley Road King is taking most of his time, and he promises to finish the Impala next.

Mark Edward Soper is president of Select Systems & Associates, Inc, a technical writing and training organization that's been in business since 1989. Mark and his company specialize in revealing the hidden power and features in PCs and their software. Select Systems has developed training courses and manuals for computer training firms, industrial, manufacturing, and media clients in print, HTML, and Adobe Acrobat formats. Mark has taught thousands of students from Maine to Hawaii computer troubleshooting and other technical subjects since 1992. Even before co-founding Select Systems, Mark's computer background was extensive, beginning with the home-computer craze of the early 1980s (his first computer was a TI-994A!) and the rise of the IBM PC. His first technical writing was a simplified instruction manual for the powerful, but almost incomprehensible Commodore 1541 disk drive, followed by a compatibility handbook he wrote for the sales force of a retail chain. As this book demonstrates, Mark is still very concerned that you get everything you paid for when you install a new hard disk or video card.

For more information about customized technical reference and training materials, contact Mark and his company:

Select Systems & Associates, Inc
1100 W. Lloyd Expy #104
Evansville, IN 47708
Phone: (812)421-1170
Fax: (812)468-4302
Email: mesoper@selectsystems.com
Web: http://selectsystems.com

Mark has been writing for major computer magazines since 1990, with more than 100 articles in publications such as *SmartComputing, PCNovice, PCNovice Guides,* and the *PCNovice Learning Series.* His early work was published in *WordPerfect Magazine, The WordPerfectionist,* and *PCToday.* Many of Mark's articles are available in back issue or electronically via the World Wide Web at www.smartcomputing.com. Select Systems maintains a subject index of all Mark's articles at http://selectsystems.com.

When he's not sweating out a writing deadline, Mark enjoys life with his wife Cheryl, a children's librarian who is also a published writer, and their four rapidly-growing children. Their computer questions and problems keep him busy, as do the computer needs of his local church, but he still finds time to watch, photograph, and (occasionally) ride trains. He's using his years of experience with photography and computers to build a personal image archive, and he has also created archiving programs for a local university.

Mark welcomes your comments and suggestions about this book. Send them to mesoper@selectsystems.com.

About the Technical Editor

In 1981 **Bruce F. Roberts** began working in an electronics technician apprenticeship program at the Long Beach Naval Shipyard where he worked on Naval Tactical Display Systems, cryptographic and test equipiment, and calibration repair. He's worked for the Federal Aviation Administration at Los Angeles International Airport on radios, radar, computers, and telephones since 1991.

Acknowledgments

Mark would like to thank the following people: Scott Mueller, whose *Upgrading and Repairing PCs* has been on his "short list" of great computer books for more than 10 years and whose latest edition provided much of the material for this book; Jill Byus and Rick Kughen at Que, whose encouragement and guidance have helped make this book a success; Cheryl, who never stopped believing that I could write; and God, who gives all of us talents and abilities and cheers us on as we develop them.

Tell Us What You Think!

As the reader of this book, *you* are our most important critic and commentator. We value your opinion and want to know what we're doing right, what we could do better, what areas you'd like to see us publish in, and any other words of wisdom you're willing to pass our way.

As the associate publisher for this book, I welcome your comments. You can fax, email, or write me directly to let me know what you did or didn't like about this book—as well as what we can do to make our books stronger.

When you write, please be sure to include this book's title and author as well as your name and phone or fax number. I will carefully review your comments and share them with the author and editors who worked on the book.

Fax: 317-817-7070
Email:hardware@mcp.com
Mail: Macmillan U.S.A.
       201 West 103rd Street
       Indianapolis, IN 46290

Introduction

If you're a computer repair technician or student, you know just how crucial it is to have concise, yet detailed technical specifications at your fingertips. It can mean the success or failure of your job.

Unfortunately, most detailed hardware books are far too large to tote around in a briefcase, book bag, or in your back pocket—where you need them.

Upgrading and Repairing PCs: Technician's Portable Reference is the exception. This concise book provides just the information you need to upgrade or repair your PC, without weighting you down.

Although you should consider this book to be a companion to Scott Mueller's best-selling opus, *Upgrading and Repairing PCs*, you'll also find that it stands quite well on its own. While much of the information is in the mother book, much of what is found here is presented in a boiled down, easy-to-digest reference that will help you get the job down quickly and efficiently. You'll also find that this portable reference contains some information not found in the main book—information that is specially geared to help the technician in the field.

I recommend that you keep *Upgrading and Repairing PCs, Eleventh Edition* (ISBN 0-7897-1903-7) on your desk or workbench and *Upgrading and Repairing PCs: Technician's Portable Reference* with your toolkit, so it's ready to go with you anytime—whether it's to a customer job site or a class.

Chapter 1

General Technical Reference

ASCII Control Codes

You'll encounter ASCII control codes primarily in the following circumstances: when you are needing to control a printer through software that lacks specific printer drivers or when you are working with data files. Depending on the situation, you might see these codes expressed by their decimal, hex, character symbol, or name values (see Figure 1.1). The most commonly-used ASCII control code is the "Escape" code (decimal 27), used by HP LaserJet and other PCL-based printers as the first character in escape sequences (printer commands).

DEC	HEX	CHAR	NAME		CONTROL CODE
0	00		Ctrl-@	NUL	Null
1	01	☺	Ctrl-A	SOH	Start of Heading
2	02	●	Ctrl-B	STX	Start of Text
3	03	♥	Ctrl-C	ETX	End of Text
4	04	♦	Ctrl-D	EOT	End of Transit
5	05	♣	Ctrl-E	ENQ	Enquiry
6	06	♠	Ctrl-F	ACK	Acknowledge
7	07	•	Ctrl-G	BEL	Bell
8	08	◘	Ctrl-H	BS	Back Space
9	09	○	Ctrl-I	HT	Horizontal Tab
10	0A	◙	Ctrl-J	LF	Line Feed
11	0B	♂	Ctrl-K	VT	Vertical Tab
12	0C	♀	Ctrl-L	FF	Form Feed
13	0D	♪	Ctrl-M	CR	Carriage Return
14	0E	♫	Ctrl-N	SO	Shift Out
15	0F	☼	Ctrl-O	SI	Shift In
16	10	►	Ctrl-P	DLE	Data Line Escape
17	11	◄	Ctrl-Q	DC1	Device Control 1
18	12	↕	Ctrl-R	DC2	Device Control 2
19	13	‼	Ctrl-S	DC3	Device Control 3
20	14	¶	Ctrl-T	DC4	Device Control 4
21	15	§	Ctrl-U	NAK	Negative Acknowledge
22	16	■	Ctrl-V	SYN	Synchronous Idle
23	17	↨	Ctrl-W	ETB	End of Transmit Block
24	18	↑	Ctrl-X	CAN	Cancel
25	19	↓	Ctrl-Y	EM	End of Medium
26	1A	→	Ctrl-Z	SUB	Substitute
27	1B	→	Ctrl-[	ESC	Escape
28	1C	∟	Ctrl-\	FS	File Separator
29	1D	↔	Ctrl-]	GS	Group Separator
30	1E	▲	Ctrl-^	RS	Record Separator
31	1FA	▼	Ctrl-_	US	Unit Separator

Figure 1.1 ASCII control codes.

Extended ASCII Line-Drawing Characters

When used with a fixed-pitch font such as Courier, Courier New, or Letter Gothic, these characters can be used to "draw" simple diagrams that can be reproduced on most non-PostScript printers (see Figure 1.2). If you create batch files for use with MS-DOS or Windows 9x, you can use these characters to highlight REMark statements onscreen. These characters are also widely used in ROM BIOS setup screens.

Note that HP LaserJet printers and others require that you change to the "IBM layout" character set (PC-8 for U.S. and Canada; PC-850 for Europe) to reproduce these characters. HP LaserJet printers default to the "Roman-8" character set, which would substitute alphanumeric characters for the line-draw characters.

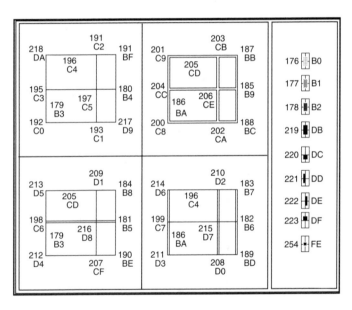

Figure 1.2 Extended ASCII line-drawing characters.

Hexadecimal/ASCII Conversions

Use Table 1.1 to look up the various representations for any character you see onscreen or want to insert into a document. You can use the Alt+keypad numbers to insert any character into an ASCII document you create with a program like the Windows Notepad or MS-DOS's Edit.

Dec	Hex	Octal	Binary	Name	Character
0	00	000	0000 0000	blank	
1	01	001	0000 0001	happy face	☺
2	02	002	0000 0010	inverse happy face	☻
3	03	003	0000 0011	heart	♥
4	04	004	0000 0100	diamond	♦
5	05	005	0000 0101	club	♣
6	06	006	0000 0110	spade	♠
7	07	007	0000 0111	bullet	•
8	08	010	0000 1000	inverse bullet	◘
9	09	011	0000 1001	circle	○
10	0A	012	0000 1010	inverse circle	○
11	0B	013	0000 1011	male sign	♂
12	0C	014	0000 1100	female sign	♀
13	0D	015	0000 1101	single note	♪
14	0E	016	0000 1110	double note	♫
15	0F	017	0000 1111	sun	☼
16	10	020	0001 0000	right triangle	▸
17	11	021	0001 0001	left triangle	◂
18	12	022	0001 0010	up/down arrow	↕
19	13	023	0001 0011	double exclamation	‼
20	14	024	0001 0100	paragraph sign	¶
21	15	025	0001 0101	section sign	§
22	16	026	0001 0110	rectangular bullet	▪
23	17	027	0001 0111	up/down to line	↨
24	18	030	0001 1000	up arrow	↑
25	19	031	0001 1001	down arrow	↓
26	1A	032	0001 1010	right arrow	→
27	1B	033	0001 1011	left arrow	←
28	1C	034	0001 1100	lower left box	∟
29	1D	035	0001 1101	left/right arrow	↔
30	1E	036	0001 1110	up triangle	▲
31	1F	037	0001 1111	down triangle	▼
32	20	040	0010 0000	space	Space
33	21	041	0010 0001	exclamation point	!
34	22	042	0010 0010	quotation mark	"
35	23	043	0010 0011	number sign	#

Table 1.1   Hexadecimal/ASCII Conversions

(continues)

Table 1.1	Hexadecimal/ASCII Conversions Continued				
Dec	**Hex**	**Octal**	**Binary**	**Name**	**Character**
36	24	044	0010 0100	dollar sign	$
37	25	045	0010 0101	percent sign	%
38	26	046	0010 0110	ampersand	&
39	27	047	0010 0111	apostrophe	'
40	28	050	0010 1000	opening parenthesis	(
41	29	051	0010 1001	closing parenthesis	)
42	2A	052	0010 1010	asterisk	*
43	2B	053	0010 1011	plus sign	+
44	2C	054	0010 1100	comma	,
45	2D	055	0010 1101	hyphen or minus sign	-
46	2E	056	0010 1110	period	.
47	2F	057	0010 1111	slash	/
48	30	060	0011 0000	zero	0
49	31	061	0011 0001	one	1
50	32	062	0011 0010	two	2
51	33	063	0011 0011	three	3
52	34	064	0011 0100	four	4
53	35	065	0011 0101	five	5
54	36	066	0011 0110	six	6
55	37	067	0011 0111	seven	7
56	38	070	0011 1000	eight	8
57	39	071	0011 1001	nine	9
58	3A	072	0011 1010	colon	:
59	3B	073	0011 1011	semicolon	;
60	3C	074	0011 1100	less-than sign	<
61	3D	075	0011 1101	equal sign	=
62	3E	076	0011 1110	greater-than sign	>
63	3F	077	0011 1111	question mark	?
64	40	100	0100 0000	at sign	@
65	41	101	0100 0001	capital A	A
66	42	102	0100 0010	capital B	B
67	43	103	0100 0011	capital C	C
68	44	104	0100 0100	capital D	D
69	45	105	0100 0101	capital E	E
70	46	106	0100 0110	capital F	F
71	47	107	0100 0111	capital G	G
72	48	110	0100 1000	capital H	H

Dec	Hex	Octal	Binary	Name	Character
73	49	111	0100 1001	capital I	I
74	4A	112	0100 1010	capital J	J
75	4B	113	0100 1011	capital K	K
76	4C	114	0100 1100	capital L	L
77	4D	115	0100 1101	capital M	M
78	4E	116	0100 1110	capital N	N
79	4F	117	0100 1111	capital O	O
80	50	120	0101 0000	capital P	P
81	51	121	0101 0001	capital Q	Q
82	52	122	0101 0010	capital R	R
83	53	123	0101 0011	capital S	S
84	54	124	0101 0100	capital T	T
85	55	125	0101 0101	capital U	U
86	56	126	0101 0110	capital V	V
87	57	127	0101 0111	capital W	W
88	58	130	0101 1000	capital X	X
89	59	131	0101 1001	capital Y	Y
90	5A	132	0101 1010	capital Z	Z
91	5B	133	0101 1011	opening bracket	[
92	5C	134	0101 1100	backward slash	\
93	5D	135	0101 1101	closing bracket	]
94	5E	136	0101 1110	caret	^
95	5F	137	0101 1111	underscore	_
96	60	140	0110 0000	grave	`
97	61	141	0110 0001	lowercase A	a
98	62	142	0110 0010	lowercase B	b
99	63	143	0110 0011	lowercase C	c
100	64	144	0110 0100	lowercase D	d
101	65	145	0110 0101	lowercase E	e
102	66	146	0110 0110	lowercase F	f
103	67	147	0110 0111	lowercase G	g
104	68	150	0110 1000	lowercase H	h
105	69	151	0110 1001	lowercase I	i
106	6A	152	0110 1010	lowercase J	j
107	6B	153	0110 1011	lowercase K	k
108	6C	154	0110 1100	lowercase L	l
109	6D	155	0110 1101	lowercase M	m
110	6E	156	0110 1110	lowercase N	n

(continues)

Table 1.1	Hexadecimal/ASCII Conversions Continued				
Dec	**Hex**	**Octal**	**Binary**	**Name**	**Character**
111	6F	157	0110 1111	lowercase O	o
112	70	160	0111 0000	lowercase P	p
113	71	161	0111 0001	lowercase Q	q
114	72	162	0111 0010	lowercase R	r
115	73	163	0111 0011	lowercase S	s
116	74	164	0111 0100	lowercase T	t
117	75	165	0111 0101	lowercase U	u
118	76	166	0111 0110	lowercase V	v
119	77	167	0111 0111	lowercase W	w
120	78	170	0111 1000	lowercase X	x
121	79	171	0111 1001	lowercase Y	y
122	7A	172	0111 1010	lowercase Z	z
123	7B	173	0111 1011	opening brace	{
124	7C	174	0111 1100	vertical line		
125	7D	175	0111 1101	closing brace	}
126	7E	176	0111 1110	tilde	~
127	7F	177	0111 1111	small house	Δ
128	80	200	1000 0000	C cedilla	Ç
129	81	201	1000 0001	u umlaut	ü
130	82	202	1000 0010	e acute	é
131	83	203	1000 0011	a circumflex	â
132	84	204	1000 0100	a umlaut	ä
133	85	205	1000 0101	a grave	à
134	86	206	1000 0110	a ring	å
135	87	207	1000 0111	c cedilla	ç
136	88	210	1000 1000	e circumflex	ê
137	89	211	1000 1001	e umlaut	ë
138	8A	212	1000 1010	e grave	è
139	8B	213	1000 1011	I umlaut	ï
140	8C	214	1000 1100	I circumflex	î
141	8D	215	1000 1101	I grave	ì
142	8E	216	1000 1110	A umlaut	Ä
143	8F	217	1000 1111	A ring	Å
144	90	220	1001 0000	E acute	É
145	91	221	1001 0001	ae ligature	æ
146	92	222	1001 0010	AE ligature	Æ
147	93	223	1001 0011	o circumflex	ô

Dec	Hex	Octal	Binary	Name	Character
148	94	224	1001 0100	o umlaut	ö
149	95	225	1001 0101	o grave	ò
150	96	226	1001 0110	u circumflex	û
151	97	227	1001 0111	u grave	ù
152	98	230	1001 1000	y umlaut	ÿ
153	99	231	1001 1001	O umlaut	Ö
154	9A	232	1001 1010	U umlaut	Ü
155	9B	233	1001 1011	cent sign	¢
156	9C	234	1001 1100	pound sign	£
157	9D	235	1001 1101	yen sign	¥
158	9E	236	1001 1110	Pt	₧
159	9F	237	1001 1111	function	f
160	A0	240	1010 0000	a acute	á
161	A1	241	1010 0001	I acute	í
162	A2	242	1010 0010	o acute	ó
163	A3	243	1010 0011	u acute	ú
164	A4	244	1010 0100	n tilde	ñ
165	A5	245	1010 0101	N tilde	Ñ
166	A6	246	1010 0110	a macron	ā
167	A7	247	1010 0111	o macron	ō
168	A8	250	1010 1000	opening question mark	¿
169	A9	251	1010 1001	upper-left box	⌐
170	AA	252	1010 1010	upper-right box	¬
171	AB	253	1010 1011	1/2	½
172	AC	254	1010 1100	1/4	¼
173	AD	255	1010 1101	opening exclamation	¡
174	AE	256	1010 1110	opening guillemets	«
175	AF	257	1010 1111	closing guillemets	»
176	B0	260	1011 0000	light block	▪
177	B1	261	1011 0001	medium block	▪
178	B2	262	1011 0010	dark block	■
179	B3	263	1011 0011	single vertical	│
180	B4	264	1011 0100	single right junction	┤
181	B5	265	1011 0101	2 to 1 right junction	╡
182	B6	266	1011 0110	1 to 2 right junction	╢
183	B7	267	1011 0111	1 to 2 upper-right	╖
184	B8	270	1011 1000	2 to 1 upper-right	╕
185	B9	271	1011 1001	double right junction	╣

(continues)

Table 1.1		Hexadecimal/ASCII Conversions Continued			
Dec	**Hex**	**Octal**	**Binary**	**Name**	**Character**
186	BA	272	1011 1010	double vertical	‖
187	BB	273	1011 1011	double upper-right	╗
188	BC	274	1011 1100	double lower-right	╝
189	BD	275	1011 1101	1 to 2 lower-right	╜
190	BE	276	1011 1110	2 to 1 lower-right	╛
191	BF	277	1011 1111	single upper-right	┐
192	C0	300	1100 0000	single lower-left	└
193	C1	301	1100 0001	single lower junction	┴
194	C2	302	1100 0010	single upper junction	┬
195	C3	303	1100 0011	single left junction	├
196	C4	304	1100 0100	single horizontal	─
197	C5	305	1100 0101	single intersection	┼
198	C6	306	1100 0110	2 to 1 left junction	╞
199	C7	307	1100 0111	1 to 2 left junction	╟
200	C8	310	1100 1000	double lower-left	╚
201	C9	311	1100 1001	double upper-left	╔
202	CA	312	1100 1010	double lower junction	╩
203	CB	313	1100 1011	double upper junction	╦
204	CC	314	1100 1100	double left junction	╠
205	CD	315	1100 1101	double horizontal	═
206	CE	316	1100 1110	double intersection	╬
207	CF	317	1100 1111	1 to 2 lower junction	╧
208	D0	320	1101 0000	2 to 1 lower junction	╨
209	D1	321	1101 0001	1 to 2 upper junction	╤
210	D2	322	1101 0010	2 to 1 upper junction	╥
211	D3	323	1101 0011	1 to 2 lower-left	╙
212	D4	324	1101 0100	2 to 1 lower-left	╘
213	D5	325	1101 0101	2 to 1 upper-left	╒
214	D6	326	1101 0110	1 to 2 upper-left	╓
215	D7	327	1101 0111	2 to 1 intersection	╫
216	D8	330	1101 1000	1 to 2 intersection	╪
217	D9	331	1101 1001	single lower-right	┘
218	DA	332	1101 1010	single upper-right	┌
219	DB	333	1101 1011	inverse space	■
220	DC	334	1101 1100	lower inverse	▄
221	DD	335	1101 1101	left inverse	▌
222	DE	336	1101 1110	right inverse	▐

Dec	Hex	Octal	Binary	Name	Character
223	DF	337	1101 1111	upper inverse	■
224	E0	340	1110 0000	alpha	α
225	E1	341	1110 0001	beta	β
226	E2	342	1110 0010	Gamma	Γ
227	E3	343	1110 0011	pi	π
228	E4	344	1110 0100	Sigma	Σ
229	E5	345	1110 0101	sigma	σ
230	E6	346	1110 0110	mu	μ
231	E7	347	1110 0111	tau	τ
232	E8	350	1110 1000	Phi	Φ
233	E9	351	1110 1001	theta	θ
234	EA	352	1110 1010	Omega	Ω
235	EB	353	1110 1011	delta	δ
236	EC	354	1110 1100	infinity	∞
237	ED	355	1110 1101	phi	φ
238	EE	356	1110 1110	epsilon	ε
239	EF	357	1110 1111	intersection of sets	∩
240	F0	360	1111 0000	is identical to	≡
241	F1	361	1111 0001	plus/minus sign	±
242	F2	362	1111 0010	greater/equal sign	≥
243	F3	363	1111 0011	less/equal sign	≤
244	F4	364	1111 0100	top half integral	⌠
245	F5	365	1111 0101	lower half integral	⌡
246	F6	366	1111 0110	division sign	÷
247	F7	367	1111 0111	approximately	≈
248	F8	370	1111 1000	degree	°
249	F9	371	1111 1001	filled-in degree	•
250	FA	372	1111 1010	small bullet	·
251	FB	373	1111 1011	square root	√
252	FC	374	1111 1100	superscript n	ⁿ
253	FD	375	1111 1101	superscript 2	²
254	FE	376	1111 1110	box	■
255	FF	377	1111 1111	phantom space	ˉ

Understanding Bits and Bytes

The foundation of all memory and disk size calculations is the byte. When storing plain-text data, a byte equals a character.

Data can also be stored or transmitted in portions of a byte. A *bit* equals 1/8 of a byte. In other words, a *byte* equals 8 bits. A *nibble* equals 1/2 of a byte, or four bits. Thus, two nibbles equals one byte. Keep the difference between bits and bytes in mind as you review the table of standard capacity abbreviations and meanings.

Standard Capacity Abbreviations and Meanings

Use Table 1.2 to translate megabytes, gigabytes, and the other abbreviations used to refer to memory, disk space, and transmission speeds into their decimal or binary values.

Unfortunately, some parts of the computer industry use the decimal values, while others use the binary values. Typically, hard disk and other drive makers rate their products in decimal megabytes or gigabytes; the ROM BIOS on most (but not all) systems and the MS-DOS and Windows 9x FDISK program use binary megabytes or gigabytes, thus creating an apparent discrepancy in disk capacity. RAM is virtually always calculated using binary values.

Modem speeds are normally given in either bits or decimal kilobits. Remember that values given in bits must be divided by eight to calculate the actual speed in bytes.

Table 1.2   Standard Abbreviations and Meanings

Abbreviation	Description	Decimal Power	Decimal Value	Binary Power	Binary Value
Kbit or Kb	Kilobit	10^3	1,000	2^{10}	1,024
K or KB	Kilobyte	10^3	1,000	2^{10}	1,024
Mbit or Mb	Megabit	10^6	1,000,000	2^{20}	1,048,576
M or MB	Megabyte	10^6	1,000,000	2^{20}	1,048,576
Gbit or Gb	Gigabit	10^9	1,000,000,000	2^{30}	1,073,741,824
G or GB	Gigabyte	10^9	1,000,000,000	2^{30}	1,073,741,824
Tbit or Tb	Terabit	10^{12}	1,000,000,000,000	2^{40}	1,099,511,627,776
T or TB	Terabyte	10^{12}	1,000,000,000,000	2^{40}	1,099,511,627,776

> **Note**
>
> For other conversion and reference tables, see the Technical Reference (found on the CD-ROM) of *Upgrading and Repairing PCs, Eleventh Edition*, published by Que (ISBN 0-7897-1903-7).

Chapter 2

System Components and Configuration

Processors and Their Data Bus Widths

> **Note**
>
> All processors Intel except as noted.

Table 2.1   Intel and Selected non-Intel Processors and Their Data Bus Widths

Processor	Data Bus Width	Notes
8088	8-bit	
8086	16-bit	
286	16-bit	
386SX	16-bit	
386DX	32-bit	
486SLC	16-bit	4
486DLC	32-bit	4
486 (all SX/DX series)	32-bit	
5X86	32-bit	5, 6
Pentium	64-bit	
K5	64-bit	1
Pentium MMX	64-bit	
K6	64-bit	1
6x86	64-bit	3
6x86MX	64-bit	3
MII	64-bit	2
Pentium Pro	64-bit	
Pentium II/III	64-bit	
Celeron	64-bit	
Pentium II/III Xeon	64-bit	

1 Designed and manufactured by Advanced Micro Devices (AMD); pin-compatible with Pentium
2 Designed and manufactured by Cyrix; pin-compatible with Pentium
3 Designed by Cyrix, produced for Cyrix by IBM. Chips may be marked as "Cyrix" or "IBM"; pin-compatible with Pentium

4 Designed by Cyrix, produced by Texas Instruments and others. Chips may be marked as "Cyrix" or "Texas Instruments". Despite names, 486SLC was similar to 386SX; 486DLC was similar to 386DX.

5 Designed and manufactured by AMD and used as an upgrade to 486SX/DX-based systems

6 Different internally than AMD's chip, but also used as an upgrade to 486SX/DX-based systems

Differences Between PC/XT and AT Systems

Systems that feature an 8-bit memory bus are called *PC/XT* systems after the pioneering IBM PC and IBM PC/XT. As you can see in Table 2.2, the differences between these systems and descendents of the IBM AT (16-bit memory bus and above) are significant. All modern systems fall into the "AT" category.

Table 2.2 Differences Between PC/XT and AT Systems		
System Attributes PC/XT Type	**(8-bit)**	**(16/32/64-bit) AT Type**
Supported processors	All x86 or x88	286 or higher
Processor modes	Real	Real/ Protected/Virtual Real[2]
Software supported	16-bit only	16- or 32-bit[2]
Bus slot width	8-bit	16/32[1]/64-bit[4]
Slot type	ISA only	ISA, EISA[1], MCA, PC-Card, Cardbus[3], VL-Bus[3], PCI[2]
Hardware interrupts	8 (6 usable)	16 (11 usable)
DMA channels	4 (3 usable)	8 (7 usable)
Maximum RAM	1MB	16MB/4GB[1] or more
Floppy controlle speedr	250 Kbit/sec	250/300/500/ 1,000 Kbit/sec
Standard boot drive	360KB or 720KB	1.2M/1.44MB/2.88MB
Keyboard interface	Unidirectional	Bidirectional
CMOS memory/clock	None standard	MC146818-compatible
Serial-port UART	8250B	16450/16550A

1 Requires 386DX-based system or above
2 Requires 386SX-based system or above
3 Requires 486SX-based system or above
4 Requires Pentium-based system or above

Intel and Compatible Processor Specifications

See Tables 2.3 and 2.4 to help determine the features of any CPU you encounter. It may be necessary to remove the heat sink or fan to see the processor markings on an older system, but many recent systems display CPU identification and speeds at startup.

Table 2.4 shows the major Pentium-class CPU's made by companies other than Intel. The newest versions of these processors can often be used to upgrade an older Pentium, provided proper voltage and system configuration information can be provided, either through adjusting the motherboard/BIOS settings or by purchasing an upgrade-type processor with third-party support.

Table 2.3   Intel Processor Specifications

Processor	CPU Clock	Voltage	Internal Register Size	Data Bus Width	Max. Memory
8088	1x	5v	16-bit	8-bit	1MB
8086	1x	5v	16-bit	16-bit	1MB
286	1x	5v	16-bit	16-bit	16MB
386SX	1x	5v	32-bit	16-bit	16MB
386SL	1x	3.3v	32-bit	16-bit	16MB
386DX	1x	5v	32-bit	32-bit	4GB
486SX	1x	5v	32-bit	32-bit	4GB
486SX2	2x	5v	32-bit	32-bit	4GB
487SX	1x	5v	32-bit	32-bit	4GB
486DX	1x	5v	32-bit	32-bit	4GB
486SL[2]	1x	3.3v	32-bit	32-bit	4GB
486DX2	2x	5v	32-bit	32-bit	4GB
486DX4	2-3x	3.3v	32-bit	32-bit	4GB
486Pentium OD	2.5x	5v	32-bit	32-bit	4GB
Pentium 60/66	1x	5v	32-bit	64-bit	4GB
Pentium 75-200	1.5-3x	3.3-3.5v	32-bit	64-bit	4GB
Pentium MMX	1.5-4.5x	1.8-2.8v	32-bit	64-bit	4GB
Pentium Pro	2-3x	3.3v	32-bit	64-bit	64GB
Pentium II MMX	3.5-4.5x	1.8-2.8v	32-bit	64-bit	64GB
Pentium II Celeron	3.5-4.5x	1.8-2.8v	32-bit	64-bit	64GB
Pentium II Celeron	3.5-7x	1.8-2v	32-bit	64-bit	64GB
Pentium II PE[3]	3.5-6x	1.6v	32-bit	64-bit	64GB
Pentium II Xeon 1MB 2MB	4-4.5x Core	1.8-2.8v FPU,MMX	32-bit	64-bit	64GB
Pentium III	4.5-6x	1.8-2v	32-bit	64-bit	64GB
Pentium III Xeon	5-6x	1.8-2v	32-bit	64-bit	64GB

Level 1 Cache	L1 Cache Type	Level 2 Cache	L2 Cache Speed	Special Features
—	—	—	—	—
—	—	—	—	—
—	—	—	—	—
—	—	—	Bus	—
0KB[1]	WT	—	Bus	—
—	—	—	Bus	—
8KB	WT	—	Bus	—
8KB	WT	—	Bus	—
8KB	WT	—	Bus	FPU
8KB	WT	—	Bus	FPU
8KB	WT	—	Bus	FPU Opt.
8KB	WT	—	Bus	FPU
16KB	WT	—	Bus	FPU
2x16KB	WB	—	Bus	FPU
2x8KB	WB	—	Bus	FPU
2x8KB	WB	—	Bus	FPU
2x16KB	WB	—	Bus	FPU, MMX
2x8KB	WB	256KB 512KB 1MB	Core	FPU
2x16KB	WB	512KB	1/2 Core	FPU, MMX
2x16KB	WB	0KB	—	FPU, MMX
2x16KB	WB	128KB	Core	FPU, MMX
2x16KB	WB	256KB	Core	FPU, MMX
2x16KB	WB	512KB		
2x16KB	WB	512KB	1/2 Core	FPU, SSE
2x16KB	WB	512KB 1MB 2MB	Core	FPU, SSE

Table 2.4   Intel-Compatible Pentium-class Processors

Processor	CPU Clock	Voltage	Internal Register Size	Data Bus Width	Max. Memory
AMD K5	1.5-1.75x	3.5v	32-bit	64-bit	4GB
AMD K6	2.5-4.5x	2.2-3.2v	32-bit	64-bit	4GB
AMD K6-2	3.5-5x	2.2-2.4v	32-bit	64-bit	4GB
AMD K6-3	4-5x	2.2-2.4v	32-bit	64-bit	4GB
AMD Athlon (K7)	2.5-3x	1.6-2.4v	32-bit	64-bit	64GB
Cyrix 6x86	2x	2.5-3.5v	32-bit	64-bit	4GB
Cyrix 6x86MX/MII	2-3.5x	2.9v	32-bit	64-bit	4GB
Nexgen Nx586	2x	4v	32-bit	64-bit	4GB
IDT Winchip	3-4x	3.3-3.5v	32-bit	64-bit	4GB
IDT Winchip2/2A	2.33-4x	3.3-3.5v	32-bit	64-bit	4GB
Rise mP6	2-3.5x	2.8v	32-bit	64-bit	4GB

FPU = Floating-Point unit (internal math coprocessor)

WT = Write-through cache (caches reads only)

WB = Write-back cache (caches both reads and writes)

Bus = Processor external bus speed (motherboard speed)

Core = Processor internal core speed (CPU speed)

MMX = Multimedia extensions, 57 additional instructions for graphics and sound processing

3DNow = MMX plus 21 additional instructions for graphics and sound processing

SSE = Streaming SIMD (Single Instruction Multiple Data) Extensions, MMX plus 70 additional instructions for graphics and sound processing

1 The 386SL contains an integral-cache controller, but the cache memory must be provided outside the chip.

2 Intel later marketed SL Enhanced versions of the SX, DX, and DX2 processors. These processors were available in both 5v and 3.3v versions and included power-management capabilities.

3 The Enhanced mobile PII has on-die L2 cache similar to the Celeron.

4 These processors physically fit into the same Socket 7 used by Intel Pentium 75MHz and above models except as noted, but might require special chipsets or BIOS settings for best operation. Check with motherboard and chip mfr. before installing them in place of your existing Pentium-class chip.

5 Pentium-class performance, but unique, non-standard pinout.

6 Cache size for initial shipments (3rd Q 1999). Athlon designed to allow cache sizes up to 8MB.

7 Athlon's cache interface is designed to handle variable speed ratios, so later versions may run L2 cache faster.

8 Athlon uses new AMD Slot A, physically similar to Slot 1 but with a different electrical pinout.

Level 1 Cache	L1 Cache Type	Level 2 Cache	L2 Cache Speed	Special Features	Similar to[4]
16+8KB	WB	—	Bus	FPU	Pentium
2x32KB	WB	—	Bus	FPU, MMX	Pentium MMX
2x32KB	WB	—	Bus	FPU, 3DNow	Pentium MMX
2x32KB	WB	256KB	Core	FPU, 3DNow	Pentium MMX
2x64KB	WB	512KB[6]	1/3[7] Core	FPU, 3D Now	Pentium III[8]
16KB	WB	—	Bus	FPU	Pentium
64KB	WB	—	Bus	FPU, MMX	Pentium MMX
2x16KB	WB	—	Bus	FPU	Pentium[5]
2x32KB	WB	—	Bus	FPU, MMX	Pentium MMX
2x32KB	WB	—	Bus	FPU, 3DNow	AMD K6-2
2x8KB	WB	—	Bus	FPU, MMX	Pentium MMX

Use Tables 2.5 and 2.6 to help determine which processors *may* fit in place of your existing CPU. Note that a replacement CPU must have the same pinout, the same electrical requirements, and be compatible with your motherboard. Many vendors sell upgrade-compatible processor versions, which have been modified from their original forms by adding a voltage regulator and other support options.

Table 2.5   Intel and Compatibles 486/Pentium-class CPU Socket Types and Specifications

Socket Number	Pins	Pin Layout	Voltage	Supported Processors
Socket 1	169	17×17 PGA	5v	486 SX/SX2, DX/DX2*, DX4 OverDrive
Socket 2	238	19×19 PGA	5v	486 SX/SX2, DX/DX2*, DX4 OverDrive, 486 Pentium OverDrive
Socket 3	237	19×19 PGA	5v/3.3v	486 SX/SX2, DX/DX2, DX4, 486 Pentium Overdrive, AMD 5x86, Cyrix 5x86
Socket 4	273	21×21 PGA	5v	Pentium 60/66, OverDrive
Socket 5	320	37×37 SPGA	3.3/3.5v	Pentium 75-133, Overdrive
Socket 6**	235	19×19 PGA	3.3v	486 DX4, 486 Pentium OverDrive
Socket 7	321	37×37 SPGA	VRM	Pentium 75-233+, MMX, OverDrive, AMD K5/K6, Cyrix M1/II
Socket 8	387	dual pattern SPGA	Auto VRM	Pentium Pro
PGA370	370	37×37 SPGA	2.0v	Celeron
Slot 1	242	Slot	Auto VRM	Pentium II/III, Celeron
Slot 2	330	Slot	Auto VRM	Pentium II/III Xeon
Slot A	242	Slot	Auto VRM	AMD Athlon (K7)

Non-overdrive DX4 or AMD 5x86 also can be supported with the addition of an aftermarket 3.3v voltage-regulator adapter.
**Socket 6 was a paper standard only and was never actually implemented in any systems.*
PGA = Pin Grid Array
SPGA = Staggered Pin Grid Array
VRM = Voltage Regulator Module

The following table lists the fastest processors you can install according to the socket type in your system. Note that newer socket designs allow faster processors, but that the bus speed of your motherboard is also a limiting factor for some CPU types.

Table 2.6	Maximum Processor Speeds by Socket
Socket Type	**Fastest Processor Supported**
Socket 1	5x86-133MHz with 3.3v adapter
Socket 2	5x86-133MHz with 3.3v adapter
Socket 3	5x86-133MHz
Socket 4	Pentium OverDrive 133MHz
Socket 5	Pentium MMX 233MHz or AMD K6 with 2.8v adapter
Socket 7	AMD K6-2, K6-3, up to 475MHz
Socket 8	Pentium Pro OverDrive (333MHz Pentium II performance)
Slot 1	Celeron 466MHz (66MHz bus)
Slot 1	Pentium III 550MHz (100MHz bus)
Slot 2	Pentium III Xeon 550MHz (100MHz bus)
Socket 370	Celeron 466MHz (66MHz bus)
Slot A	600MHz AMD Athlon (K7)

Troubleshooting Processor Problems

Table 2.7 provides a general troubleshooting checklist for processor-related PC problems.

Table 2.7	Troubleshooting Processor-Related Problems	
Problem Identification	**Possible Cause**	**Resolution**
System is dead, no cursor, no beeps, no fan	Power cord failure	Plug in or replace power cord. Power cords can fail even though they look fine.
	Power supply failure	Replace the power supply. Use a known, good spare for testing.
	Motherboard failure	Replace motherboard. Use a known, good spare for testing.
	Memory failure	Remove all memory except 1 bank and retest. If the system still won't boot replace bank 1.
System is dead, no beeps, or locks up before POST begins	All components either not installed or incorrectly installed	Check all peripherals, especially memory and graphics adapter. Reseat all boards and socketed components.
System beeps on startup, fan is running, no cursor onscreen.	Improperly seated or failing graphics adapter	Reseat or replace graphics adapter. Use known, good spare for testing.
Locks up during or shortly after POST	Poor heat dissipation	Check CPU heat sink/fan; replace if necessary, use one with higher capacity.
	Improper voltage settings	Set motherboard for proper core processor voltage.

(continues)

Table 2.7	Troubleshooting Processor-Related Problems Continued	
Problem Identification	**Possible Cause**	**Resolution**
	Wrong motherboard bus speed	Set motherboard for proper speed.
	Wrong CPU clock multiplier	Jumper motherboard for proper clock multiplier.
Improper CPU identification during POST	Old BIOS	Update BIOS from manufacturer.
	Board is not configured properly	Check manual and jumper board accordingly to proper bus and multiplier settings.
Operating system will not boot	Poor heat dissipation	Check CPU fan replace if necessary, may need higher capacity heat sink.
	Improper voltage settings	Jumper motherboard for proper core voltage.
	Wrong motherboard bus speed	Jumper motherboard for proper speed.
	Wrong CPU clock multiplier	Jumper motherboard for proper clock multiplier.
	Applications will not install or run	Improper drivers or incompatible hardware. Update drivers and check for compatibility issues.
System appears to work but no video is displayed	Monitor turned off or failed	Check monitor and power to monitor. Replace with known-good spare for testing.

If during POST the processor is not identified correctly, your mother-board settings may be incorrect or your BIOS may need to be updated. Check that the motherboard is jumpered or configured correctly for the processor that you have, and make sure that you have the latest BIOS for your motherboard.

If the system seems to run erratically after it warms up, try setting the processor to a lower speed. If the problem goes away, the processor might be defective or overclocked.

Many hardware problems are really software problems in disguise. Make sure you have the latest BIOS for your motherboard and the latest drivers for your peripherals. Also it helps to use the latest version of your given operating system because there will normally be fewer problems.

> ## Note
>
> For more information about processors, see Chapter 3 of *Upgrading and Repairing PCs, Eleventh Edition*, also published by Que.

Motherboard Form Factors

While many PC users have extended the life span of their systems by changing the CPU, any system that will be kept for a long time could be a candidate for a motherboard replacement. Use the following charts to determine whether your system uses one of these standard form factors, which will allow you the choice of many vendors for a replacement. A replacement motherboard provides you with these benefits:

- Access to faster, more advanced CPUs

- "Free" updated BIOS with support for large hard drives, Y2K, and boot from LS-120, Zip, and CD-ROM drives

- Newer I/O features such as USB ports, UDMA-66 hard disk interfacing, and AGP video

Baby-AT Motherboard

Until mid-1996, this descendent of the original IBM/XT motherboard was the dominant design. While limited numbers of these motherboards are still available for use with both Pentium-class and Pentium II/Celeron processors, the lack of built-in ports and cooling problems make this an obsolescent design. If you are trying to upgrade a system that uses this motherboard design, consider purchasing a new ATX-style case; power supply; and motherboard, and moving the CPU; RAM; drives; and cards from your existing system to the new "box." See Figure 2.1.

LPX Motherboard

Since 1987, many low-cost systems have used variations on this layout, which features a single slot used for a riser card. The expansion cards for video, audio, and so forth are connected to the riser card, not the motherboard. Most LPX systems have built-in video, audio, and other I/O ports. Unfortunately, because its details were never standardized, it is virtually impossible to upgrade. Systems with this motherboard are essentially "disposable". See Figure 2.2.

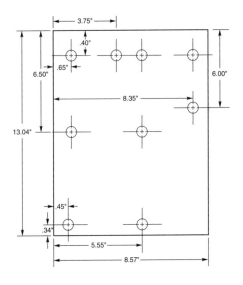

Figure 2.1 Baby-AT motherboard form factor dimensions.

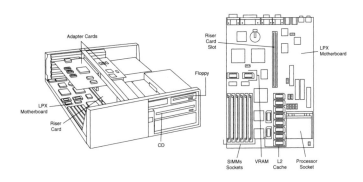

Figure 2.2 Typical LPX system chassis and motherboard.

ATX Motherboard

Since mid-1996, the ATX motherboard has become the standard for most systems using non-proprietary motherboards (see Figure 2.3). Compared to Baby-AT, it's also an industry standard. Compared to LPX, it also features built-in ports. Compared to both, it offers much greater ease of upgrading and servicing. ATX motherboards are rotated 90 degrees when compared to Baby-ATs, and also use a different power supply for advanced power management features. Because of its built-in ports and differences in layout, ATX motherboards require an ATX case. ATX cases can also be used for Baby-AT motherboards, though. Figure 2.3 shows a full-size ATX layout, though there are now several smaller versions including mini-ATX, micro-ATX, and flex-ATX.

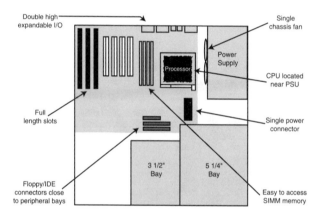

Figure 2.3 ATX system chassis layout and features.

NLX Motherboard

The replacement for the old LPX low-profile motherboard is the NLX motherboard (see Figure 2.4). NLX also features built-in ports and a riser card, but its standard design means that replacement motherboards should be easier to purchase than for LPX systems. A major advantage of NLX systems is that the motherboard is easy to remove for servicing through a side panel, a feature that makes NLX-based systems popular as corporate network client PCs.

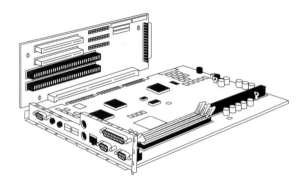

Figure 2.4 NLX motherboard and riser combination.

Which Motherboard Is Which?

Use Table 2.8 to help determine whether a system is a Baby-AT, LPX, ATX, or an NLX-based system.

Table 2.8   Comparison of Major Motherboard Form Factors

	Baby-AT	LPX	ATX	NLX
Ports built into chassis	No	Yes	Yes	Yes
Riser Card	No	Yes	No	Yes
Single row of ports at rear	n/a	Yes	No	No
Two rows of ports at rear	n/a	No	Yes	Yes
Slots on both sides of riser card	n/a	Opt	No	No
Riser card location	n/a	Middle	n/a	Side near power supply on MB

Power Supplies

Power supplies actually convert high-voltage AC (alternating current) into low-voltage DC (direct current) for use by PCs. Power supplies come in several different form factors, and also feature different motherboard connectors to correspond with the newer motherboard designs on the market. Table 2.9 illustrates which power supplies are most likely to be used with different motherboards.

Table 2.9 Matching Power Supplies and Motherboards		
Motherboard Form Factor	**Most Common PS Form Factor Used**	**Other PS Form Factors Used**
Baby-AT	LPX style	Baby-AT, AT/Tower, or AT/Desk
LPX	LPX style	None
ATX	ATX style	None
Micro-ATX	ATX style	SFX style
NLX	ATX style	None

LPX Versus ATX Power Supplies

Some motherboards are designed to handle either LPX or ATX power supplies. The ATX is a preferred design, because it provides the lower voltage needed by today's CPUs, offers foolproof installation, and also provides better cooling than older designs.

Table 2.10 compares two of the more common power supply form factors used in computers today.

Table 2.10 Comparing ATX and LPX Power Supplies			
Power Supply Type	**Voltage Output**	**Motherboard Power Connectors**	**Other Features Notes**
LPX	5v, 12v	Two—6 pins each (P8/P9)	Easy to reverse plug due to poor keying
ATX	3.3v, 5v, 12v	One—20 pins	Keyed to go in only one way; allows hibernation via operating system or keyboard command

> **Caution**
>
> To get the cables oriented correctly, keep the ground wires (black) next to each other. Although most connectors are keyed to prevent improperly plugging them in, some connectors can easily be inserted incorrectly. This will cause your motherboard to be destroyed the first time you switch on the power and could possibly cause a fire.

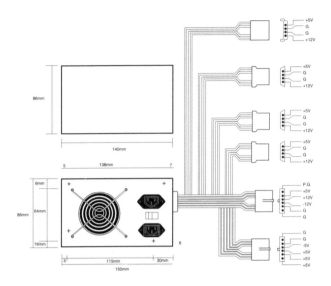

Figure 2.5 LPX form factor power supply.

Table 2.11	Typical LPX Power Supply Connections	
Connector	**Voltage**	**Standard Color/Notes**
P8-1	Power_Good (+5v)	Orange
P8-2	+5v	Red
P8-3	+12v	Yellow
P8-4	-12v	Blue
P8-5	Ground (0)	Black
P8-6	Ground (0)	Black
P9-1	Ground (0)	Black
P9-2	Ground (0)	Black
P9-3	-5v	White
P9-4	+5v	Red
P9-5	+5v	Red
P9-6	+5v	Red

Power Connectors for the Drive(s)

These might not be labeled, but can easily be distinguished by the four-wire cable and color-coding. The same colors are used for drive power connectors on ATX power supplies.

Connector	Voltage	Standard Color/Notes
P10-1	+12v	Yellow
P10-2	Ground (0)	Black
P10-3	Ground (0)	Black
P10-4	+5v	Red

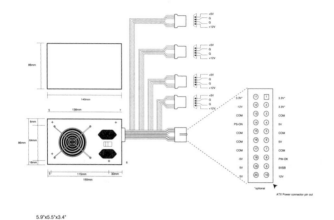

5.9"x5.5"x3.4"

Figure 2.6 ATX form factor power supply, used with both ATX and NLX systems. The pinout for the motherboard power is given at lower right. Note the single square pin used for keying.

Table 2.12   ATX Power Supply Connections

Color	Signal	Pin	Pin	Signal	Color
Orange	+3.3v	11	1	+3.3v	Orange
Blue	-12v	12	2	+3.3v	Orange
Black	GND	13	3	GND	Black
Green	PS_On	14	4	+5v	Red
Black	GND	15	5	GND	Black
Black	GND	16	6	+5v	Red
Black	GND	17	7	GND	Black
White	-5v	18	8	Power_Good	Gray
Red	+5v	19	9	+5VSB (Standby)	Purple
Red	+5v	20	10	+12v	Yellow

Quick-Reference Chart for Troubleshooting Power Supplies

Table 2.13 Troubleshooting Power Supplies		
Symptom	**Cause(s)**	**Tests & Solution(s)**
Overheating	Inadequate system cooling	Check ventilation around system; clean system internally; check for missing slot covers.
	Higher load on system in watts than power supply rating	Replace power supply with higher rated unit
System reboots itself	Incorrect power level on Power_Good; can indicate overloaded power supply or otherwise bad unit	Use DC-voltage digital multimeter (DMM) to test P8-1 (orange wire) on LPX and older power supplies or Pin 8 (gray wire) on ATX and newer power supplies; rated voltage is +5v; acceptable is +3.0v to +6.0v
		Replace failed power supply with higher rated unit
Fan turns for only a moment then stops	Wrong voltage (PS set to 220/230v in U.S.)	Turn off system; reset PS to correct voltage (110/115v in U.S.) and restart. Using 220/230v power on a PS set for 110/115v will destroy it!
	Dead short in system	Short can be caused by loose screws, failed hard drives, or add-on cards.
		Turn off and unplug system; disconnect hard drive and see if system starts; if system still fails; plug drive in and remove add-on card; repeat until each card and drive has been checked; also check Y-adapter cables, because bad cables can cause shorts
		Replace faulty component(s).

> **Note**
>
> For more information on power supplies, wattage ratings, and testing, see Chapter 21 of *Upgrading and Repairing PCs, Eleventh Edition*, published by Que (ISBN 0-7897-1903-7).

Memory Types

RAM (random access memory) provides the work area that processors use to create and modify data. While RAM was sometimes found on expansion boards on old XT-class and early AT-class systems, all standard 486-based and Pentium-class systems have their memory modules attached to the motherboard.

- Features common to all SIMMs

- Pins numbered from left to right

- Same pins on both sides of the module

> **Tip**
>
> Note that all dimensions for both SIMMs and DIMMs in the fol-
> lowing figures are in both inches and millimeters (in parentheses).

30-Pin SIMM

The 30-pin SIMM is the oldest type of memory module still in use
(see Figure 2.7). It was popular on 386-based and early 486-based
systems. While its capacities are extremely small compared to more
modern memory designs, the unpopularity of the 30-pin SIMM
means that it's the most expensive memory per megabyte. If you
are supporting systems that use this type of module, look for
sources of used memory or replace the motherboard with one that
uses newer memory rather than buy new modules.

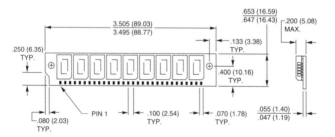

Figure 2.7 A typical 30-pin SIMM. The one shown here is 9-bit, although
the dimensions would be the same for 8-bit.

72-Pin SIMM

The 72-pin SIMM was the most popular for a number of years, but
has now been superseded on newer systems by DIMM modules.
They are commonly found on late-model 486-based systems, most
Pentium, and most early Pentium-compatible systems. Because
these modules are also becoming very expensive per megabyte, try
to salvage or swap memory to populate older systems rather than
purchase new. 72-pin SIMMs can be either fast-page or EDO
(extended data out), and should not be mixed. See Figure 2.8.

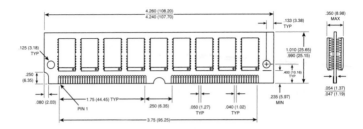

Figure 2.8 A typical 72-pin SIMM, although the dimensions would be the same for 32-bit.

DIMMs

Dual Inline Memory Modules became popular with the rise of the Pentium II/III/Celeron family of processors and can also be found on many late-model Pentium and "Super Socket 7" motherboards used with AMD K6-series and Cyrix 6x86MX/MII processors (see Figure 2.9). DIMMs are the most popular and fastest type of memory module in widespread use. Most DIMMs are Synchronous DRAM (SDRAM). On motherboards with both SIMM and DIMM sockets, SDRAMs cannot be used in conjunction with SIMMs, but EDO DIMMs can be used along with EDO SIMMs.

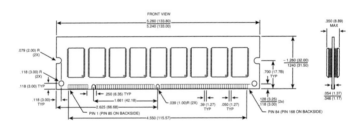

Figure 2.9 A typical 168-pin DIMM. The one shown here is 72-bit, although the dimensions would be the same for 64-bit.

RDRAM

The *RDRAM*, or *Rambus DRAM*, is a radical new memory design that is expected to appear in high-end PC systems in late 1999. It is endorsed by Intel and is supported in most of their new PC motherboard chipsets for 1999 and beyond.

RDRAM differs from previous memory devices in that it provides multiple high-speed (800MHz), narrow-channel (16-bit-wide) data transfers to and from a 128-bit memory bus instead of the slower

(100MHz or 66MHz), 32-bit or 64-bit data transfers of SDRAM and previous memory types.

RDRAM modules are called RIMMs (Rambus Inline Memory Module), and any unused RIMM slots on a motherboard must be filled with a continuity module (see Figure 2.10) to permit a continuous high-speed data pathway through the RIMMs. Each RIMM represents multiple memory banks, and thus a single RIMM at a time can be added to a system, much the way installation of DIMMs works; although, the memory types are not interchangeable.

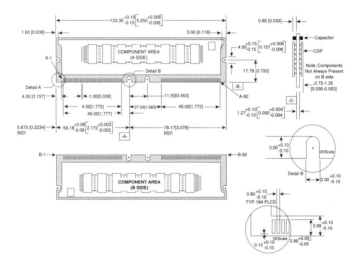

Figure 2.10 Typical RDRAM bus layout, showing two RIMMs and one continuity module installed.

Parity Versus Non-Parity Memory

Virtually all 386-based and older systems, and most 486-based systems require parity-checked memory, which can detect memory errors. Parity-checked RAM uses units of 8 memory bits plus 1 parity bit, for a total of 9 bits. Most Pentium-class and higher systems don't require parity-checked RAM, but will ignore the parity bit(s) if present. Use the following suggestions to determine whether existing memory is likely to be parity checked. Parity-checked memory *must* be used on systems that require it, and *should* be used on systems that can be configured to use the parity bits, *especially* if the systems support ECC (Error Correction Code) operation, which uses the parity bit as a means of *correcting* a faulty memory bit.

"Divide by 3" Rule

Count the chips on a SIMM or DIMM. If you can divide the number of chips by 3, the module is most likely a parity-checked module. However, some memory manufacturers created memory modules with fake parity chips.

Note

See *Upgrading and Repairing PCs, Eleventh Edition*, Chapter 6, for more information about how to detect "logic parity" module.

A similar "divide by 9"rule can also be used to determine parity checking if you know the number of memory bits in the module. Note in Table 2.14 that the number of bits in parity-checked modules can be divided by 9, but the number of bits in non-parity modules can only be divided by 8.

Table 2.14   SIMM and DIMM Capacities

30-Pin SIMM Capacities

Capacity	Parity SIMM	Non-Parity SIMM
256KB	256KB×9	256KB×8
1MB	1MB×9	1MB×8
4MB	4MB×9	4MB×8
16MB	16MB×9	16MB×8

72-Pin SIMM Capacities

Capacity	Parity SIMM	Non-Parity SIMM
1MB	256KB×36	256KB×32
2MB	512KB×36	512KB×32
4MB	1MB×36	1MB×32
8MB	2MB×36	2MB×32
16MB	4MB×36	4MB×32
32MB	8MB×36	8MB×32
64MB	16MB×36	16MB×32
128MB	32MB×36	32MB×32

168-Pin DIMM Capacities

Capacity	Parity DIMM	Non-Parity DIMM
8MB	1MB×72	1MB×64
16MB	2MB×72	2MB×64
32MB	4MB×72	4MB–64
64MB	8MB×72	8MB×64
128MB	16MB×72	16MB×64
256MB	32MB×72	32MB×64

Expanding Memory on a System

Memory must be added to a system in "banks". Simply put, a *bank of memory* is the amount of RAM in bits equal to the data bus width of the computer's CPU (see Table 2.15). Thus, a Pentium's data bus is 64 bits, and memory module(s) used with a Pentium must have a total width of 64 bits for non-parity memory, and 72 bits for parity-checked or ECC memory.

Table 2.15		**Memory Bank Widths on Different Systems**				
Processor	Data Bus	Memory Bank Size (No Parity)	Memory Bank Size (Parity)	30-Pin SIMMs per Bank	72-Pin SIMMs per Bank	168-Pin SIMMs per Bank
8088	8-bit	8-bits	9-bits	1	n/a	n/a
8086	16-bit	16-bits	18-bits	2	n/a	n/a
286	16-bit	16-bits	18-bits	2	n/a	n/a
386SX, SL, SLC	16-bit	16-bits	18-bits	2	n/a	n/a
386DX	32-bit	32-bits	36-bits	4	1	n/a
486SLC, SLC2	16-bit	16-bits	18-bits	2	n/a	n/a
486SX, DX, DX2, DX4, 5x86	32-bit	32-bits	36-bits	4	1	n/a
Pentium, K5, K6, 6x86, 6x86MX, MII	64-bit	64-bits	72-bits	8*	2	1
Pentium Pro, PII, PIII, Celeron, Xeon	64-bit	64-bits	72-bits	8*	2	1

Very few motherboards for these processors acFtually use this type of memory

The number of bits for each bank can be made up of single chips, SIMMs, or DIMMs. Modern systems don't use individual chips; instead, they use only SIMMs or DIMMs. If the system has a 16-bit processor such as a 386SX, it would probably use 30-pin SIMMs and have two SIMMs per bank. All the SIMMs in a single bank must be the same size and type.

Memory Troubleshooting

Figure 2.11 provides basic steps that allow you to effectively test and troubleshoot your system RAM. First, let's cover the memory testing and troubleshooting procedures.

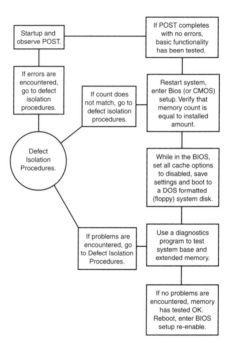

Figure 2.11 Testing and troubleshooting memory.

After you've determined that the system's memory is defective, you need to determine which memory module is at fault. Follow the procedure in Figure 2.12 to isolate the module for replacement.

Memory Usage Within the System

The original PC had a total of 1MB of addressable memory, and the top 384KB of that was reserved for use by the system. Placing this reserved space at the top (between 640KB and 1,024KB instead of at the bottom, between 0KB and 640KB) led to what is often called the *conventional memory barrier*. Systems with more than 1MB of RAM treat the additional RAM as extended memory, beginning at 1MB.

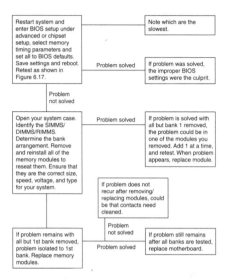

Figure 2.12 Follow these steps if you are still encountering memory errors after completing the steps in Figure 2.11.

Thus, there is a "hole" in memory usage between 640KB and 1MB. Some standard add-on cards and motherboard devices use part of this memory area for RAM and ROM addresses, leaving the remainder of this space free for additional card usage.

Hardware and Firmware Devices that Use Memory Addresses

The listing of hardware and firmware devices that use memory addresses is relatively short when compared to IRQ, DMA, and I/O port address usage, but it is no less important. No two devices can share a memory address. Table 2.16 shows memory usage in the 640KB to 1MB memory range for standard devices.

Table 2.16 Memory Usage in the 640KB–1MB Range		
Device	**Address Range**	**Notes**
Graphics Mode Video RAM	0A0000–0AFFFF	
Monochrome Text Mode Video RAM	0B0000–0B7FFF	
Color Text Mode Video RAM	0B8000–0BFFFF	
Video ROM for VGA, Super VGA	0C0000–0C7FFF	
Unassigned	0C8000–0DFFFF	Available for use by BIOS or RAM chips on add-on cards or by memory managers such as QEMM or EMM386
Motherboard ROM can be BIOS extension space (IBM PS/2s, most Pentium-class and newer systems)	0E0000–0EFFFF	If not used by BIOS extensions, treated as additional unassigned
Motherboard ROM BIOS (all systems)	0F0000–0FFFFF	

If you are using an add-on card that uses a ROM BIOS chip onboard to overcome IDE hard drive limitations, Y2K date rollover problems, or provides support for bootable SCSI hard drives, the BIOS chips on those cards must be placed in the unassigned memory range listed earlier. If you have two or more add-on cards that use memory address ranges, for best system performance, set the cards to use adjacent memory addresses.

Here are the typical memory uses for some common IDE and SCSI interface cards that use ROM BIOS chips:

Table 2.17 Memory Addresses Used by Different Adapter Cards		
Adapter Type	**Onboard BIOS Size**	**BIOS Address Range**
Most XT compatible controllers	8KB	0C8000–0C9FFF
Most AT controllers	None	Drivers in motherboard BIOS
Most standard IDE hard disk adapters	None	Drivers in motherboard BIOS
Most enhanced[1] IDE hard disk adapters	16KB	0C8000–0CBFFF
Some SCSI host adapters	16KB	0C8000–0CBFFF
Some SCSI host adapters	16KB	0DC000–0DFFFF

1 This type of adapter supplements the motherboard's IDE interface by supporting drives beyond 528MB (decimal) or 504MB (binary) in size. Some of these adapters can also provide Y2K-date rollover support. Cards that combine both functions may have larger BIOS sizes.

Some older network cards also used memory addresses for RAM buffers or for ROM BIOS chips that permit diskless workstations to use a network copy of the operating system for booting. Network cards that use memory addresses are seldom used today.

Using Memory Addresses Beyond 1MB (0FFFFF)

Some older Super VGA cards, notably those from ATI, could also be set to use a 1MB extended memory address starting at 15MB for moving video data. This so-called *memory aperture* technique made the video cards using it faster, but could not be used on systems with 16MB of RAM or above. If you use a video card that uses a memory aperture on a system with less than 16MB of RAM, disable the memory aperture feature before you upgrade the RAM.

Determining Memory Address Ranges in Use

On a system with Windows 9x or Windows 2000, use the Device Manager's System Properties sheet to see overall memory address usage (see the following).

Use add-on card documentation or a memory viewer such as those included with AMIDiag, CheckIt, or Microsoft's MSD.EXE to see memory usage on systems running Windows 3.1 or MS-DOS.

Note

To learn more about memory modules, see Chapter 6 of
Upgrading and Repairing PCs, Eleventh Edition, published by Que.

Other Add-On Card Configuration Issues

When a card is installed into an expansion slot or a PCMCIA/PC card device is installed into a PC card slot, the card must use at least one of four different hardware resources to be accessible to the system. All add-on cards must use at least an I/O port address range or ranges; most cards use an IRQ (interrupt request line); fewer cards use DMA (Direct Memory Access);Memory addresses are used least of all. Many cards use two or more of these hardware resources.

Note

See "Hardware and Firmware Devices that Use Memory Addresses," earlier in this chapter.

If an add-on card is set to use the same hardware resource as an existing card, it will not work unless that resource is designed to be shared between cards. While the capability to share IRQs has existed (at least in theory) since the Micro Channel Architecture of the late 1980s, even today the best rule of thumb for adding cards is "each card has its own settings".

Plug-and-Play (PnP) configuration, introduced with Windows 95 and also present with Windows 98 and Windows 2000, is designed to minimize much of the grief of adding cards, but this technology has been in a state of flux since it was introduced. To help you add cards, the following tables of standard settings also list software and hardware tools that can help you find the settings already in use before you install your next card.

IRQs

Interrupt request channels (IRQs), or hardware interrupts, are used by various hardware devices to signal the motherboard that a request must be fulfilled. Most add-on cards use IRQs, and because systems today have the same number of IRQs available with the first IBM PC/AT systems built in 1984, IRQs frequently cause trouble in add-on card installations.

Table 2.18 shows IRQ assignments for 16-bit ISA and 32-bit VL-Bus/PCI expansion slots, listed by priority. Technically speaking, PCI interrupts can be shared, but in practice, many older Pentium systems must use a unique IRQ value for each PCI card, as with ISA and VL-Bus cards.

Table 2.18	16/32-Bit ISA/VL-Bus/PCI Default Interrupt Assignments			
IRQ	**Standard Function**	**Bus Slot**	**Card Type**	**Recommended Use**
0	System Timer	No	—	—
1	Keyboard Controller	No	—	—
2^1	Second IRQ Controller Cascade	No	—	—
8	Real-time Clock	No	—	—
9	Available (appears as IRQ 2)	Yes	8/16-bit	Network Interface Card
10	Available	Yes	16-bit	USB
11	Available	Yes	16-bit	SCSI Host Adapter
12	Motherboard Mouse Port Available	Yes	16-bit	Motherboard Mouse Port
13	Math Coprocessor	No	—	—
14	Primary IDE	Yes	16-bit	Primary IDE (Hard disks)
15	Secondary IDE/ Available	Yes	16-bit	Secondary IDE (CD-ROM/Tape)
3^4	Serial Port 2 (COM 2:)	Yes	8/16-bit	COM 2:/ Internal Modem
4^3	Serial Port 1 (COM 1:)	Yes	8/16-bit	COM 1:
5^2	Sound/Parallel Port 2 (LPT2:)	Yes	8/16-bit	Sound Card

IRQ	Standard Function	Bus Slot	Card Type	Recommended Use
6	Floppy Disk Controller	Yes	8/16-bit	Floppy Controller
7	Parallel Port 1 (LPT1:)	Yes	8/16-bit	LPT1:

1 *The original IBM PC/XT and compatible systems with 8-bit ISA slots did not assign any standard device to IRQ 2. When the 16-bit ISA slot was introduced, along with a second range of IRQs (8–15), this permitted the "cascading" of these interrupts via IRQ 2. Older cards that have IRQ 2 as a setting actually use IRQ 9 instead on 286-based and higher systems.*

2 *On original XT-class systems with 8-bit ISA slots, IRQ 5 was assigned to the hard disk controller card. While IRQ 5's "official" assignment is to handle LPT2 on systems with 16-bit ISA slots, only EPP and ECP (IEEE-1284) parallel port modes actually use an IRQ. This permits the use of IRQ 5 for sound cards in most systems without interfering with the use of LPT2.*

3 *Systems with COM 3 default to "sharing" COM 1's IRQ 4. This will cause system lockups in Windows if a serial mouse is used on COM 1 with a modem on COM 3. Use the modem, and the IRQ conflict crashes the system. To avoid problems, set the device using COM 3 to a different IRQ, or disable COM 2 and use COM 2 for the modem.*

4 *Systems with COM 4 default to "sharing" COM 2's IRQ 3. This will cause system lockups in Windows if a serial mouse is used on COM 2 with a modem on COM 4. Use the modem, and the IRQ conflict crashes the system. To avoid problems, set the device using COM 4 to a different IRQ, or disable COM 2 and use COM 2 for the modem.*

DMA

Direct Memory Access permits high-speed data transfer between I/O devices and memory without CPU management. This method of data transfer boosts performance for devices that use it, but because there is no CPU management, the possibility of data corruption is higher than for non-DMA transfers. Although DMA channels can theoretically be "shared" between devices that are not in use at the same time, this is not a recommended practice.

PCI cards don't use these DMA channels, with the exception of sound cards, which are emulating the ISA-based Sound Blaster or compatibles —the major users of DMA channels today. See Table 2.19.

Table 2.19 16/32-Bit ISA/PCI Default DMA-Channel Assignments					
DMA	Standard Function	Bus Slot	Card Type	Transfer	Recommended Use
0	Available	Yes	16-bit	8-bit	Integrated Sound
1	Available	Yes	8/16-bit	8-bit	8-bit Sound
2	Floppy Disk Controller	Yes	8/16-bit	8-bit	Floppy Controller
3	Available	Yes	8/16-bit	8-bit	LPT1: in ECP Mode
4	1st DMA Controller Cascade	No	—	16-bit	—
5	Available	Yes	16-bit	16-bit	16-bit Sound
6	Available	Yes	16-bit	16-bit	ISA SCSI Adapter
7	Available	Yes	16-bit	16-bit	Available

Note that PCI adapters don't use these ISA DMA channels; these are only for ISA cards.
On PC/XT systems with only 8-bit ISA slots, only DMA channels 1–3 are available. DMA channel 2 was used for the floppy controller, as it is today, but channels 1 and 3 were not assigned to standard devices.

Determining Actual IRQ and DMA Usage

While these tables provide the "official" guidelines for IRQ and DMA usage, these settings might not be true for all systems at all times.

Add-on network, sound, serial, parallel, and SCSI cards can often be moved to different IRQ and DMA channels to work around conflicts. Non-standard settings can be done manually with some cards and is a virtual certainty with PnP cards used with Windows 9x and Windows 2000. Well-designed PnP cards already installed in a system are designed to automatically move to non-conflicting settings when less-flexible PnP cards are inserted. Late-model Pentium-class systems using Windows 95 OSR 2.x and Windows 98 can also use an "IRQ-steering" feature that allows multiple PCI devices to use a single IRQ, if the BIOS is designed to support it.

To view the current IRQ and DMA settings for systems using Windows 9x, use the Device Manager (a tab on the System Properties sheet). View the properties for the "Computer" icon at the top of the device list and you can choose from IRQ, DMA, I/O port, and Memory address information. See Figure 2.13.

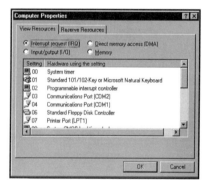

Figure 2.13 The Windows 9x Device Manager and Computer Properties sheet showing IRQs in use; available IRQs are not listed.

For other operating systems, I recommend an interface card with signal lights for IRQ and DMA usage. The Discovery Card, developed by John Rourke, pioneered this diagnostic category, and many vendors offer cards with this feature.

To use an IRQ/DMA card, turn off the system, insert the card into an open slot, and turn on the system. As devices that use an IRQ or a DMA are activated, the corresponding signal light on the card is displayed. Most cards have a reset switch, which permits the card lights to be cleared, allowing you to test for possible conflicts. When combined with information from a system configuration template (see the following), this helps provide accurate IRQ and DMA usage information.

I/O Port Addresses

Your computer's I/O ports enable communications between devices and software in your system. They are equivalent to two-way radio channels. If you want to talk to your serial port, you need to know what I/O port (radio channel) it is listening on. Similarly, if you want to receive data from the serial port, you need to listen on the same channel it is transmitting on.

One confusing issue is that I/O ports are designated by hexadecimal addresses similar to memory addresses. They are not memory; they are ports.

Motherboard and chipset devices are normally set to use I/O port addresses from 0h to FFh, and all other devices use from 100h to FFFFh. Table 2.20 shows motherboard and chipset-based I/O port usage.

Table 2.20 Motherboard and Chipset-based Device Port Addresses		
Address (hex)	**Size**	**Description**
0000–000F	16 bytes	Chipset - 8237 DMA 1
0020–0021	2 bytes	Chipset - 8259 interrupt controller 1
002E–002F	2 bytes	Super I/O controller Configuration registers
0040–0043	4 bytes	Chipset - Counter/Timer 1
0048–004B	4 bytes	Chipset - Counter/Timer 2
0060	1 byte	Keyboard/Mouse controller byte - reset IRQ
0061	1 byte	Chipset - NMI, speaker control
0064	1 byte	Keyboard/Mouse Controller, CMD/STAT Byte
0070, bit 7	1 bit	Chipset - Enable NMI
0070, bits 6:0	7 bits	MC146818 - Real-time clock, Address
0071	1 byte	MC146818 - Real-time clock, Data
0078	1 byte	Reserved - Board configuration
0079	1 byte	Reserved - Board configuration
0080–008F	16 bytes	Chipset - DMA page registers
00A0–00A1	2 bytes	Chipset - 8259 interrupt controller 2
00B2	1 byte	APM control port
00B3	1 byte	APM status port
00C0–00DE	31 bytes	Chipset - 8237 DMA 2
00F0	1 byte	Math Coprocessor Reset Numeric Error

To find out exactly what port addresses are being used on your motherboard, consult the board documentation or look the settings up in the Windows Device Manager.

Bus-based devices (I/O devices found on the motherboard or on add-on cards) normally use the addresses from 100h on up. Table 2.21 lists the commonly used bus-based device addresses and some common adapter cards and their settings.

Table 2.21	Bus-based Device Port Addresses	
Address (hex)	**Size**	**Description**
0130–0133	4 bytes	Adaptec SCSI adapter (alternate)
0134–0137	4 bytes	Adaptec SCSI adapter (alternate)
0168–016F	8 bytes	Fourth IDE interface
0170–0177	8 bytes	Secondary IDE interface
01E8–01EF	8 bytes	Third IDE interface
01F0–01F7	8 bytes	Primary IDE/AT (16-bit) hard disk controller
0200–0207	8 bytes	Gameport or joystick adapter
0210–0217	8 bytes	IBM XT expansion chassis
0220–0233	20 bytes	Creative Labs Sound Blaster 16 audio (default)
0230–0233	4 bytes	Adaptec SCSI adapter (alternate)
0234–0237	4 bytes	Adaptec SCSI adapter (alternate)
0238–023B	4 bytes	MS bus mouse (alternate)
023C–023F	4 bytes	MS bus mouse (default)
0240–024F	16 bytes	SMC Ethernet adapter (default)
0240–0253	20 bytes	Creative Labs Sound Blaster 16 audio (alternate)
0258–025F	8 bytes	Intel above board
0260–026F	16 bytes	SMC Ethernet adapter (alternate)
0260–0273	20 bytes	Creative Labs Sound Blaster 16 audio (alternate)
0270–0273	4 bytes	Plug-and-Play I/O read ports
0278–027F	8 bytes	Parallel Port 2 (LPT2)
0280–028F	16 bytes	SMC Ethernet adapter (alternate)
0280–0293	20 bytes	Creative Labs Sound Blaster 16 audio (alternate)
02A0–02AF	16 bytes	SMC Ethernet adapter (alternate)
02C0–02CF	16 bytes	SMC Ethernet adapter (alternate)
02E0–02EF	16 bytes	SMC Ethernet adapter (alternate
02E8–02EF	8 bytes	Serial Port 4 (COM 4)
02EC–02EF	4 bytes	Video, 8514 or ATI standard ports
02F8–02FF	8 bytes	Serial Port 2 (COM 2)
0300–0301	2 bytes	MPU-401 MIDI Port (secondary)
0300–030F	16 bytes	SMC Ethernet adapter (alternate)

Address (hex)	Size	Description
0320–0323	4 bytes	XT (8-bit) hard disk controller
0320–032F	16 bytes	SMC Ethernet adapter (alternate)
0330–0331	2 bytes	MPU-401 MIDI port (default)
0330–0333	4 bytes	Adaptec SCSI adapter (default)
0334–0337	4 bytes	Adaptec SCSI adapter (alternate)
0340–034F	16 bytes	SMC Ethernet adapter (alternate)
0360–036F	16 bytes	SMC Ethernet adapter (alternate)
0366	1 byte	Fourth IDE command port
0367, bits 6:0	7 bits	Fourth IDE status port
0370–0375	6 bytes	Secondary floppy controller
0376	1 byte	Secondary IDE command port
0377, bit 7	1 bit	Secondary floppy controller disk change
0377, bits 6:0	7 bits	Secondary IDE status port
0378–037F	8 bytes	Parallel Port 1 (LPT1)
0380–038F	16 bytes	SMC Ethernet adapter (alternate)
0388–038B	4 bytes	Audio - FM synthesizer
03B0–03BB	12 bytes	Video, Mono/EGA/VGA standard ports
03BC–03BF	4 bytes	Parallel Port 1 (LPT1) in some systems
03BC–03BF	4 bytes	Parallel Port 3 (LPT3)
03C0–03CF	16 bytes	Video, EGA/VGA standard ports
03D0–03DF	16 bytes	Video, CGA/EGA/VGA standard ports
03E6	1 byte	Third IDE command port
03E7, bits 6:0	7 bits	Third IDE status port
03E8–03EF	8 bytes	Serial Port 3 (COM 3)
03F0–03F5	6 bytes	Primary floppy controller
03F6	1 byte	Primary IDE command port
03F7, bit 7	1 bit	Primary Floppy controller disk change
03F7, bits 6:0	7 bits	Primary IDE status port
03F8–03FF	8 bytes	Serial Port 1 (COM 1)
04D0–04D1	2 bytes	Edge/level triggered PCI interrupt controller
0530–0537	8 bytes	Windows sound system (default)
0604–060B	8 bytes	Windows sound system (alternate)
0678–067F	8 bytes	LPT2 in ECP mode
0778–077F	8 bytes	LPT1 in ECP mode
0A20–0A23	4 bytes	IBM Token-Ring adapter (default)
0A24–0A27	4 bytes	IBM Token-Ring adapter (alternate)
0CF8–0CFB	4 bytes	PCI Configuration address Registers

(continues)

Table 2.21	Bus-based Device Port Addresses Continued	
Address (hex)	Size	Description
0CF9	1 byte	Turbo and Reset control register
0CFC–0CFF	4 bytes	PCI configuration data registers
FF00–FF07	8 bytes	IDE bus master registers
FF80–FF9F	32 bytes	Universal Serial Bus (USB)
FFA0–FFA7	8 bytes	Primary bus master IDE registers
FFA8–FFAF	8 bytes	Secondary bus master IDE registers

Determining Actual I/O Address Ranges in Use

To find out exactly what your devices are using, consult the documentation for the device or look the device up in the Windows 9x Device Manager. Note that some device documentation might list only the starting I/O address and not the full range of addresses used.

Virtually all devices on your system buses use I/O port addresses. Most of these are fairly standardized, meaning you won't often have conflicts or problems with these settings.

Troubleshooting Add-on Card Resource Conflicts

The resources in a system are limited. Unfortunately, the demands on those resources seem to be unlimited. As you add more and more adapter cards to your system, you will find that the potential for resource conflicts increases.

Symptoms of a Potential Resource Conflict

- A device transfers data inaccurately.

- Your system frequently locks up.

- Your sound card doesn't sound quite right.

- Your mouse doesn't work.

- Garbage appears on your video screen for no apparent reason.

- Your printer prints gibberish.

- You cannot format a floppy disk.

- The PC starts in Safe mode (Windows 95).

Spotting Resource Conflicts with Windows 9x/2000

Windows 9x and Windows 2000 also show conflicts by highlighting a device in yellow or red in the Device Manager representation. By using the Windows Device Manager, you can usually spot the conflicts quickly (see Figure 2.14).

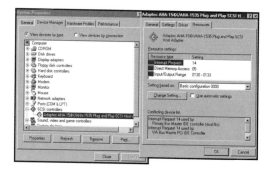

Figure 2.14 The yellow circle next to the Adaptec 154x SCSI card indicates a conflict; view the card resources (right window) to see the conflicting device.

Keep in mind that many computer viruses can also cause symptoms similar to hardware resource conflicts. Scan your system for viruses before you start working on it.

Recording System Settings

Use a System Configuration Template to record system settings. This sheet is resource-oriented, not device-oriented, to make finding conflicts easier to do. You can make a printout of the System Summary from the Windows 9x/Windows 2000 Device Manager to get a lot of this information. For other operating systems, use the methods listed earlier.

The first system resource map is provided as a model for your use; it lists fixed resources on a modern PC. Add the other resources used on your PC.

System Resource Map

PC Make and Model: _____
Serial Number: _____
Date: _____

Interrupts (IRQs):	I/O Port Addresses:

0 - Timer Circuits_____   040-04B _____
1 - Keyboard/Mouse Controller ____   060 & 064_____
2 - 2nd 8259 IRQ Controller _____   0A0-0A1 _____
8 - Real-time Clock/CMOS RAM ___   070-071 _____
9 - _____   _____
10 - _____   _____
11 - _____   _____
12 - _____   _____
13 - Math Coprocessor _____   0F0 _____
14 - _____   _____
15 - _____   _____
3 - _____   _____
4 - _____   _____
5 - _____   _____
6 - _____   _____
7 - _____   _____

Devices not using Interrupts: I/O Port Addresses:

Mono/EGA/VGA Standard Ports ____   3B0-3BB _____
EGA/VGA Standard Ports _____   3C0-3CF_____
CGA/EGA/VGA Standard Ports_____   3D0-3DF _____
_____   _____
_____   _____
_____   _____
_____   _____
_____   _____
_____   _____

DMA Channels:

0 - _____
1 - _____
2 - _____
3 - _____
4 - DMA Channel 0-3 Cascade_____
5 - _____
6 - _____
7 - _____

System Resource Map

PC Make and Model: Intel SE440BX-2_____
Serial Number: 100000_____
Date: 06/09/99 _____

Interrupts (IRQs):   I/O Port Addresses:

0 - Timer Circuits _____   040-04B _____
1 - Keyboard/Mouse Controller_____   060 & 064 ____
2 - 2nd 8259 IRQ Controller _____   0A0-0A1_____
8 - Real-time Clock/CMOS RAM_____   070-071 _____
9 - SMC EtherEZ Ethernet card_____   340-35F _____
10 - _____   _____
11 - Adaptec 1542CF SCSI Adapter (scanner)   334-337*_____
12 - Motherboard Mouse Port _____   060 & 064 ____
13 - Math Coprocessor _____   0F0 _____
14 - Primary IDE (hard disk 1 and 2)_____   1F0-1F7, 3F6___
15 - Secondary IDE (CD-ROM/tape)_____   170-177, 376__
3 - Serial Port 2 (Modem) _____   3F8-3FF_____
4 - Serial Port 1 (COM1) _____   2F8-2FF_____
5 - Sound Blaster 16 Audio _____   220-233 _____
6 - Floppy Controller _____   3F0-3F5 _____
7 - Parallel Port 1 (Printer) _____   378-37F _____

Devices not using interrupts: I/O Port Addresses:

Mono/EGA/VGA Standard Ports _____   3B0-3BB _____
EGA/VGA Standard Ports _____   3C0-3CF_____
CGA/EGA/VGA Standard Ports_____   3D0-3DF_____
ATI Mach 64 video card additional ports ___   102,1CE-1CF,2EC-2EF _
Sound Blaster 16 MIDI port _____   330-331 _____
Sound Blaster 16 Game port (joystick) ___   200-207 _____
Sound Blaster 16 FM synthesizer (music)__   388-38B_____

DMA Channels:

0 - _____
1 - Sound Blaster 16 (8-bit DMA)_____
2 - Floppy Controller _____
3 - Parallel Port 1 (in ECP mode) _____
4 - DMA Channel 0-3 Cascade_____
5 - Sound Blaster 16 (16-bit DMA)_____
6 - Adaptec 1542CF SCSI adapter* ___
7 - _____

Represents a resource setting that had to be changed to resolve a conflict.

After you've completed your system resource map by recording the current settings for hardware, you're ready to solve conflicts.

Resolving Conflicts by Card and Operating System Type

Table 2.22   Guide to Resolving Conflicts

Operating System	Card Type	Notes
Windows 9x/2000	PnP	Use Device Manager to change card settings if possible; remove and reinstall card to redetect card and use new settings if card can't be set manually; if new card can't be detected when installed, remove other PnP cards and install new card first.
	Non-PnP	Use Device Manager to see conflicting devices; manually configure cards to non-conflicting settings by changing jumpers, DIP switches, or rerunning configuration programs.
Other operating systems	Any	*When did the conflict first become apparent?* If the conflict occurred after you installed a new adapter card, that new card probably is causing the conflict. If the conflict occurred after you started using new software, chances are good that the software uses a device that is taxing your system's resources in a new way.
		Are there two similar devices in your system that do not work? For example, if your modem, integrated serial ports, or mouse devices that use a COM port do not work, chances are good that these devices are conflicting with each other.
		Have other people had the same problem? And if so, how did they resolve it? Public forums such as those on CompuServe, Internet newsgroups, and America Online are great places to find other users who might be able to help you solve the conflict. Also check vendor forums for help.
		After you research these questions, make 1 (one!) change to your system configuration, reboot the computer and see if the problem is now resolved. Repeat with a different setting until the problem is solved.
		Test all components to make sure that "fixing" one component didn't cause a conflict with another.

Expansion Slots

If you want to add network, SCSI, modem, or sound capabilities to an existing system or upgrade your video card, you need to understand expansion slots. Expansion slots act as an extension of the system bus and permit you to connect cards with different features to your system.

ISA

ISA (Industry Standard Architecture) expansion slots are the oldest expansion slot design found in current PCs. Eight-bit versions go all the way back to the original IBM PC of 1981. While 8-bit–only ISA slots have faded away, 16-bit ISA slots (introduced with the IBM PC/AT in 1984) are fully pin-compatible with 8-bit ISA cards. See Figures 2.15 and 2.16.

Signal	Pin	Pin	Signal
Ground	B1	A1	-I/O CH CHK
RESET DRV	B2	A2	Data Bit 7
+5 Vdc	B3	A3	Data Bit 6
IRQ 9	B4	A4	Data Bit 5
-5 Vdc	B5	A5	Data Bit 4
DRQ 2	B6	A6	Data Bit 3
-12 Vdc	B7	A7	Data Bit 2
-0 WAIT	B8	A8	Data Bit 1
+12 Vdc	B9	A9	Data Bit 0
Ground	B10	A10	-I/O CH RDY
-SMEMW	B11	A11	AEN
-SMEMR	B12	A12	Address 19
-IOW	B13	A13	Address 18
-IOR	B14	A14	Address 17
-DACK 3	B15	A15	Address 16
DRQ 3	B16	A16	Address 15
-DACK 1	B17	A17	Address 14
DRQ 1	B18	A18	Address 13
-Refresh	B19	A19	Address 12
CLK(8.33MHz)	B20	A20	Address 11
IRQ 7	B21	A21	Address 10
IRQ 6	B22	A22	Address 9
IRQ 5	B23	A23	Address 8
IRQ 4	B24	A24	Address 7
IRQ 3	B25	A25	Address 6
-DACK 2	B26	A26	Address 5
T/C	B27	A27	Address 4
BALE	B28	A28	Address 3
+5 Vdc	B29	A29	Address 2
OSC(14.3MHz)	B30	A30	Address 1
Ground	B31	A31	Address 0

Signal	Pin	Pin	Signal
-MEM CS16	D1	C1	-SBHE
-I/O CS16	D2	C2	Latch Address 23
IRQ 10	D3	C3	Latch Address 22
IRQ 11	D4	C4	Latch Address 21
IRQ 12	D5	C5	Latch Address 20
IRQ 15	D6	C6	Latch Address 19
IRQ 14	D7	C7	Latch Address 18
-DACK 0	D8	C8	Latch Address 17
DRQ 0	D9	C9	-MEMR
-DACK 5	D10	C10	-MEMW
DRQ5	D11	C11	Data Bit 8
-DACK 6	D12	C12	Data Bit 9
DRQ 6	D13	C13	Data Bit 10
-DACK 7	D14	C14	Data Bit 11
DRQ 7	D15	C15	Data Bit 12
+5 Vdc	D16	C16	Data Bit 13
-Master	D17	C17	Data Bit 14
Ground	D18	C18	Data Bit 15

Figure 2.15 Pinouts for the 16-bit ISA bus.

Figure 2.16 shows the orientation and relation of 8-bit and 16-bit ISA bus slots.

8/16-bit ISA Bus Pinouts.

8-bit PC/XT Connector:

Signal	Pin Numbers		Signal
GROUND	B1	A1	-I/O CHK
RESET DRV	B2	A2	DATA 7
+5 Vdc	B3	A3	DATA 6
IRQ 2	B4	A4	DATA 5
-5 Vdc	B5	A5	DATA 4
DRQ 2	B6	A6	DATA 3
-12 Vdc	B7	A7	DATA 2
-CARD SLCT	B8	A8	DATA 1
+12 Vdc	B9	A9	DATA 0
GROUND	B10	A10	-I/O RDY
-SMEMW	B11	A11	AEN
-SMEMR	B12	A12	ADDR 19
-IOW	B13	A13	ADDR 18
-IOR	B14	A14	ADDR 17
-DACK 3	B15	A15	ADDR 16
DRQ 3	B16	A16	ADDR 15
-DACK 1	B17	A17	ADDR 14
DRQ 1	B18	A18	ADDR 13
-REFRESH	B19	A19	ADDR 12
CLK (4.77MHz)	B20	A20	ADDR 11
IRQ 7	B21	A21	ADDR 10
IRQ 6	B22	A22	ADDR 9
IRQ 5	B23	A23	ADDR 8
IRQ 4	B24	A24	ADDR 7
IRQ 3	B25	A25	ADDR 6
-DACK 2	B26	A26	ADDR 5
T/C	B27	A27	ADDR 4
BALE	B28	A28	ADDR 3
+5 Vdc	B29	A29	ADDR 2
OSC (14.3MHz)	B30	A30	ADDR 1
GROUND	B31	A31	ADDR 0

16-bit AT Connector:

Signal	Pin Numbers		Signal
GROUND	B1	A1	-I/O CHK
RESET DRV	B2	A2	DATA 7
+5 Vdc	B3	A3	DATA 6
IRQ 9	B4	A4	DATA 5
-5 Vdc	B5	A5	DATA 4
DRQ 2	B6	A6	DATA 3
-12 Vdc	B7	A7	DATA 2
-OWS	B8	A8	DATA 1
+12 Vdc	B9	A9	DATA 0
GROUND	B10	A10	-I/O RDY
-SMEMW	B11	A11	AEN
-SMEMR	B12	A12	ADDR 19
-IOW	B13	A13	ADDR 18
-IOR	B14	A14	ADDR 17
-DACK 3	B15	A15	ADDR 16
DRQ 3	B16	A16	ADDR 15
-DACK 1	B17	A17	ADDR 14
DRQ 1	B18	A18	ADDR 13
-REFRESH	B19	A19	ADDR 12
CLK (8.33MHz)	B20	A20	ADDR 11
IRQ 7	B21	A21	ADDR 10
IRQ 6	B22	A22	ADDR 9
IRQ 5	B23	A23	ADDR 8
IRQ 4	B24	A24	ADDR 7
IRQ 3	B25	A25	ADDR 6
-DACK 2	B26	A26	ADDR 5
T/C	B27	A27	ADDR 4
BALE	B28	A28	ADDR 3
+5 Vdc	B29	A29	ADDR 2
OSC (14.3MHz)	B30	A30	ADDR 1
GROUND	B31	A31	ADDR 0

Signal	Pin Numbers		Signal
-MEM CS16	D1	C1	-SBHE
-I/O CS16	D2	C2	LADDR 23
IRQ 10	D3	C3	LADDR 22
IRQ 11	D4	C4	LADDR 21
IRQ 12	D5	C5	LADDR 20
IRQ 15	D6	C6	LADDR 19
IRQ 14	D7	C7	LADDR 18
-DACK 0	D8	C8	LADDR 17
DRQ 0	D9	C9	-MEMR
-DACK 5	D10	C10	-MEMW
DRQ 5	D11	C11	DATA 8
-DACK 6	D12	C12	DATA 9
DRQ 6	D13	C13	DATA 10
-DACK 7	D14	C14	DATA 11
DRQ 7	D15	C15	DATA 12
+5 Vdc	D16	C16	DATA 13
-MASTER	D17	C17	DATA 14
GROUND	D18	C18	DATA 15

Figure 2.16 The 8-bit and 16-bit ISA bus connectors.

EISA—A 32-bit Version of ISA

The EISA (Enhanced ISA) bus was developed from the ISA architecture to provide 32-bit data transfers. The EISA expansion slot (introduced in 1988) is a deeper version of ISA, providing a second, offset row of connectors that allows EISA slots to support ISA cards. Figure 2.17 shows the locations of the pins.

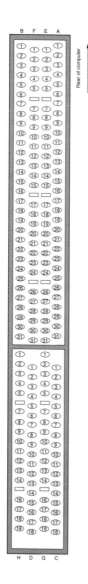

Figure 2.17 The card connector for the EISA bus. The inner connectors were used for the EISA cards, while the outer connectors supported 8-bit and 16-bit ISA cards.

Because of its high cost and limited performance boost over ISA, EISA bus systems have primarily been used for network file servers using 386, 486, and occasionally Pentium-class CPUs.

EISA was introduced as a response to IBM's MicroChannel architecture, which was used primarily on more-advanced models of IBM's PS/2 line from 1987 until the early 1990s. It is now obsolete.

VL-Bus—A Faster 32-bit Version of ISA

Introduced in 1992, the VL-Bus (VESA Local-Bus) was an improved 32-bit version of ISA designed originally to provide faster video card performance on 486-based systems. VL-Bus hard disk adapter cards were also popular. While a few early Pentium-based systems also used VL-Bus slots, the decline of 486-based systems has made this once-popular expansion slot design a dead end.

While most VL-Bus slots were added to an ISA slot, the VL-Bus connector could also be added to an EISA slot. Thus, any VL-Bus slot is also an ISA or an ISA/EISA slot. See Figure 2.18.

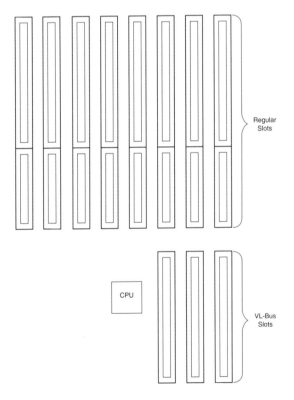

Figure 2.18 An example of VL-Bus slots in an ISA system.

PCI

Intel developed PCI (Peripheral Component Interconnect) in 1992 to eventually replace ISA and its variations. Most PCI slots provide 32-bit transfers, with a 64-bit version of PCI being used in many late-model file servers.

While PCI slots will replace ISA in the near future, virtually all PCs with PCI slots also have ISA slots, as in Figure 2.19.

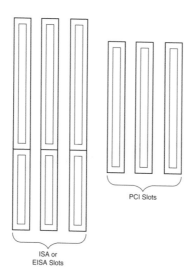

Figure 2.19 Possible configuration of PCI slots in relation to ISA or EISA slots.

AGP

The latest expansion slot design is AGP (Accelerated Graphics Port), introduced in 1996 to provide faster video performance in a dedicated slot. AGP doesn't replace PCI for general purposes, but AGP video cards offer much faster performance than similar PCI cards, and can also "borrow" from main memory for 3D texturing.

A typical Pentium II/III or Super Socket 7 system includes a single AGP slot as well as a mixture of PCI and ISA slots, as Figure 2.20.

Table 2.23 provides a visual quick reference for expansion slots found in modern PCs.

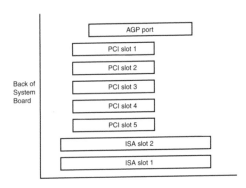

Figure 2.20 The AGP slot is located at the first (inside) slot position on motherboards with an AGP slot. Note the lack of space between the last PCI slot and the first ISA slot. This is called a "combo" or "shared" slot; only one of the slots can actually be used.

Table 2.23	Expansion Slot Quick-Reference Table		
Slot Type	**Bus Speed**	**Bus Width**	**Best Use**
ISA	8.33MHz	8-bit or 16-bit	Modems, serial, parallel ports; will be phased out by early 2000s
EISA	8.33MHz	32-bit with EISA cards; compatible with ISA cards	Obsolete for most uses; works well with server-optimized NIC cards
MCA	10MHz	16-bit or 32-bit	Introduced with IBM MicroChannel PS/2s in 1987; obsolete
VL-Bus	25–33MHz typical; can be run up to 40MHz on some systems	32-bit; slot also usable as ISA	Obsolete; was popular for video cards and IDE hard disk interfaces
PCI	25–33MHz (depends on speed of motherboard)	Most are 32-bit; some 64-bit implementations used on file servers	Video, SCSI, sound, modems. Replacing ISA as general-purpose bus
AGP	66MHz	64-bit	Dedicated high-speed video

Chapter 3

BIOS Configurations and Upgrades

What the BIOS Is and What It Does

The BIOS (basic input/output system) chip on the computer's mother-board is designed to provide the essential interfacing between hardware (such as drives, the clock, the CPU, the chipset, and video) and software (the operating system). While video, some SCSI, and a few IDE add-on cards might also have BIOS chips that help manage those devices, whenever I refer to the computer's *BIOS chip*, I mean the one on the motherboard. The BIOS chip is often referred to as the *ROM BIOS*, because in its traditional form it was a read-only memory chip with contents that could not be changed. Later versions could be reprogrammed with an EEPROM programmer, and beginning in the early 1990s, BIOSes using flash memory (*Flash BIOS*) began to appear. Flash BIOSes can be reprogrammed through software, and virtually all BIOSes on Pentium-class machines and beyond are flash-upgradable.

When a BIOS Update Is Necessary

The following list shows the primary benefits of a ROM BIOS upgrade:

- Adds LS-120 (120MB) floppy drive support (also known as a SuperDrive)

- Adds support for hard drives greater than 8GB

- Adds support for Ultra-DMA/33 or faster IDE hard drives

- Adds support for bootable ATAPI CD-ROM drives

- Adds or improves Plug-and-Play support and compatibility

- Corrects year-2000 and leap-year bugs

- Corrects known bugs or compatibility problems with certain hardware and software

- Adds support for newer types of processors

In general, if your computer is incapable of using all the features of new software or hardware, you might need a BIOS upgrade.

Specific Tests to Determine if Your BIOS Needs an Update

To determine if your BIOS needs to be updated because of hard-drive capacity limitations, see Chapter 4, "Hard Drives".

To determine if your BIOS needs to be updated because of Y2K date-handling problems, see the following section "Y2K BIOS Tests".

To determine if your BIOS needs to be updated because of operating system issues, consult the technical-support Web sites for the operating system.

Y2K BIOS Tests

The number one reason many people are looking into BIOS upgrades right now may be the well-known Y2K problem, which involves the misinterpretation of *00* as a valid date other than *2000*. Systems with a Y2K BIOS problem might see the date 1/1/00 as being 1900 or 1980.

The problem results from the lack of century support in virtually all RTC (real-time clock) chips found in PCs. These RTCs keep dates stored as MM/DD/YY, and the motherboard BIOS is responsible for properly interpreting 1/1/00 as 1/1/2000. A BIOS that does not interpret 1/1/00 correctly will send erroneous dates to the operating system (which may or may not be capable of correcting them) and to applications.

While there are many commercial test programs available from many online and commercial sources, you can perform preliminary screening tests yourself if you don't have test software available. A system that passes these tests might still have obscure Y2K BIOS problems which need addressing; these tests do nothing about Y2K problems that are widespread in both old and new operating systems and application programs. However, any system that fails one or more of these tests needs a Y2K BIOS fix immediately.

Before you perform the following Y2K tests, create an MS-DOS or Windows 9x boot diskette and always start your system with the boot diskette rather than from the hard disk. Because these tests involve changing dates, software licenses could expire and date/time stamps on temporary files will show "illegal" dates if you allow your operating system to boot normally. I suggest using MS-DOS 6.x if possible, because Windows 9x might be capable of compensating for non-compliant dates, especially if it's been updated for Y2K compliance.

After each test, return the date and time to the current correct values.

Perform the tests in the order listed, because they are structured to screen out varying levels of problems.

Power-On BIOS Date Rollover Test

Enter your computer's BIOS setup screens and move to the Date and Time fields.

Enter the following date: 12/31/(19)99

Enter the following time: 23:59:50

Watch the date-rollover. If the date rolls over to 1/1/(20)00, continue to the next test. If the date rolls over to 1/1/1980 or 1/1/1900, the system fails. Get a BIOS update or use alternative fixes listed here.

Power-Off BIOS Date Rollover Test

Enter your computer's BIOS setup screens and move to the Date and Time fields.

Enter the following date: 12/31/(19)99

Enter the following time: 23:58:00

Save the BIOS changes and exit. Leave the system off for at least three minutes. Start up the system, enter the BIOS setup screens and immediately proceed to the date and time fields. If the date is now 1/1/(20)00, continue to the next test. If the date is now 1/1/1980 or 1/1/1900, the system fails. Get a BIOS update or use alternative fixes listed here.

Power-On DOS Date Rollover Test

Insert the boot diskette and boot the computer to an A:> command prompt.

Enter the Date and Time commands and verify that the date and time are set to current values.

Use the Date command to enter the following date: 12/31/(19)99

Use the Time command to enter the following time: 23:59:30

Wait one minute and run Date again. If the date displayed is any value other than 1/1/2000, the system fails.

Power-Off DOS Date Rollover Test

Insert the boot diskette and boot the computer to an A:> command prompt.

Enter the Date and Time commands and verify that the date and time are set to current values.

Use the Date command to enter the following date: 12/31/(19)99

Use the Time command to enter the following time: 23:58:00

Shut down the computer immediately. Leave the boot diskette in the drive and wait three minutes before rebooting the system from the boot diskette.

After rebooting, use the `Date` command to view the computer date. If it is any date other than 1/1/2000 , the system fails.

To test for year 2000 leap-year compliance, use the same tests given earlier, but substitute `2/28/2000` for `12/31/1999`. A system that performs proper leap-year rollover will roll to 2/29/2000. A system that fails the leap-year rollover will roll to 3/1/2000.

Fixing BIOS Limitations—BIOS Fixes and Alternatives

Use Table 3.1 to determine what options you can follow if a BIOS update isn't possible, depending on the BIOS problem noted.

Table 3.1	Alternatives to BIOS Upgrades		
Problem	**Alternative Fix**	**Benefits of Alternative Fix**	**Limitations of Alternative Fix**
Y2K date rollover	Install Y2K-compliant BIOS card	Provides hardware solution to non-compliant BIOS; can be combined with fix for hard disk capacity limitations	Uses an ISA slot; doesn't handle problems with direct access to RTC that may be performed by some operating systems and applications
	Install Y2K-compliant BIOS and RTC card	Provides hardware solution for both BIOS and RTC Y2K	Uses an ISA slot; some versions require that drivers be installed for operating system in use
	Install Y2K -compliant TSR or device driver	Low-cost or free solution that avoids opening system	Can be bypassed by booting off floppy; may not handle all Y2K clock rollover problems; can be removed from boot process; not available for all operating systems
IDE hard disk capacity limitations	See Chapter 4 for details of these fixes		
Complete solution	Replace motherboard	Provides both brand-new BIOS and new motherboard features at a price often just slightly higher than a third-party BIOS upgrade	System must use standard MB form factor; mix of ISA and PCI/AGP slots may mean some existing cards won't fit since latest motherboards have more PCI than ISA slots; time-consuming hardware install; requires time-consuming redetection and configuration of hardware drivers in operating system

How BIOS Updates Are Performed

There are two different ways of updating a motherboard BIOS:

With older systems, a physical *chip swap* (also called a *BIOS upgrade*) is necessary. The original BIOS chip is removed, and a new BIOS is inserted in its place. The new BIOS must be customized to match the old system's motherboard and chipset, use its existing CPU, and provide the enhanced features specified by the upgrade BIOS maker. The typical cost range is around $60–90 for a single BIOS chip.

With newer systems that have a flash-upgradable BIOS, the update software is downloaded and installed onto a diskette, which is used to boot the computer. Then, the new BIOS code is copied to the BIOS chip in a process that takes about three to five minutes. If the BIOS update comes from a source *other* than the original system or motherboard maker, it will also cost as much as $90 for the update.

In either case, the system might need to be reconfigured, especially if the new BIOS was physically installed, or if either a chip-based or flash-based BIOS is a different brand of BIOS than the original.

Where BIOS Updates Come From

The best (and cheapest!) place to get a BIOS update is from your motherboard or system vendor. Most major system manufacturers offer free BIOS updates for their systems with flash BIOS chips on their Web sites. For *clone* systems with motherboards from various producers, see the "Determining What BIOS You Have" section later in this chapter.

A second source for BIOS updates is from one of the following companies:

For systems that originally used the Phoenix BIOS, contact Micro Firmware (www.firmware.com or 800-767-5465). Micro Firmware typically supplies updated Phoenix flash BIOS code on diskette for systems they support. See the Web site for the current list of supported systems and motherboards.

For systems that originally used the Award, AMI, MR BIOS, or Phoenix BIOS (including systems not supported by Micro Firmware), contact Unicore Software (www.unicore.com or 800-800-BIOS). Unicore may supply the update on diskette or as a replacement MR BIOS chip. Contact these vendors for details and prices, which vary by system.

Precautions to Take Before Updating a BIOS

Use the following checklist to be safe, not sorry, when updating a BIOS.

First, back up your data. An "almost working" BIOS that doesn't quite work with your hard drive can blow away your data.

Back up your current BIOS code if you can. Some BIOS update loaders offer this option but others don't. As an alternative, some BIOS chips keep a "mini-BIOS" onboard that can be reactivated in the event that a botched update destroys the main BIOS. Some motherboards have a jumper that can be used to switch to the backup; check your system documentation. For others, check the Micro Firmware Web site for its "Flash BIOS Recovery Disks" page and see if your motherboard is listed. If the BIOS update isn't completed properly, you could have a dead system that will need a trip to the manufacturer. See "How to Recover from a Failed BIOS Update Procedure" later in this chapter for a typical recovery procedure.

Record your hard drive configuration information, including the following:

- Cylinders

- Heads

- Sectors per Track

- Translation (Normal, LBA [greater than 504MB], Large, etc.)

If you are switching to a different brand of BIOS, you might need to re-enter this information.

Record other non-standard BIOS settings, such as hard disk transfer rate settings, built-in serial and parallel port settings, etc.

Read carefully and completely the information provided with the flash BIOS download or chip-type BIOS update kit. Check online or call the BIOS manufacturer if you have any questions before you ruin your BIOS.

Check to see if your system has a *write-protect* setting jumper on the motherboard that must be adjusted to allow a BIOS update to take place. Some motherboards disable BIOS updates by default to protect your system's BIOS from unauthorized changes. Set your mother-board to allow the change before you install the flash BIOS update, and reset the protection after the update is complete.

How to Recover from a Failed BIOS Update Procedure

Most motherboards with soldered-in flash ROMs have a special BIOS Recovery procedure that can be performed. This hinges on a special unerasable part of the flash ROM that is reserved for this purpose.

In the unlikely event that a flash upgrade is interrupted catastrophically, the BIOS may be left in an unusable state. Recovering from this condition requires the following steps. A minimum of a power supply, a speaker, and a floppy drive configured as drive A: should be attached to the motherboard for this procedure to work.

1. Change the Flash Recovery jumper to the recovery mode position. Virtually all Intel motherboards and many third-party motherboards have a jumper or switch for BIOS recovery, which is normally labeled "Recover/Normal".

2. Install the bootable BIOS upgrade disk you previously created to do the flash upgrade into drive A: and reboot the system.

   Because of the small amount of code available in the nonerasable flash boot block area, no video prompts are available to direct the procedure. In other words, you will see nothing onscreen. In fact, it is not even necessary for a video card to be connected for this procedure to work. The procedure can be monitored by listening to the speaker and looking at the floppy drive LED. When the system beeps and the floppy drive LED is lit, the system is copying the BIOS recovery code into the flash device.

3. As soon as the drive LED goes off, the recovery should be complete. Power the system off.

4. Change the flash recovery jumper back to the default position for normal operation.

When you power the system back on, the new BIOS should be installed and functional. However, you might want to leave the BIOS upgrade floppy in drive A: and check to see that the proper BIOS version was installed.

> **Note**
>
> Note that this BIOS recovery procedure is often the fastest way to update a large number of machines, especially if you are performing other upgrades at the same time. This is how it is normally done in a system assembly or production environment.

Plug-and-Play BIOS

The role of the traditional BIOS was to manage the essential devices in the system: the hard drive, floppy drive, video, parallel and serial ports, and keyboard and system timer. Other devices were left to fight for the remaining IRQs and other hardware resources listed in Chapter 2, " System Components and Configuration". When Windows 95 was introduced, the role of the BIOS changed dramatically. To support Windows 95, the Plug-and-Play BIOS was introduced, changing how cards were installed and managed. Table 3.2 compares a Plug-and-Play (PnP) BIOS to a conventional BIOS.

Table 3.2   Plug-and-Play BIOS Versus Conventional BIOS

Task	Conventional BIOS	Plug-and Play BIOS
Hardware configuration	Motherboard-based devices and video only	All PnP devices as well as motherboard devices
Configuration type	Static (fixed settings)	Dynamic (settings can be altered as different devices are installed)
Configuration method	Manual configuration	Manual, BIOS-assisted, or operating system assisted
Operating system relationship to BIOS	Accepts all BIOS settings without alteration	Receives PnP device information from BIOS and may alter settings as required

PnP BIOS Configuration Options

While PnP BIOSes vary widely in their features, the following settings are typical. Use the list in Table 3.3 along with the tables that follow to help you make configuration changes when necessary.

Resource Configuration

The Resource Configuration menu is used for configuring the memory and interrupt usage of non–Plug-and-Play (legacy) ISA bus-based devices. Table 3.3 shows the functions and options found in a typical modern BIOS.

Table 3.3   Typical Resource Configuration Menu*

Feature	Options	Description
Memory Reservation	C800 CBFF Available (default) I Reserved CC00 CFFF Available (default) I Reserved D000 D3FF Available (default) I Reserved D400 D7FF Available (default) I Reserved D800 DBFF Available (default) I Reserved DC00 DFFF Available (default) I Reserved	Reserves specific upper memory blocks for use by legacy ISA devices.

Feature	Options	Description
IRQ	IRQ 3 Available (default) I Reserved	Reserves specific IRQs
Reservation	IRQ 4 Available (default) I Reserved	for use by legacy ISA
	IRQ 5 Available (default) I Reserved	devices. An asterisk (*)
	IRQ 7 Available (default) I Reserved	displayed next to an IRQ
	IRQ 10 Available (default) I Reserved	indicates an IRQ conflict.
	IRQ 11 Available (default) I Reserved	

Based on the Phoenix BIOS used by the Intel SE440BX2 motherboard. Used by permission of Intel Corporation.

Note that these settings are only for legacy (non–Plug-and-Play) ISA devices. For all Plug-and-Play ISA devices as well as PCI devices (which are Plug and Play by default), these resources are instead configured by the operating system or by software that comes with the cards.

Setting these resources here does not actually control the legacy ISA device; that usually must be done by moving jumpers on the card. By setting the resource as reserved here, you are telling the Plug-and-Play operating system that the reserved resources are off-limits, so it won't accidentally set a Plug-and-Play device to use the same resource as a legacy ISA device. Reserving resources in this manner is sometimes required because the Plug-and-Play software cannot detect all legacy ISA devices and therefore won't know what settings the device might be using.

In a system with no legacy devices, it is not necessary to reserve any resources via this menu.

Some boards have additional configuration options for the Plug-and-Play (PnP) BIOS features as well as the PCI bus. These features are largely chipset dependent, but some common examples are shown in Table 3.4.

Table 3.4 Typical PnP and PCI Options*	
DMA n Assigned to	When resources are controlled manually, assign each system DMA channel as one of the following types, depending on the type of device using the interrupt:
	• Legacy ISA devices compliant with the original PC AT bus specification, requiring a specific DMA channel
	• PCI/ISA PnP devices compliant with the Plug-and-Play standard, whether designed for PCI or ISA bus architecture.
PCI IRQ Activated by	Leave the IRQ trigger set at Level unless the PCI device assigned to the interrupt specifies edge-triggered interrupts.
PCI IDE IRQ Map to	This field enables you to select PCI IDE IRQ mapping or PC AT (ISA) interrupts. If your system does not have one or two PCI IDE connectors on the system board, select values according to the type of IDE interface(s) installed in your system (PCI or ISA). Standard ISA interrupts for IDE channels are IRQ 14 for primary and IRQ 15 for secondary.

(continues)

Table 3.4   Typical PnP and PCI Options* Continued

Primary/Secondary IDE INT#	Each PCI peripheral connection is capable of activating up to four interrupts: INT# A, INT# B, INT# C, and INT# D. By default, a PCI connection is assigned INT# A. Assigning INT# B has no meaning unless the peripheral device requires two interrupt services rather than one. Because the PCI IDE inter-face in the chipset has two channels, it requires two interrupt services. The primary and secondary IDE INT# fields default to values appropriate for two PCI IDE channels, with the primary PCI IDE channel having a lower interrupt than the secondary.

Note that all single-function PCI cards normally use INT# A, and each of these must be assigned to a different and unique ISA interrupt request (IRQ). |
Used Mem base addr	Select a base address for the memory area used by any peripheral that requires high memory.
Used Mem Length	Select a length for the memory area specified in the previous field. This field does not appear if no base address is specified.
Assign IRQ for USB	Select Enabled if your system has a USB controller and you have one or more USB devices connected. If you are not using your system's USB controller, select Disabled to free the IRQ resource.

*Based on the Phoenix BIOS used by the Intel SE440BX2 motherboard. Used by permission of Intel Corporation.

When to Use the PnP BIOS Configuration Options

In an ideal situation involving PnP-aware operating systems such as Windows 9x or 2000, a computer with a PnP BIOS and a PnP device, the BIOS detects the PnP device and Windows configures it without user intervention. Table 3.5 lists the circumstances under which you might need to use PnP BIOS configuration options.

Table 3.5   Solving Configuration Problems with the PnP BIOS Configuration Options

Problem	Solution	Notes
Legacy (non-PnP) card needs particular IRQ or DMA setting already in use by PnP device	Set DMA and IRQ used by legacy card to "ISA" option in BIOS	This prevents PnP devices from using the resource; verify legacy card setting matches BIOS selections
Windows 9x/2000 is not detecting and configuring PnP devices not needed at boot time (such as modems, printers, etc.)	Set "Plug and Play Aware Operating System" option to "Yes" in BIOS	
PCI video card is assigned an IRQ that you need for another device	Set "Assign IRQ to VGA" option to "No" in BIOS	This frees up the IRQ with-out ill effects in most cases; may not work if the video card is used for MPEG movie playback
New PnP device cannot be detected by system	Set "PCI Slot x IRQ Priority" to desired (unused) IRQ; install card into designated PCI slot	If setting the IRQ for the PCI slot doesn't work, remove all non-essential PnP cards, install new PnP card first, and then reinstall others

Other BIOS Troubleshooting Tips

Use Table 3.6 to help solve some other typical system problems through BIOS configuration settings.

Table 3.6 Troubleshooting Common BIOS-related System Problems		
Problem	**Solution**	**Notes**
Can't access system because password(s) for startup or setup access aren't known	Passwords are stored in CMOS non-volatile RAM (NVRAM) and are configured through BIOS	Remove battery on motherboard and wait for all CMOS settings to be lost or use MB jumper called "clear CMOS"; before clearing CMOS, view bootup configuration information and note hard drive and other configuration information, because all setup information must be re-entered after CMOS is cleared
System wastes time detecting hard drives at every bootup	Disable automatic drive detection in BIOS; "lock in" settings for drives by using "detect drives" option in BIOS	
System drops network or modem connection when system is idle	Power management not set correctly for IRQs in use by modem or network card	Determine which IRQs are used by devices and adjust power management for those devices; disable power management in BIOS
Parallel or serial port conflicts	Change configuration in BIOS	See Chapters 6 and 7 for details

For more about troubleshooting and adjusting BIOS configuration settings, see Chapter 5 of *Upgrading and Repairing PCs, Eleventh Edition*, published by Que.

Determining What BIOS You Have

It's important to know what BIOS brand and version a computer has for the following reasons:

In the event of a boot failure, BIOS error codes, which vary by brand and model, can be used to help you find the cause of the problem and lead you to a solution.

Knowing what BIOS brand and version you have can help you get help from the BIOS or system vendor for certain chipset configuration issues.

To determine what BIOS you have, use the following methods:

- Watch your system startup screen for information about the BIOS brand and version, such as "Award BIOS v4.51PG".

- Use a hardware test-and-reporting utility such as Microsoft's venerable MSD.EXE, AMIDiag, CheckIt, or others.

Note that the best source for machine-specific information about error codes and other BIOS issues is your system manufacturer. Major vendors such as IBM, Dell, Compaq, Gateway, Hewlett-Packard, and others maintain excellent Web sites that list specific information for your system. However, if you are working with a "white-box" clone system made from generic components, BIOS-level information might be the best information you can get.

Determining the Motherboard Manufacturer for BIOS Upgrades

While knowing the BIOS brand and version is sufficient for troubleshooting a system that won't start, solving problems with issues such as year-2000 compliance, large hard disk support, and power management requires knowing exactly which motherboard you have and who produced it. Because motherboard manufacturers tailor BIOS code to the needs of each motherboard model, the motherboard or system vendor, not the BIOS vendor, is the source to turn to for BIOS upgrades and other BIOS configuration issues.

Identifying Motherboards with AMI BIOS

Motherboards using AMI BIOS versions built from 1991 to the present (AMI's High-Flex BIOS or WinBIOS) display a long string of numbers at the bottom of the first screen displayed when the system is powered on or restarted:

    51-0411-001771-00111111-071595-82439HX-F

Interpret a number such as this one with the following numerical key (see Table 3.7):

    AB-CCCC-DDDDDD-EFGHIJKL-mmddyy-MMMMMMMM-N

Table 3.7 AB-CCcc-DDDDDD-EFGHIJKL-mmddyy-MMMMMMMM-N	
Position	**Description**
A	Processor Type:
	0 = 8086 or 8088
	2 = 286
	3 = 386
	4 = 486
	5 = Pentium
	6 = Pentium Pro/II

Position	Description
B	Size of BIOS:
	0 = 64K BIOS
	1 = 128K BIOS
CCcc	Major and minor BIOS version number
DDDDDD	Manufacturer license code reference number
	0036xx = AMI 386 motherboard, xx = Series #
	0046xx = AMI 486 motherboard, xx = Series #
	0056xx = AMI Pentium motherboard, xx = Series #
	0066xx = AMI Pentium Pro motherboard, xx = Series #
	(for other numbers see the following note)
E	1 = Halt on POST Error
F	1 = Initialize CMOS every boot
G	1 = Block pins 22 and 23 of the keyboard controller
H	1 = Mouse support in BIOS/keyboard controller
I	1 = Wait for F1 key on POST errors
J	1 = Display floppy error during POST
K	1 = Display video error during POST
L	1 = Display keyboard error during POST
mmddyy	BIOS Date, mm/dd/yy
MMMMMMMM	Chipset identifier or BIOS name
N	Keyboard controller version number

Note

Use the following resources to determine the manufacturer of non-AMI motherboards using the AMI BIOS:

AMI has a listing of U.S. and non-U.S. motherboard manufacturers at: http://www.ami.com/amibios/support/bios.strings.html.

A more detailed listing, including complete identification of particular motherboard models, is available at Wim's BIOS page: www.ping.be/bios. This site also has links to motherboard manufacturers for BIOS upgrades.

Identifying Motherboards with Award BIOS

Motherboards with the Award Software BIOS also use a numerical code, although the structure is different than that for the AMI Hi-Flex BIOS

A typical Award BIOS ID:

> 2A59I**AB**DC-00

The sixth and seventh characters (bolded for emphasis)indicate the motherboard manufacturer, while the eighth character can be used for the model number or the motherboard family (various motherboards using the same chipset).

Note

For lookup tables of these codes, see the following Web sites:

Award Software's official table for manufacturers only is available at: www.phoenix.com/pcuser/bios-award-vendors.html.

An expanded list, also containing chipset information (stored in the first five characters of the Award BIOS ID), is available at: www.ping.be/bios/numbers.shtml.

Identifying Motherboards with Phoenix or Microid Research BIOS

Unfortunately, neither Phoenix nor Microid Research (MR BIOS) use any type of a standardized motherboard ID number system.

For systems using a Phoenix BIOS, see if your motherboard or system is listed on the Micro Firmware BIOS upgrades page. Links from this page for Intel and Micronics motherboards list the codes that show up onscreen during boot. Match these codes to your system and you might be able to use a Micro Firmware upgrade. Most MR BIOS (Microid Research BIOS) installations are done as upgrades rather than in original equipment. See the list of supported chipsets (identified by chipset brand and model, not motherboard vendor) and motherboards using the Intel's Triton-series chipsets to see if your system can use an MR BIOS.

Accessing the BIOS Setup Programs

The BIOS is configured in one of several ways. Early computers such as the IBM PC and PC/XT used DIP switches on the motherboard to set a limited range of BIOS options, including memory size and the number of floppy disk drives. The IBM PC/AT introduced a diskette-based configuration utility to cope with the many additional options on 286-based CPUs. Since the late 1980s, most computers have had their BIOS Setup programs incorporated into the BIOS chip itself. The Setup program is accessed on these systems by pressing a key or key combination early in the system startup procedure. Most recent computers display the correct keystroke(s) to use during the system startup. If not, use Table 3.8 to learn the keystrokes used to start common BIOS types.

Table 3.8	Common Keystrokes Used to Access BIOS Setup Program	
BIOS	**Keystrokes**	**Notes**
Phoenix BIOS	Ctrl+Alt+Esc	
	Ctrl+Alt+F1	
	Ctrl+Alt+S	
	Ctrl+Alt+Enter	
	Ctrl+Alt+F11	
	Ctrl+Alt+Ins	
Award BIOS	Ctrl+Alt+Esc	
	Esc	
AMI BIOS	Del	
IBM BIOS	Ctrl+Alt+Ins*F1	*Early notebook models; press when cursor is in upper-right corner of screen
Compaq BIOS	F10*	Keystroke actually loads Compaq Setup program from hard disk partition; press when cursor is in upper-right corner of screen

---

Note

See Chapter 5 of *Upgrading and Repairing PCs, Eleventh Edition*, published by Que, to see how a typical BIOS Setup program operates.

How the BIOS Reports Errors

The BIOS will use three methods for reporting errors:

Beep codes, error/status codes, and onscreen messages. Error/status codes must be read with a special interface board, whereas the others require no special equipment.

BIOS Beep Codes and Their Purposes

Virtually all systems make a polite "beep" noise when started, but most systems have a special series of beep codes that serve the following purposes:

Beeps alert you to serious system problems, many of which can prevent your system from even starting (a so-called *fatal errors*) or from working to its full potential (a so-called *non-fatal error).

Because most fatal and many non-fatal errors take place before the video subsystem is initialized (or may indicate the video isn't work-ing), beeps can be used to determine the cause of the problem.

A system that can't start and is reporting a problem with beep codes will give the code once, and then halt. To hear the code again, restart the computer.

Use the following tables of beep codes to determine why your system will not start. To solve the problem reported by the beep codes, repair or replace the device listed in the description. If your repair or replacement has solved the problem, the beep code will no longer sound when you restart the system.

For errors involving removable devices (socketed chips, memory, or video), an easy fix is to remove and replace the item, because a device that's not securely in its socket will cause the test to fail.

AMI BIOS Beep Codes

Note

AMI BIOS beep codes used by permission of American Megatrends, Inc.

Beeps	Error Message	Description
1	DRAM Refresh Failure	The memory refresh circuitry on the motherboard is faulty.
2	Parity Error	A parity error occurred in system memory.
3	Base 64K (First Bank) Memory Failure	Memory failure in the first bank of memory.
4	System Timer Failure	Memory failure in the first bank of memory, or Timer 1 on the motherboard is not functioning.
5	Processor Error	The processor on the motherboard generated an error.
6	Keyboard Controller Gate A20 Failure	The keyboard controller might be bad. The BIOS cannot switch to protected mode.
7	Virtual Mode Processor Exception Interrupt Error	The processor generated an exception interrupt.
8	Display Memory Read/Write Error	The system video adapter is either missing or its memory is faulty.
9	ROM Checksum Error	ROM checksum value does not match the value encoded in BIOS.
10	CMOS Shutdown Register Read/Write Error	The shutdown register for CMOS RAM failed.
11	Cache Error/L2 Cache Bad	The L2 cache is faulty.
1 long, 3 short	Conventional/extended memory failure	The motherboard memory is faulty.
1 long, 8 short	Display/retrace test failed	The video card is faulty; try reseating or moving to a different slot.

Award BIOS Beep Codes

Currently there is only one beep code in the Award BIOS. A single long beep followed by two short beeps indicates that a video error has occurred and the BIOS cannot initialize the video screen to display any additional information.

Phoenix BIOS Beep Codes

Note

Phoenix BIOS beep codes used by permission of Phoenix Technologies, Ltd.

Beeps	Port 80h Code	Explanation
1-2-2-3	16h	BIOS ROM checksum
1-3-1-1	20h	Test DRAM refresh
1-3-1-3	22h	Test keyboard controller
1-3-3-1	28h	Autosize DRAM
1-3-3-2	29h	Initialize POST memory manager
1-3-3-3	2Ah	Clear 512KB base RAM
1-3-4-1	2Ch	RAM failure on address line xxxx
1-3-4-3	2Eh	RAM failure on data bits xxxx of low byte of memory bus
1-4-1-1	30h	RAM failure on data bits xxxx of high byte of memory bus
2-1-2-2	45h	POST device initialization
2-1-2-3	46h	Check ROM copyright notice
2-2-3-1	58h	Test for unexpected interrupts
2-2-4-1	5Ch	Test RAM between 512 and 640KB
1-2	98h	Search for option ROMs. One long, two short beeps on checksum failure

IBM BIOS Beep and Alphanumeric Error Codes

After completing the power-on self test (POST), an audio code indicates either a normal condition or that one of several errors has occurred.

Note

IBM BIOS and Alphanumeric error codes used by permission of IBM.

Audio Code	Sound Graph	Description
1 short beep	•	Normal POST—system okay
2 short beeps	••	POST error—error code on display

(continues)

Audio Code	Sound Graph	Description
No beep		Power supply, system board
Continuous beep	——————	Power supply, system board
Repeating short beeps	••••••	Power supply, system board
1 long, 1 short beep	—•	System board
1 long, 2 short beeps	—••	Video adapter (MDA/CGA)
1 long, 3 short beeps	—•••	Video adapter (EGA/VGA)
3 long beeps	– – –	3270 keyboard card

Microid Research Beep Codes

The MR BIOS generates patterns of high and low beeps to signal an error condition.

> **Note**
>
> MR BIOS beep codes used by permission of Phoenix Technologies, Ltd.

Port 80h Code	Beep Codes	Error Messages
03h	LH-LLL	ROM-BIOS Checksum Failure
04h	LH-HLL	DMA Page Register Failure
05h	LH-LHL	Keyboard Controller Selftest Failure
08h	LH-HHL	Memory Refresh Circuitry Failure
09h	LH-LLH	Master (16 bit) DMA Controller Failure
09h	LH-HLH	Slave (8 bit) DMA Controller Failure
0Ah	LH-LLLL	Base 64K Pattern Test Failure
0Ah	LH-HLLL	Base 64K Parity Circuitry Failure
0Ah	LH-LHLL	Base 64K Parity Error
0Ah	LH-HHLL	Base 64K Data Bus Failure
0Ah	LH-LLHL	Base 64K Address Bus Failure
0Ah	LH-HLHL	Base 64K Block Access Read Failure
0Ah	LH-LHHL	Base 64K Block Access Read/Write Failure
0Bh	LH-HHHL	Master 8259 (Port 21) Failure
0Bh	LH-LLLH	Slave 8259 (Port A1) Failure
0Ch	LH-HLLH	Master 8259 (Port 20) Interrupt Address Error
0Ch	LH-LHLH	Slave 8259 (Port A0) Interrupt Address Error
0Ch	LH-HHLH	8259 (Port 20/A0) Interrupt Address Error
0Ch	LH-LLHH	Master 8259 (Port 20) Stuck Interrupt Error
0Ch	LH-HLHH	Slave 8259 (Port A0) Stuck Interrupt Error

Port 80h Code	Beep Codes	Error Messages
0Ch	LH-LHHH	System Timer 8254 CH0/IRQ 0 Interrupt Failure
0Dh	LH-HHHH	8254 Channel 0 (System Timer) Failure
0Eh	LH-LLLLH	8254 Channel 2 (Speaker) Failure
0Eh	LH-HLLLH	8254 OUT2 (Speaker Detect) Failure
0Fh	LH-LHLLH	CMOS RAM Read/Write Test Failure
0Fh	LH-HHLLH	RTC Periodic Interrupt/IRQ 8 Failure
10h	LH-LLHLH	Video ROM Checksum Failure at Address XXXX, Mono Card Memory Error at Address XXXX, Mono Card Memory Address Line Error at Address XXXX, Color Graphics Card Memory Error at Address XXXX, Color Graphics Card Address Line Error at Address XXXX
11h	none	Real Time Clock (RTC) Battery is Discharged
11h	none	Battery Backed Memory (CMOS) is Corrupt
12h	LH-HLHLH	Keyboard Controller Failure
14h 18h 19h	LH-LHHLH	Memory Parity Error
14h 18h 19h	LH-HHHLH	I/O Channel Error
14h 18h 19h	none	RAM Pattern Test Failed at XXXX, Parity Circuit Failure in Bank XXXX, Data Bus Test Failed: Address XXXX, Address Line Test Failed at XXXX, Block Access Read Failure at Address XXXX, Block Access Read/Write Failure: Address XXXX, Banks Decode to Same Location: XXXX and YYYY
12h 15h	none	Keyboard Error - Stuck Key Keyboard Failure or no Keyboard Present
17h	LH-LLLHH	A20 Test Failure Due to 8042 Timeout
17h	LH-HLLHH	A20 Gate Stuck in Disabled State (A20=0)
17h	none	A20 Gate Stuck in Asserted State (A20 Follows CPU)
1Ah	LH-LHLHH	Real Time Clock (RTC) is Not Updating
1Ah	none	Real Time Clock (RTC) Settings are Invalid
1Eh	none	Diskette CMOS Configuration is Invalid, Diskette Controller Failure, Diskette Drive A: Failure, Diskette Drive B: Failure
1Fh	none	Fixed Disk CMOS Configuration is Invalid, Fixed Disk C:(80) Failure, Fixed Disk D:(81) Failure, Please Wait for Fixed Disk to Spin Up
20h	none	Fixed Disk, Diskette, Serial Port, Parallel Port, Video, Memory, or Numeric Coprocessor Configuration Change
21h	none	System Key is in Locked Position - Turn Key to Unlocked Position
29h	none	Adapter ROM Checksum Failure at Address XXXX

Note for beep codes: L=low tone and H=high tone

Reading BIOS Error Codes

Because beep codes can indicate only some of the problems in a system at startup, most BIOSes also output a series of status codes during the boot procedure. These codes are sent to an I/O port address that can be read by specialized diagnostic cards which you can purchase from many different vendors. These "POST cards" (so named from the power-on self test) feature a two-digit LED panel that will display the status codes output by the BIOS. The simpler POST cards are "hard-wired" to pick up signals from the most commonly used I/O port address 80hex, but more expensive models can be adjusted with jumper blocks to use other addresses used by certain BIOSes (such as Compaq).

These cards are normally sold with manuals that list the error/status codes. While the cards are durable, the codes can go out of date. To get an updated list of codes, contact the system or BIOS vendor's Web site.

Most POST cards have been based on the ISA bus, but the latest models are now being made to fit into PCI slots, because ISA is becoming obsolete.

Onscreen Error Messages

An onscreen error message is often the easiest of the error methods to understand, because you don't need to count beeps or open the system to install a POST card. However, since some systems use numeric error codes, and even "plain English" codes need interpretation, these messages can still be a challenge to interpret. Because the video circuits are tested after components like the motherboard, CPU, and BIOS, an onscreen error message is usually indicative of a less-serious error than one that is reported with beep codes.

Interpreting Error Codes and Messages

Since beep codes, error/status codes, and onscreen messages vary a great deal by BIOS vendor (and sometimes BIOS model), you must know what BIOS a system has before you can choose the correct table. With major-brand systems (and some others), you'll typically find a list of error codes and messages in the system documentation. You can also contact the BIOS or system vendors' Web sites for this information, or check on the CD included with *Upgrading and Repairing PCs, Eleventh Edition*, published by Que.

Chapter 4

Hard Drives and Interfaces

Understanding Hard Disk Terminology

When installing IDE hard disks in particular, three parameters must be indicated in the BIOS Setup program to define a hard disk.

> **Note**
>
> Understanding how hard drives store data is an enormous topic. If you'd like to learn more, see Chapters 9 and 10 of *Upgrading and Repairing PCs, Eleventh Edition*.

Heads, Sectors per Track, and Cylinders

If this information is not accurately listed in the BIOS configuration, the full capacity of the drive will not be available unless special hard disk drivers or supplementary BIOS cards are used. Whenever possible, the computer's own ROM BIOS should fully support the drive's capacity.

Hard Drive Heads

A hard drive is comprised of one or more platters, normally made of aluminum but occasionally made of glass. These platters are covered with a thin rigid film of magnetized material. The magnetic structures of the platters are read or changed by read/write heads that move across the surface of the platters but are separated from it by a thin cushion of air. Virtually all platters are read from both sides.

Sectors per Track

The magnetic structures stored on the hard disk platters are organized into sectors of 512 data bytes each, plus additional areas in each sector for identifying the sector location on the hard disk. These sectors form concentric circles numbering from the outside of each platter to the hub area of the platter.

Cylinders

The third factor used to calculate the size of the hard disk is the number of cylinders on the hard disk. The identically positioned tracks on each side of every platter together make up a cylinder.

The BIOS calculates the size of the hard disk in MB or more often today, GB from the number of cylinders, the number of heads, and the number of sectors per track. Most BIOSes make this calculation in binary MB or GB (the same way as the hard disk preparation program FDISK does), but a few make the calculation in decimal MB or GB (see Chapter 1, "General Technical Reference," for the differences in these numbering methods). BIOSes that use decimal MB or GB calculations will report the size of the drive the same way that drive manufacturers do. Either way, the same number of bytes will be available *if* the drive is fully and accurately handled by the ROM BIOS and operating system. Most recent and current drives print the cylinder, head, and sectors per track information (collectively called the drive's *geometry*) on a label on the top of the drive for easy reference during installation.

Note that all three elements of the drive geometry are in reality logical, not physical, on IDE drives. This factor explains why the geometry can be translated (see the following), and why some IDE drives in older machines are working, despite being installed with "incorrect" geometries.

IDE Hard Drive Identification

IDE (Integrated Drive Electronics), more properly called ATA drives (AT Attachment), are the overwhelming favorite for client PC installations. While SCSI hard drives (see the following) offer benefits for network and high-performance workstation use, the combination of constantly-improving performance, rock bottom pricing per MB (under 2 cents and falling!), and enormous capacities (up to 20GB and climbing) will continue to make IDE/ATA drives the choice of most users. Figure 4.1 shows the typical IDE drive connectors.

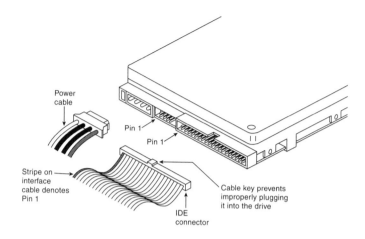

Figure 4.1 Typical ATA (IDE) hard drive connectors.

Master and Slave Drives

As Figure 4.2 demonstrates, virtually every IDE drive interface is designed to handle two drives with a single 40-pin interface cable.

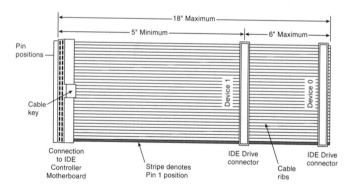

Figure 4.2 ATA (IDE) cable.

Because the cable has no twist, unlike a typical 34-pin floppy inter-face cable, jumper blocks must be used on each hard drive to dis-tinguish between the first, or "master," drive on the cable and the second, or "slave," drive on the cable.

Most IDE drives can be configured with four possible settings:

- Master (single-drive), also called Single

- Master (dual-drive)

- Slave (dual-drive)

- Cable Select

For virtually all systems, the Cable Select setting can be ignored, because it must be used with a non-standard IDE cable. Thus, there are only three settings that are really used, as seen in the Table 4.1.

| **Table 4.1   Jumper Settings for Typical ATA IDE-Compatible Drives** | | | |
Jumper Name	Single-Drive	Dual-Drive Master	Dual-Drive Slave
Master (M/S)	On	On	Off
Slave Present (SP)	Off	On	Off

Use Table 4.1 as a general guideline only. Follow your drive manufacturer's recommendations if they vary.

The jumpers on the hard drive may be located on the back of the drive (between the power and data connectors) or on the bottom of the drive. Typical hard disk jumpers are shown in Figure 4.3.

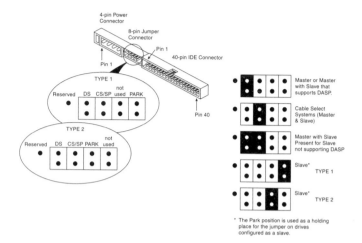

Figure 4.3 ATA (IDE) drive jumpers.

Breaking the 504MB (528 Million Byte) Drive Barrier

Because IDE was developed in the late 1980s, the combination of MS-DOS's limit of 1,024 cylinders, the standard BIOS's limit of 16 heads, and the IDE interface's limitation of 63 sectors per track limited the original size of IDE drives to 504MB (about 528 Million bytes). This limit was merely theoretical until 1994, when IDE drives larger than this began to appear. A revised version of the IDE/ATA standard, ATA-2 (also called *enhanced IDE*) defined an enhanced BIOS to avoid these limits.

An enhanced BIOS circumvents the limits by using a different geometry when talking to the drive than when talking to the software. What happens in between is called *translation*. For example, if your drive has 2,000 cylinders and 16 heads, a translating BIOS will make programs think that the drive has 1,000 cylinders and 32 heads. The most common translation methods are listed in Table 4.2. These methods are also followed by newer versions of the ATA specification, such as ATA-3 and above.

Table 4.2   ATA-2 Translation Methods

BIOS Mode	Operating System to BIOS	BIOS to Drive Ports
Standard CHS	Logical CHS Parameters	Logical CHS Parameters
Extended CHS	Translated CHS Parameters	Logical CHS Parameters
LBA	Translated CHS Parameters	LBA Parameters

A BIOS that supports only Standard CHS will recognize only 1,024 cylinders, 16 heads, and 63 sectors per track maximum for any IDE/ATA drive. Thus, if you install a 6.4GB IDE/ATA drive in a system with this type of BIOS, it will recognize only 504MB. On systems that provide translation, this BIOS mode is called "Normal," because the geometry isn't changed. Configuring a drive to use Normal mode is correct for operating systems such as UNIX, Linux, and Novell NetWare, but not for systems that use MS-DOS file structures, including MS-DOS itself, Windows 9x/NT/2000, and OS/2.

The other two modes, Extended CHS and LBA (Logical Block Addressing), do translate the geometry. Extended CHS is also called "Large" mode, and is recommended only for >504MB drives that cannot be operated in LBA mode. Most enhanced BIOSes don't offer Large mode, but all offer LBA mode, although a few (such as older Acer BIOSes) may call it something different, such as "DOS mode" or ">504MB" mode.

Using LBA Mode

LBA mode can be enabled in two different ways, depending on the BIOS. On most current BIOSes, using the "automatic detection" option in the BIOS or during system boot will detect the basic hard drive geometry and select LBA mode automatically. On some BIOSes, the automatic detection sets up the basic cylinder-head-sectors per track drive geometry, but doesn't enable LBA mode unless you set it yourself. A BIOS that performs LBA translation should allow you to use an IDE hard drive as large as 8.4GB with MS-DOS. If you find that you can use a 2.1GB hard disk, but not larger ones, the version of LBA mode supported by your BIOS is a very early version, and your BIOS should be updated. Support for drives larger than 8.4GB is discussed later in this chapter.

When LBA Mode Is Needed—and When Not to Use It

Use Table 4.3 to determine when to use LBA mode.

Table 4.3	Using LBA Mode		
Drive Size	**Operating System**	**Use LBA Mode**	**Reason**
<=504MB	Any	No	Not needed
>504MB	MS-DOS, Windows 9x/ NT/2000, OS/2	Yes	Drive will be limited to 504MB without LBA mode because of 1,024 cylinder limit
>504MB	Linux, UNIX, Novell NetWare	No	No 1,024 cylinder limit with these operating systems

Problems with LBA Support in the BIOS

Ideally, LBA mode would be automatically enabled in a clearly understood way on every system with an enhanced BIOS. And, it would also be easy to know when you did *not* need to use it. Unfortunately, this is often not the case.

Many 1994–1996 versions of the AMI text-based and graphical ("WinBIOS") BIOSes listed the basic hard drive geometry on one screen and listed the LBA mode option on a different screen altogether. To make matters worse, the automatic drive setup options on many of these BIOSes didn't set the LBA mode for you; you had to find it and then set it. But perhaps the worst problem of all was for users who had carefully set the LBA mode, and then ran into problems with other BIOS configurations. Most AMI BIOS versions offer a feature called *Automatic configuration* with either "BIOS"/"Optimal" defaults (high performance) or "Power-On"/"Fail-Safe" defaults (low performance). In AMI BIOSes where the LBA mode was *not* listed on the same screen with the hard disk geometry, *any* automatic configuration would reset LBA mode to its default setting—off.

Dangers of Altering Translation Settings

Depending on the operating system and drive configuration, one of several unpleasant events takes place when LBA translation is turned off after a drive is configured using LBA. Table 4.4 summarizes these problems—some of which can be fatal to data!

Table 4.4 Problems Associated with Disabling LBA Mode			
Drive Configuration	**Operating System**	**Symptom**	**End Result**
C: and D: partitions on single physical drive	MS-DOS	Can't access D: because part of it is beyond cylinder 1024	Usually no harm to data, because drive is inaccessible until LBA mode is reset
C: or C:, D:, etc.	Windows 9x	Can't boot drive because of incorrect geometry	Usually no harm to data, since drive is inaccessible until LBA mode is reset
C: only	MS-DOS	System boots and operates normally until data is written to a cylinder beyond 1024	Drive wraps around to Cylinder 0 (location of partition table and other vital disk structures) since LBA translation to access cylinders past 1024 is absent; drive overwrites beginning of disk, causing loss of all data!

I used the last scenario in a computer troubleshooting class a few times, and it was quite a surprise to see a hard disk "eat" itself! It is never a good idea to "play" with LBA translation once it's been set in a system.

Detecting Lack of LBA Mode Support in Your System

To determine if your system lacks LBA support or doesn't have LBA support enabled, do the following:

1. Install the hard drive set for master, slave, or cable select as appropriate.

2. Turn on the computer and detect the drive in the BIOS Setup program. Note the size of the drive reported.

3. Boot the computer from a floppy diskette containing the operating system and FDISK.

4. Select the drive you want to view with option #5.

5. Use the #4 option—"View Current Partitions"—and check what capacity FDISK reports.

6. If FDISK reports the drive size as only 504MB and the drive is larger, LBA support is lacking or is not enabled.

7. Enable LBA mode and try steps 2–5 again. If FDISK reports the same or similar size to what the BIOS reports, your drive is being translated correctly by the BIOS, if your hard disk is <=8.4.GB. If FDISK still reports a size significantly less than your hard disk's actual capacity, see the Table 4.5 for solutions.

8. If your hard disk is >8.4GB *and* you are using Windows 9x, the size that FDISK should report will be *greater* than what the BIOS displays. If FDISK reports only 8.4GB and the hard disk is larger, see the Table 4.5 for solutions.

Note

Remember that hard drive makers rate their hard disks in decimal MB or GB, and most BIOS follow the FDISK standard for rating drives in binary MB or GB. See the MB, GB, TB translation table (Table 1.2) in Chapter 1 for equivalents.

---

9. If you can't start the computer after installing the new hard drive, the BIOS is incapable of handling the drive's geometry. See Table 4.8 for solutions.

Using FDISK to Determine Compatibility Problems Between Hard Disk and BIOS

A mismatch between the capacity that FDISK reports for a hard disk and what the BIOS reports for the hard disk indicates a problem with LBA translation or with support for hard disks above 8.4GB.

FDISK can also be used to determine when the dangerous "DOS wraparound" condition exists, in which a drive prepared with LBA translation has the LBA translation turned off.

I've included a mock-up of how the FDISK "Display Partition Information" screen appears. See the discussion of LBA mode earlier in this chapter for solutions. In Figure 4.7, FDISK indicates no problems, because the values for "X" (size of hard disk partition) and "Y" (total size of drive) are equal.

```
Display Partition Information    Current fixed
disk drive: 1
Label  Mbytes   System   Usage     C: 1
A    PRI DOS
Partition  Status   Type    Volume
W95US1U        1626  FAT16        100%
                     X

     Total disk space is 1626 Mbytes (1 Mbyte =
1048576 bytes)               Y

     Press Esc to continue
```

X=Size of hard disk partition (drive has already been FDISKed)

Y=Total disk space (as seen by FDISK)

Use Table 4.5 to determine what the FDISK "total disk space" figure is telling you about your system.

Table 4.5 FDISK "Disk Space Detected" as a Guide to Disk Problem			
X Value1	**Y Value2**	**Drive Size**	**Underlying Cause**
>504MB	=504MB	>504MB Binary /FDISK (528MB Decimal)	Drive was prepared with LBA mode enabled, but LBA mode has been disabled in BIOS. See "Dangers of Altering Translation Settings" earlier in this chapter.
Not listed	=504MB	>504MB	LBA mode not enabled in BIOS.or not present
Not listed	8192MB	>8192MB (8.38 billion bytes)	BIOS supports LBA mode, but not Extended Int13h modes.

1 The "X" value appears only when a drive has already been FDISKed.

2 The "Y" value will appear on any drive being viewed through FDISK, whether the FDISK process has been completed or not.

For more information about using FDISK, see the "Using FDISK" section later in this chapter.

Getting LBA and Extended Int13h Support for Your System

If your computer is incapable of detecting the full capacity of your hard disk or locks up after you install the hard drive, your BIOS is not compatible with your hard drive. Use Table 4.6 to determine the causes and solutions that will help you get full capacity from your new hard disk with maximum safety.

Table 4.6	**Why IDE Drive Not Detected at Full Capacity**			
Symptom	**Drive Size**	**Operating System**	**Cause**	**Solution**
System locks up after installing new drive	>2.1GB	Any	BIOS cannot handle 4,096 cylinders or more even with LBA enabled	Upgrade BIOS (see Table 4.7)
Full capacity not available	>504MB – 8.4GB	MS-DOS, Windows 9x/NT/2000, OS/2	No LBA mode or inadequate LBA support in BIOS	Upgrade BIOS (see Table 4.7)
	>8.4GB	Windows NT	Atapi.sys not correct version; BIOS lacks Enhanced Int13h support, required for large drives	Update Atapi.sys (included in SP3 or above of NT 4.0) and upgrade BIOS if necessary (see Table 4.7)
	>8.4GB	Novell NetWare4.11	Drivers are needed to support drive at full capacity	Contact Novell for drivers; NetWare 5 will support >8.4GB drives; upgrade BIOS if necessary
	>8.4GB	IBM OS/2 Warp	Patch needed file; upgrade BIOS if drive at full capacity	Contact IBM for to support necessary
	>8.4GB	Windows 9x	Windows 9x has Enhanced Int13h support for drive, but BIOS lacks support	Upgrade BIOS (see Table 4.7)
	>8.4GB	MS-DOS	MS-DOS can't use IDE drives above 8.4GB; lacks Enhanced Int13h support	Buy 8.4GB or below; update to Windows 9x; use SCSI drives; use big drive as only 8.4GB

Note that 8.4GB represents a second "barrier" to drive capacity for MS-DOS, and one that cannot be overcome without changing to a different type of drive (SCSI) or making the move to Windows 9x.

Even if you have Windows 9x or updated versions of other operating systems that support IDE capacities beyond 8.4GB, your BIOS must also offer this support. This support is not "visible" in the BIOS; there is no "Enhanced Int13h" option to enable as there is with LBA mode; neither does the reported geometry change. An 8.4GB hard disk reports a geometry to the BIOS of 16 heads, 16,383 cylinders, and 63 sectors per track. A 20.4GB hard disk reports the same geometry! Support of hard disks beyond 8.4GB breaks the "rule" about the BIOS configuration matching the drive's capacity.

Sources for BIOS Upgrades and Alternatives for Large IDE Hard Disk Support

If your BIOS doesn't support the full capacity of your hard disk, use Table 4.7 to choose your best solution.

Table 4.7 Sources for BIOS and Alternative Support for Large Hard Drives			
Solution	**Benefits**	**Cost**	**Concerns**
Upgrade BIOS	Best all-around solution to hard disk and other support issues	Free if BIOS is Flash type and is supported by motherboard or system mfr.

If BIOS is no longer supported by MB or manufacturer, purchase upgrade | Be sure to correctly identify your system or motherboard before installing the upgrade; test after ward (see Chapter 3 for details)

See Chapter 3 for sources and system details |
| Purchase BIOS upgrade card | May be less expensive than purchasing BIOS replacement or new motherboard; fast, easy install | $35–75; can be combined with Y2K date-rollover support or UDMA 33/66 features | Make sure card is designed for full capacity of your hard disk; many early versions had 2.1GB or 8.4GB limits; requires open ISA or PCI slot |
| Use BIOS replacement feature in hard disk installation software supplied with drive | You probably received a copy of it with your drive | Download it from your hard disk vendor if your drive didn't come with a copy | Worst choice for large hard disk support because software drivers and non-standard disk structures can be altered and destroyed very easily |

Once you decide on a strategy for handling the full capacity of your hard disk, don't change it! Don't use a BIOS replacement option in a program such as Disk Manager or EZ-Drive, and then decide to install a BIOS upgrade (flash, chip, or card). The BIOS support won't be capable of working with your drive because it's already being translated by the software. Make your choice before you finish your drive installation.

Standard and Alternative Jumper Settings

If you decide to use the BIOS replacement software shipped with the hard drive instead of downloading or purchasing a BIOS upgrade, you might need to use alternative jumper settings on your hard disk. An example of these settings as used by some Western Digital drives with capacities at 2.5GB or above is shown in Figure 4.4. Many other drive makers use similar approaches to deal with this problem.

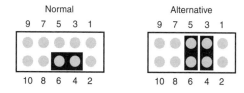

Figure 4.4 Standard (full capacity) and Alternative (Limited Capacity plus EZ-Drive) jumpers for Western Digital Hard Disks with 10-pin jumper blocks.

The Normal Single Drive configuration (at left) is used for drives installed in systems whose BIOSes can handle drives with over 4,096 cylinders (2.1GB). The BIOS may provide full access to the drive's capacity, or a program such as EZ-Drive may be necessary.

The Alternate Single Drive configuration (at right) is used to limit the drive's reported geometry to 4,092 cylinders (about 2.1GB). This configuration is required when installing a drive with over 4,096 cylinders causes the system to lock up because of BIOS incompatibilities. A drive configured this way requires the use of EZ-Drive or other Western Digital-supplied disk utility programs to access the full capacity of the drive. This jumper position is not for use with Windows NT, UNIX, Linux, or Novell NetWare.

Improving Hard Disk Speed

While the ATA-2/EIDE standard is best known for establishing LBA mode as a means of allowing larger hard drives to be used on the IDE interface, a second major benefit of ATA-2/EIDE was improving data transfer rates, as shown in the following Table 4.8.

Table 4.8	PIO Modes and Transfer Rates		
PIO Mode	**Cycle Time (ns)**	**Transfer Rate (MB/sec)**	**Specification**
0	600	3.33	ATA
1	383	5.22	ATA
2	240	8.33	ATA
3	180	11.11	ATA-2, EIDE, fast-ATA
4	120	16.67	ATA-2, EIDE, fast-ATA

PIO modes 0–2 could be achieved with the original 16-bit motherboard or expansion slot-based IDE/ATA host adapters, but PIO modes 3 and above require a local-bus connection, either VL-Bus, PCI card, or most often, a PCI motherboard connection.

The first ATA-2/EIDE hard drives introduced in 1994 were capable of PIO 3 transfer rates, but newer drives run at PIO 4 transfer rates or above. Most recent BIOSes will detect the correct PIO mode as well as the basic drive geometry and set it for you. On BIOSes that offer a PIO mode setting that you must make manually, consult the drive vendor for the correct mode. Setting the PIO mode to too high a setting will cause data corruption.

Ultra DMA

The newest hard drives and motherboards support an even faster method of data transfer called Ultra DMA, or UDMA for short. See Table 4.9 for common Ultra DMA modes.

Table 4.9	Common Ultra DMA Modes		
UDMA Mode	**Cycle Time (ns)**	**Transfer Rate (MB/sec)**	**Specification**
2	120	33.33	ATA-4, ultra-ATA/33
4	60	66.67	ATA-5, ultra-ATA/66

With both PIO and UDMA modes, the transfer rates listed are maximum (burst) transfer rates; sustained rates are much slower. Nevertheless, you will want to run your hard disk at the highest PIO or UDMA mode it's capable of.

UDMA/66 Issues

Many of the greater than 10GB hard drives now on the market are designed to support UDMA/66 (a.k.a. Ultra ATA-66) *if* certain requirements are met. Table 4.10 lists the requirements needed for UDMA/66 compliance.

Table 4.10 Ultra DMA/66 Requirements		
Item	**Features**	**Notes**
Drive	Drive must have UDMA/66 firmware	Some drives automatically sense UDMA/66 compliance; others require you run a configuration program to enable UDMA/66 mode; consult drive vendor
Motherboard chipset	Must have UDMA/66 support	May require BIOS upgrade; check system or MB vendor for compliance
Cable	Cable must be 80-wire cable (40 data wires separated by 40 ground wires)	UDMA/66 data cable has blue end to attach to motherboard

Any system that cannot run the drive at UDMA/66 can use the drive at the system's maximum speed (UDMA/33, PIO 4, etc.).

Benefits of Manual Drive Typing

Even though virtually every BIOS used the last few years supports automatic drive detection (a.k.a. "drive typing") at startup, there are a couple of benefits to performing this task within the BIOS configuration screen.

- In the event that you need to move the drive to another system, you'll know the drive geometry and translation scheme (such as LBA) that was used to access the drive. If the drive is moved to another computer, the identical drive geometry (cylinder, head, sectors per track) and translation scheme must be used in the other computer, or the data on the drive will not be accessible and can be lost. Because many systems with auto-configuration don't display these settings during the startup process, performing the drive-typing operation yourself might be the only way to get this information.

- If you want to remove a drive that is already in use and the BIOS displays the drive geometry, write it down! Because the IDE interface allows a drive to work with *any* defined geometry that doesn't exceed the drive's capacity, the current BIOS configuration for any given drive may *not* be what the manufacturer recommends (and what would be detected by the BIOS, using the IDE identify drive command). I ran a 203MB Conner drive successfully for years with an incorrect BIOS setting that provided 202MB, because technical information about drives in the early days of IDE wasn't always easy to get. Drives working with the "wrong" geometry should *not* be "corrected," because this would require a complete backup of the drive, resetting the geometry in the BIOS, FDISK, FORMAT, and restore. Just label the drive with the actual head, cylinder, and sectors per track it uses now.

Troubleshooting IDE Installation

In addition to the BIOS capacity and PIO/UDMA mode configuration issues, you may run into other problems during an IDE drive installation. Use Table 4.11 to determine problems, causes, and solutions.

Table 4.11 Other IDE Drive Installation Problems and Solutions		
Problem	**Causes**	**Solution**
Drive not recognized by BIOS but system will boot from floppy (drive is spinning)	Drive cabling installed incorrectly	Make sure pin 1 on IDE interface and IDE drive are connected to pin 1 (colored edge) of IDE cable; some cables are keyed with a plugged hole at pin 20 or with a "bump" over the middle of the cable that corresponds with a cutout in the plastic skirt that surrounds the cable On non-skirted motherboard IDE connectors, make sure pins are connected to both rows of the cable, without any offsets
Drive not recognized by BIOS but system will boot from floppy (drive is not spinning)	Drive power cable is not connected or defective	If a Y-splitter or power extender is in use, check it for damage or remove it and plug drive directly to power supply; make sure Molex power connector is tightly inserted into drive; use a Digital Multimeter (DMM) to check power leads; drive may be defective if power checks out okay
One or both IDE drives on a single cable are not recognized by system (drives are spinning)	Drives may be jumpered as master or as slave	Jumper boot drive as master, second drive as slave

Problem	Causes	Solution
One or both IDE drives on a single cable are not recognized by system (drives are spinning and are jumpered correctly)	Drives may not be 100 percent compliant with ATA standards (very likely when trying to mix different brands of IDE drives, especially older ones)	Reverse master and slave jumpering; move second drive to other IDE connector and jumper both drives accordingly

SCSI

SCSI, the Small Computer System Interface, is a very flexible and high-performance drive and device interface. In addition to supporting hard drives, it can also support non-bootable optical and tape storage, scanners, and many other device types.

SCSI Types and Data Transfer Rates

While many different types of SCSI exist, different SCSI types can be mixed on the same host adapter. For best results, you should buy a host adapter capable of running your fastest devices at their top speeds *and* one that allows different types of devices to run without slowing each other down. Use Table 4.12 to learn common SCSI types and their characteristics.

Table 4.12   SCSI Data-Transfer Rates

Bus Width	Standard SCSI	Fast SCSI[1]	Fast-20 (Ultra)[2]	Fast-40 (Ultra2)[2]	Fast-80 (Ultra3)[2]	Cable Type
8-bit (narrow)	5MB/sec	10MB/sec	20MB/sec	40MB/sec	80MB/sec	A (50-pin)
16-bit (wide)	10MB/sec	20MB/sec	40MB/sec	80MB/sec	160MB/sec[3]	P (68-pin)

1 SCSI-2
2 SCSI-3
3 Ultra2Wide

> ### Note
>
> The A cable is the standard 50-pin SCSI cable, whereas the P cable is a 68-pin cable designed for 16-bit. Maximum cable length is 6 meters (about 20 feet) for standard speed SCSI, and only 3 meters (about 10 feet) for Fast/Fast-20/Fast-40 (Ultra) SCSI. Ultra2Wide allows cable lengths up to 12 meters (about 40 feet!).

Single-Ended Versus Differential SCSI

SCSI is not only a flexible interface, it's also a multi-platform interface. Traditionally, PCs have used single-ended SCSI, while other platforms use differential SCSI. Since these two types of SCSI are not interchangable, you should never mix them on a host adapter designed for single-ended SCSI. Use the markings in Figure 4.5 to distinguish between these.

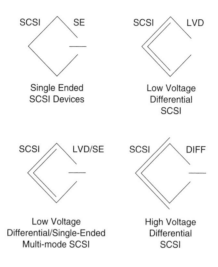

Figure 4.5 Single-ended and differential SCSI universal symbols.

LVD (Low-Voltage Differential) Devices

Ultra2Wide SCSI devices, which run at 80MB/sec maximum transfer rates, use a modified version of differential SCSI called LVD (Low-Voltage Differential). Workstation-oriented cards such as Adaptec's AHA-2940U2W allow the use of LVD Ultra2Wide devices and standard single-ended SCSI devices on the same card. Cards with this feature use two buses—one for LVD and one for standard SCSI devices.

Note

If you do need to use single-ended and differential SCSI devices on the same cable, there are adapters available that will safely handle the connection. Paralan Corporation—4655 Ruffner St., San Diego, CA 92111, Tel.: (858) 560-7266; Fax: (858) 560-8929, www.paralan.com—offers the SD10B and SD16B adapters.

Recognizing SCSI Interface Cables and Connectors

Because SCSI is actually a family of standards, each with its own cable and connector, matching cables and connectors to the appropriate SCSI "family member" is important. Use the following figures to determine this information.

8-Bit SCSI Centronics 50-pin Connector

Older narrow (8-bit) SCSI adapters and external devices use a full size Centronics type connector that normally has wire latches on each side to secure the cable connector. Figure 4.6 shows what the low-density 50-pin SCSI connector looks like.

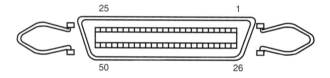

Figure 4.6 Low-density, 50-pin SCSI connector.

SCSI-2 High-Density Connector

The SCSI-2 revision added a high-density, 50-position, D-shell connector option for the A-cable connectors. This connector now is called Alternative 1. Figure 4.7 shows the 50-pin high-density SCSI connector.

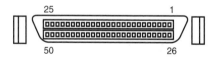

Figure 4.7 High-density, 50-pin SCSI connector.

The Alternative 2 Centronics latch-style connector remains unchanged from SCSI-1.

SCSI-3 68-pin P Cable

A new 68-conductor P cable was developed as part of the SCSI-3 specification. Shielded and unshielded high-density D-shell connectors are specified for both the A and P cable. The shielded high-density connectors use a squeeze-to-release latch rather than the

wire latch used on the Centronics-style connectors. Active termination for single-ended buses is specified, providing a high level of
signal integrity. Figure 4.8 shows the 68-pin high density SCSI
connector.

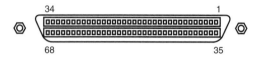

Figure 4.8 High-density, 68-pin SCSI connector.

RAID Array, Hot Swappable 80-pin Connector

Drive arrays normally use special SCSI drives with what is called an
80-pin Alternative-4 connector, which is capable of wide SCSI and
also includes power signals as well. Drives with the 80-pin connector are normally *hot swappable*—they can be removed and installed
with the power on—in drive arrays. The 80-pin Alt-4 connector is
shown in Figure 4.9.

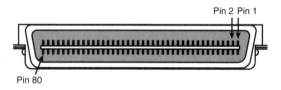

Figure 4.9 80-pin Alt-4 SCSI connector.

Apple and some other non-standard implementations from other
vendors (such as Iomega SCSI Zip drives) used a 25-pin cable and
connector for SCSI devices.

They did this by eliminating most of the grounds from the cable,
which unfortunately resulted in a noisy, error prone connection. I
don't recommend using 25-pin cables and connectors; you should
avoid them if possible. The connector used in these cases was a standard female DB-25 connector, which looks exactly like a PC parallel
port (printer) connector. Unfortunately, it is possible to damage
equipment by plugging printers into DB-25 SCSI connectors or by
plugging SCSI devices into DB-25 printer connectors. So, if you use
this type of SCSI connection, be sure it is marked well, as there is no
way to tell DB-25 SCSI from DB-25 parallel printer connectors by
looking at them. The DB-25 connector is shown in Figure 4.10.

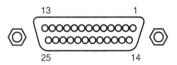

Figure 4.10 DB-25 SCSI connector.

Again I recommend you avoid making SCSI connections using this type of cable or connector.

SCSI Drive and Device Configuration

SCSI drives (and other devices) are not too difficult to configure, but they are more complicated than IDE drives. The SCSI standard controls the way the drives must be set up. You need to set two items when you configure a SCSI drive or device:

- SCSI ID setting (0–7 or 0–15)

- Terminating resistors

The number of SCSI IDs available on a host adapter depends on its design: 0–7 on SCSI adapters with an 8-bit bus; 0–15 on SCSI adapters with a 16-bit bus; two groups of 0–15 on a 16-bit bus with a dual-processor host bus adapter.

SCSI Device ID

Up to seven SCSI devices (plus the adapter for a total of eight) can be used on a single narrow SCSI bus (8-bit) or up to 15 devices (plus the adapter for a total of 16) on a wide (16-bit) SCSI bus. There are now dual-processor 16-bit host adapters that can operate up to 30 devices plus the host adapter. In every case, each device must have a unique SCSI ID address. The host adapter takes one address, so the rest are free for up to seven SCSI peripherals (or more as defined by the host adapter). Most SCSI host adapters are factory-set to ID 7 or 15, which is the highest priority ID. All other devices must have unique IDs that do not conflict with one another. Some host adapters boot only from a hard disk set to a specific ID. Older Adaptec host adapters required the boot hard disk to be ID 0; newer ones can boot from any ID. A SCSI device containing multiple drives (such as a CD-ROM tower or changer) will have a single ID, but each physical drive or logical drive will also be known by a LUN (Logical Unit Number). For example, a five-CD changer is SCSI ID #3. Each "virtual drive" or disc position within SCSI ID #3 has a LUN, 0–4. So the last "drive" has drive letter "J" and is also identified by Windows as "SCSI ID#3, LUN 4."

Setting the SCSI ID

The methods for setting the SCSI ID vary with the device. For internal drives, the settings are made with jumper blocks. Use Table 4.13 to set the jumpers. Note that the column to the left is the lowest numbered ID jumper, which may be identified as "A0" or "SCSI ID0", depending on the drive vendor.

Table 4.13	SCSI ID Jumper Settings				
SCSI	**A0**	**A1**	**A2**	**A3**	**(Seagate Markings)**
ID#	**ID0**	**ID1**	**ID2**	**ID3**	**(WD Markings)**
0	0	0	0	0	
01	1	0	0	0	
02	0	1	0	0	
03	1	1	0	0	
04	0	0	1	0	
05	1	0	1	0	
06	0	1	1	0	
07	1	1	1	0	
8	0	0	0	1	
9	1	0	0	1	
10	0	1	0	1	
11	1	1	0	1	
12	0	0	1	1	
13	1	0	1	1	
14	0	1	1	1	
15	1	1	1	1	

1 = Jumper On, 0 = Jumper Off
For SCSI hard drives that support device IDs up to 15, see the manufacturer's documentation.

SCAM—Automatic ID Setting

Some SCSI hard drives and host adapters support SCAM (SCSI Configure AutoMagically), which automatically assigns the drive a unique SCSI ID number. To use SCAM, both the host adapter and drive must support SCAM, and SCAM must be enabled (usually by a jumper on the drive).

SCSI ID Setting for External Devices

SCSI drives and devices can be used both internally and externally, often with the same interface card. For external devices, one of the following methods will apply for each device in the SCSI daisy-chain. Use Table 4.14 as a general reference. Typically, the ID setting control is at the back of the device, near the SCSI interface cable. Depending on the device, the device ID may be set by a rotary dial, a push-button control, or a sliding switch. Not all SCSI ID numbers are available with every device; many low-cost devices allow a choice of only two or three numbers. Regardless of the setting method, each internal and external device on a single SCSI daisy-chain of devices must have a unique ID! If you use Adaptec SCSI interface cards, use the SCSI Interrogator program before you add a new SCSI device to determine what device IDs you have remaining. If you are adding a new SCSI device with limited ID choices (such as the Iomega Zip 100 SCSI drive), you might need to move an existing device to another ID to make room for the new device.

For high-performance SCSI cards that offer multiple buses, you should be able to reuse device number 0–7 for each separate bus on the card. If you have problems with duplicate ID numbers on different buses, the device drivers for either the device or the interface card may not be up-to-date. Contact the device and card maker for assistance.

SCSI Termination

SCSI termination is simple. Termination is required at both ends of the bus; there are no exceptions. If the host adapter is at one end of the bus, it must have termination enabled. If the host adapter is in the middle of the bus, and if both internal and external bus links are present, the host adapter must have its termination disabled, and the devices at each end of the bus must have terminators installed. Unfortunately, the majority of problems that I see with SCSI installations are the result of improper termination.

Terminators can be external or internal (set with a jumper block or with switches or sliders). Some devices also terminate themselves automatically.

The pass-through models are required when a device is at the end of the bus and only one SCSI connector is available.

SCSI Configuration Troubleshooting

When you are installing a chain of devices on a single SCSI bus, the installation can get complicated very quickly. Here are some tips for getting your setup to function quickly and efficiently:

- *Start by adding one device at a time.* Rather than plug numerous peripherals into a single SCSI card and then try to configure them at the same time, start by installing the host adapter and a single hard disk. Then you can continue installing devices one at a time, checking to make sure that everything works before moving on.

- *Keep good documentation.* When you add an SCSI peripheral, write down the SCSI ID address and any other switch and jumper settings, such as SCSI Parity, Terminator Power, and Delayed or Remote Start. For the host adapter, record the BIOS addresses, IRQ, DMA channel, and I/O Port addresses used by the adapter, and any other jumper or configuration settings (such as termination) that might be important to know later.

- *Use proper termination.* Each end of the bus must be terminated, preferably with active or Forced Perfect (FPT) terminators. If you are using any Fast SCSI-2 device, you must use active terminators rather than the cheaper passive types. Even with standard (slow) SCSI devices, active termination is highly recommended. If you have only internal or external devices on the bus, the host adapter and last device on the chain should be terminated. If you have external and internal devices on the chain, you generally will terminate the first and last of these devices but not the SCSI host adapter (which is in the middle of the bus).

- *Use high-quality shielded SCSI cables.* Make sure that your cable connectors match your devices. Use high-quality shielded cables, and observe the SCSI bus-length limitations. Use cables designed for SCSI use, and if possible, stick to the same brand of cable throughout a single SCSI bus. Different brands of cables have different impedance values; this situation sometimes causes problems, especially in long or high-speed SCSI implementations.

- *Have the correct driver for your SCSI host adapter, and for each device.* SCSI, unlike IDE, is not controlled by your computer's motherboard BIOS, but by software drivers. An SCSI device cannot be used unless the appropriate software drivers are installed for it. As with any other software-driven peripheral, these drivers are often updated periodically. Check for improved drivers and install them as needed.

Following these tips will help minimize problems and leave you with a trouble-free SCSI installation.

Use Table 4.14 to help you record SCSI information. Table 4.15 shows a form I use to record data about my system. You can attach this information to the System Template referred to in Chapter 2, "System Components and Configurations."

Table 4.14   SCSI Device Data Sheet

Interface Card	IRQ	DMA	I/O Port Address	Slot Type
Interface Card Notes and Details				
Device Information				

Include SCSI interface card and all devices

Device ID	Device Name	Internal or External	Cable/ Connector Type	Terminated? Y/N
0				
1				
2				
3				
4				
5				
6				
7				

Table 4.15   Completed SCSI Device Data Sheet

Interface Card	IRQ	DMA	I/O Port Address	Slot Type
Adaptec AHA-1535	10	5	0130h-0133h	ISA
Interface Card Notes and Details	Bus-mastering card with internal and external cable connectors; allows pass-through so that both connectors can be used at once			
Device Information				

Include SCSI interface card and all devices.

Device ID Y/N	Device Name/ Type	Internal or External	Cable/ Connector Type	Terminated?
0				
1				
2	Epson Expression 636 flatbed scanner with transparency adapter	External	50-pin Centronics	No
3	Polaroid SprintScan 35Plus slide and filmstrip scanner	External	50-pin Centronics and DB-25 25-pin	Yes
4	Philips CDD2600 CD-Recorder (CD-R)	Internal	50-pin ribbon cable	Yes
5				
6	Iomega Zip 100 Zip drive	External	DB-25 25-pin	No
7	Adaptec AHA-1535 SCSI host adapter card	Internal	50-pin ribbon (internal)	
			50-pin high-density (external)	No

Note that both ends of the daisy-chain are terminated, and that the actual end of the internal daisy-chain is *not* the AHA-1535 SCSI host adapter, but the Philips CDD2600 drive! Also note that some SCSI devices support different types of cables.

Hard Disk Preparation

There are three major steps in the formatting process for a hard disk drive subsystem:

1. Low-level formatting
2. Partitioning
3. High-level formatting

Table 4.16 outlines the steps for preparing a drive for use after installation.

Table 4.16   Comparing the Steps in the Formatting Process

Process Step	When Necessary	How Performed
Low-level formatting (LLF)	IDE and SCSI hard drives are low-level formatted at the factory; reformat only to correct errors.	
	With SCSI only, to configure drive for use with a specified host adapter and its driver software. This is usually required for Windows 3.x/MS DOS systems, but not for	Use factory-supplied LLF or diagnostic utilities; use Ontrack Disk Manager (generic or OEM version); use MicroScope version 7 software for IDE For SCSI, use the host adapter's BIOS or software Windows 9x systems routines (such as Adaptec's EZ-SCSI) if necessary
Partitioning	Always required for both SCSI and IDE hard drives; indicates what portion of the drive will be used for each operating system and how the drive letters will be defined	Use operating system utility (FDISK or equivalent) if BIOS provides full support for drive capacity; EZ-Drive, Disk Manager, and similar products can be used for both FDISK and FORMAT options
		With SCSI drives under Windows 3.x/MS-DOS, host-adapter–specific partitioning and format-ting routines are normally used
High-level formatting	Always required for all drive letters defined by FDISK or partitioning utility	Use operating system utility (FORMAT or equivalent); EZ-Drive, Disk Manager, and similar products can be used for both FDISK and FORMAT options With SCSI drives under Windows 3.x/MS-DOS, host-adapter–specific partitioning and formatting routines are normally used

Using FDISK

FDISK is the partitioning utility used with MS-DOS, Windows 95 and above, and has equivalents in all other operating systems. In most cases with SCSI and all cases with IDE drives, it's the first software program you run after you physically install a hard disk and properly detect it in the BIOS.

FDISK is used to set aside disk space (or an entire physical drive) for use by an operating system, and to specify how many and what size the logical drives will be within that space. By default, the MS-DOS and Windows 9x versions of FDISK will prepare a single physical drive as a single drive letter (up to the limits listed), but FDISK can also be used to create multiple drives. By not preparing all of a hard disk's capacity with FDISK, you can use the remaining room on the hard disk for another operating system.

Drive-Letter Size Limits

We've already considered the physical drive size limits caused by BIOS limitations and how to overcome them. Those limits define the maximum size a *physical* hard drive can be. However, depending on the version of Windows in use (and with any version of MS-DOS), it might be necessary to subdivide a hard drive through the use of FDISK to allow its full capacity to be used through the creation of multiple logical drive letters.

The original release of Windows 95 and all versions of MS-DOS from DOS 3.3x support FAT16, which allows no more than 65,536 files per drive and a single drive letter of no more than 2.1GB in size. Thus, a 8.4GB hard disk prepared with MS-DOS or the original Windows 95 must have at a minimum four drive letters and could have more. See Figure 4.11.

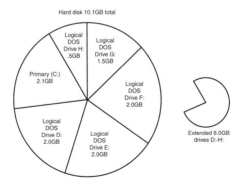

Figure 4.11 Adding a hard drive above 2.1GB in size to an MS-DOS or original Windows 95 computer forces the user to create multiple drive letters to use the entire drive capacity. The logical DOS drives are referenced like any other drive, although they are portions of a single physical hard disk.

Large Hard Disk Support

If you use the Windows 95B or above (Win95 OSR 2.x) or Windows 98 versions of FDISK with a hard drive greater than 512MB, FDISK will offer to enable large hard disk support.

Choosing to enable large hard disk support provides several benefits:

- You can use a large hard disk (greater than 2.1GB) as a single drive letter; in fact, your drive can be as large as 2TB and still be identified by a single drive letter. This is because of the FAT32 file system, which allows for many more files per drive than FAT16.

- Because of the more efficient storage methods of FAT-32, your files will use less hard disk space. FAT-32 is not supported by Windows NT 4.0 or earlier, but is supported by Windows 2000.

- Note that a FAT-32 drive cannot be accessed by older versions (pre-OSR 2.x) of Windows 95, by Windows 3.1x/MS-DOS, or any other operating system. If you occasionally need to run older applications that cannot run under Windows 95B or Windows 98 and you want to store those applications on a hard drive, make sure you create a hard drive letter that uses FAT-16. This way you can boot your older operating system and still access your program files.

Benefits of Hard-Disk Partitioning

While it may seem like a lot of trouble to partition a single physical hard disk into multiple drive letters, especially with FAT-32, there are several good reasons for both FAT-16 and FAT-32 users to partition their hard disks.

- Multiple partitions can be used to separate the operating system, application programs, and data for easier backup and greater security. This method for dividing a hard disk into C: (Windows and drivers), D: (applications), and E: (data) is recommended by PowerQuest, makers of the popular PartitionMagic disk utility, and I've followed their advice for some time. Recently, I lost both C: and D: drives to a completely unexpected disk crash, but my data, on E:, stayed safe!

- For FAT-16 operating systems in particular (MS-DOS, Windows 95/95a, and others using FAT-16), partitioning the drive results in significantly less disk space wasted. Because files are actually stored in clusters (or allocation units) that are multiples of the 512-byte disk sector, a small file must occupy an entire cluster. As Table 4.17 indicates, the bigger the drive, the greater the space wasted.

Table 4.17   FAT-16 Cluster Sizes

Drive Size (defined by FDISK) Binary MB/GB	Drive Size (Defined by Drive Maker) Decimal MB/GB	Cluster Size in Binary KB	Cluster Size in Bytes
0–127MB*	0–133MB*	2KB	2,048
128–255MB	134–267MB	4KB	4,096
256–511MB	268–537MB	8KB	8,192
512MB–1023MB	538MB–1073MB	16KB	16,384
1024MB (1GB)–2048MB (2GB)	1074MB–2113MB	32KB	32,768

If you create a partition under 15MB (binary) in size, the operating system actually uses the old FAT-12 file system, which results in a cluster size of 8KB!

FAT-32 Versus FAT-16 Cluster Sizes

FAT-32 is far more efficient than FAT-16, and is used by virtually every recent system with a preinstalled copy of Windows 95 OSR 2.x (95B/95C) or Windows 98. If you are installing an additional hard disk on a system that uses these operating systems, use Table 4.18 to determine the relative efficiencies of FAT-16 versus FAT-32, since you can choose either FAT type for the entire new drive or any partitions on it. This chart uses binary (FDISK/BIOS) sizes only.

Table 4.18   FAT-16 Versus FAT-32

Cluster Size	FAT-16 Partition Size	FAT-32 Partition Size
4KB	128MB–255MB	260MB–8GB
8KB	256MB–511MB	8GB–16GB
16KB	512MB–1024MB	16GB–32GB
32KB	1025MB–2048MB	32GB–2TB

Converting FAT-16 Partition to FAT-32

If your existing hard disk uses FAT-16, you can convert any partition on it to FAT-32 *if* one of the following is true:

- You have Windows 95B or above (OSR 2.x) *and* PowerQuest's PartitionMagic v3.x or newer. PartitionMagic has a FAT-16 to FAT-32 converter, which can also reverse the process (FAT-32 to FAT-16)

- You have Windows 98. Windows 98 comes with its own FAT-16 to FAT-32 converter, and it can also use PartitionMagic version 4.x or newer.

How FDISK and the Operating System Create and Allocate Drive Letters

There are two types of partitions that can be created with the FDISK in Windows 9x and MS-DOS: *primary* and *extended*. The primary partition can be bootable and can occupy all, part, or none of a hard disk's capacity. If you have only one hard disk in a system and it's bootable, at least a portion of that drive's partition is primary.

An extended partition is like a "pocket" that holds one or more "logical DOS drives" inside it. Table 4.19 shows how FDISK identifies these different disk structures as they might be found in a typical 13GB hard disk divided up into three drives: C:, D:, and E:

Table 4.19   FDISK Primary, Extended, and Logical DOS Drives Compared (13GB Hard Disk)

Partition Type	Size	Contained Within	Bootable?	% of total Disk Space	% of *Partition*
Primary	4GB	n/a	Yes	32.5%	
Drive C:	4GB	Primary	Yes	32.5%	100% of *primary*
Extended	9GB	n/a	No	67.5%	
Logical DOS drive D: partition	4GB	Extended	No	32.5%	44.4% of *extended*
Logical DOS drive E: partition	5GB	Extended	No	35.0%	55.6% of *extended*

With the MS-DOS and Windows 9x FDISK, the partitions shown earlier must be created in the following order:

1. Create the primary partition to occupy less than 100 percent of disk space at the size you choose.

2. Create an extended partition to use the *remainder* of disk space unused by the primary partition.

3. Create one or more logical DOS drives to occupy the extended partition.

4. Before leaving FDISK, make the primary partition (C:) active to allow it to boot.

Assigning Drive Letters with FDISK

There are many ways to use FDISK, depending on the number of hard drives you have in your system and the number of drive letters you want to create.

With a single drive, creating a primary partition (C:) and an extended partition with two logical DOS drives within it will result in the following drives, as you saw earlier:

Partition Type	Contains drive letter(s)
Primary	C:
Extended	D: and E:

A second drive added to this system should have drive letters that follow the E: drive.

However, you need to understand how drive letters are allocated by the system to know how to use FDISK correctly in this situation. Table 4.20 shows how FDISK assigns drive letters by drive and partition type.

Table 4.20	Drive Letter Allocations by Drive and Partition Type		
Drive	**Partition**	**Order**	**First drive letter**
1st	Primary	1st	C:
2nd	Primary	2nd	D:
1st	Extended	3rd	E:
2nd	Extended	4th	F: or higher

How does this affect you when you add another hard drive? If you prepare the second hard drive with a primary partition and your first hard drive has an extended partition on it, the second hard drive will take the primary partition's D: drive letter. This moves all the drive letters in the first hard drive's extended partition up at least one drive letter.

This example lists a drive with C:, D:, and E: as the drive letters (D: and E: were in the extended partition). Table 4.21 indicates what happens if a second drive is added with a primary partition on it.

Table 4.21	Drive Letter Changes Caused by Addition of Second Drive with Primary Partition			
Drive	**Partition Type**	**Order**	**Original drive letter(s) (first drive only)**	**New drive letter(s) after adding second drive**
1st	Primary	1st	C:	C:
2nd	Primary	2nd	—	D:
1st	Extended	3rd	D:, E:	E:, F:

This principle extends to third and fourth physical drives as well: the primary partitions on each drive get their drive letters first, followed by logical DOS drives in the extended partitions.

How can you avoid the problem of changing drive letters? If you're installing an additional hard drive (not a replacement), remember that it can't be a bootable drive. If it can't be bootable, there's no reason to make it a primary partition. FDISK will allow you to create an extended partition using 100 percent of the space on any drive.

Table 4.22 shows the same example used in the preceding table with the second drive installed as an extended partition:

Table 4.22	Drive Letter Allocations After Addition of Second Drive with Extended Partition Only			
Drive	Partition Type	Order	Original drive letter(s) (first drive only)	New drive letter(s) after adding second drive
1st	Primary	1st	C:	C:
1st	Extended	2nd	D:, E:	D:, E:
2nd	Extended	3rd	—	F:

This operating system behavior also explains why some of the first computers with IDE-based (ATAPI) Iomega Zip drives had the Zip drive as D:, with a single 2.5GB or larger hard disk identified as C: and E:; the Zip drive was treated as the second hard drive with a primary partition.

High-Level (DOS) Format

The final step in the installation of a hard disk drive is the high-level format. Like the partitioning process, the high-level format is specific to the file system you've chosen to use on the drive. On Windows 9x and DOS systems, the primary function of the high-level format is to create a FAT and a directory system on the disk so the operating system can manage files. You must run FDISK before formatting a drive. Each drive letter created by FDISK must be formatted before it can be used for data storage. This process may be automated with setup programs for some operating systems such as Windows 9x retail versions. In the following notes, I provide the steps for a manual drive preparation in which you'll install a full operating system copy later.

Usually, you perform the high-level format with the FORMAT.COM program or the formatting utility in Windows 9x Explorer. FORMAT. COM uses the following syntax:

```
FORMAT C:  /S  /V
```

This command high-level formats drive C:, writes the hidden operating system files in the first part of the partition (/S), and prompts
for the entry of a volume label (/V) to be stored on the disk at the
completion of the process.

The FAT high-level format program performs the following functions
and procedures:

1. Scans the disk (read only) for tracks and sectors marked as bad
   during the LLF and notes these tracks as being unreadable.

2. Returns the drive heads to the first cylinder of the partition,
   and at that cylinder (Head 1, Sector 1) writes a DOS volume
   boot sector.

3. Writes a FAT at Head 1, Sector 2. Immediately after this FAT, it
   writes a second copy of the FAT. These FATs essentially are
   blank except for bad-cluster marks noting areas of the disk that
   were found to be unreadable during the marked-defect scan.

4. Writes a blank root directory.

5. If the /S parameter is specified, copies the system files,
   IO.SYS and MSDOS.SYS (or IBMBIO.COM and IBMDOS.COM,
   depending on which DOS you run) and COMMAND.COM to
   the disk (in that order).

6. If the /V parameter is specified, prompts the user for a volume
   label, which is written as the fourth file entry in the root
   directory.

Now, the operating system can use the disk for storing and retrieving
files, and the disk is a bootable disk.

Note

Because the high-level format doesn't overwrite data areas
beyond the root directory of the hard disk, it's possible to use
programs such as Norton Utilities to unformat the hard disk that
contains data from previous operations, provided no programs
or data has been copied to the drive after high-level formatting.
Unformatting can be performed because the data from the
drive's previous use is still present.

If you create an extended partition, the logical DOS drive letters located in the extended partition need a simpler FORMAT command, because system files aren't necessary. For example, FORMAT D:/V for drive D: and FORMAT E:/V for drive E:, etc.

Replacing an Existing Drive

Previous sections discuss installing a single hard drive or adding a new hard drive to a system. While formatting and partitioning a new hard disk can be challenging, replacing an existing drive and moving your programs and files to it can be a lot more challenging.

Drive Migration for MS-DOS Users

When MS-DOS 6.x was dominant, many users used this straight-forward method to transfer the contents of their old hard drive to their new hard drive:

1. The user created a bootable disk containing FDISK, FORMAT, and XCOPY.

2. The new hard drive was prepared with a primary partition (and possibly an extended partition, depending on the user's desires).

3. The new hard drive was formatted with system files, although the operating system identifies it as D:.

4. The XCOPY command was used to transfer all non-hidden files from C:\ (the old hard drive) to D:\ thus:

   ```
   XCOPY C:\ D:\/S/E
   ```

   The XCOPY command also was used as necessary to transfer files from any remaining drive letters on the old hard drive to the corresponding drive letters on the new drive.

Because the only hidden files such a system would have were probably the operating system boot files (already installed) and the Windows 3.1 permanent swap file (which could be recreated after restarting Windows), this "free" data transfer routine worked well for many people.

After the original drive was removed from the system, the new drive would be jumpered as master and assigned C:. You will need to run FDISK from a floppy and set the primary partition on the new C: drive as Active. Then exit FDISK and the drive will boot.

Drive Migration for Windows 9x Users

Windows 95 and 98 have complicated the once simple act of data transfer to a new system by their frequent use of hidden files and folders (such as \Windows\Inf, where Windows 9x hardware drivers are stored). The extensive use of hidden files was a major reason for a greatly enhanced version of XCOPY to be included in Windows 9x.

> **Note**
>
> XCOPY32 is automatically used in place of XCOPY when XCOPY is started within a DOS session under Windows.

XCOPY32 for Windows 9x Data Transfer

Compared to "classic" XCOPY, XCOPY32 can copy hidden files; preserve file attributes such as system, hidden, read-only, and archive; automatically create folders, and is compatible with long filenames. Thus, it is possible to use it to duplicate an existing drive, but with these cautions:

1. The XCOPY32 command is much more complex.

2. There may be errors during the copy process because of Windows' use of temporary files during normal operation, but XCOPY32 can be forced to continue.

This command line will call XCOPY32 and transfer all files and folders with their original attributes intact from the original drive (C:) to the new drive (D:). *This command must be run from an MS-DOS session under Windows 95 or 98.*

```
xcopy32 c:\. d:\/s/c/h/e/r/k
```

The command switches are explained here:

- /S. Copies folders beneath the starting folder

- /C. Continues to copy after errors (The Windows swap file can't be copied due to being in use.)

- /H. Copies hidden and system files

- /E. Copies folders, even if empty

- /R. Overwrites read-only files

- /K. Preserves file attributes

Repeat the command with appropriate drive-letter changes for any additional drive letters on your old drive.

After the original drive is removed from the system, the new drive needs to be jumpered as master (or single) and the operating system will assign it C:. You will need to run FDISK from a floppy and set the primary partition on the new C: drive as Active. Then exit FDISK, and the drive will boot.

This process can take a long time because of the overhead of running an MS-DOS session beneath Windows.

If your hard disk comes with a disk-preparation utility such as EZ-Drive, Disk Manager, Disc Wizard, or others, it may include a fast data-transfer utility that you can use in place of this procedure. I also recommend the PowerQuest utility DriveCopy, which uses a special method called "SmartSector copying" to copy hundreds of megabytes of data from the old to the new drive in just a few minutes.

Hard Disk Drive Troubleshooting and Repair

Hard disk problems fall into two categories, hard and soft. "Hard" problems are triggered by mechanical problems that cause the drive to emit strange grinding or knocking noises (or no noise at all!), while "soft" problems are read and write errors that occur in a drive that sounds normal. See Table 4.23.

Table 4.23   Hard and Soft Problems and Solutions

Symptom	Cause	Solution
Drive makes banging noise on initial power up; may not boot without restarting the computer a couple of times; usually found on very old (under 100MB) RLL or MFM hard disks only; these drives use two (20-pin and 34-pin) data and signal cables.	*Stiction* (Static friction) is causing the heads to stick to the media because of an aging mechanism and lubrication problems internally.	If drive "hangs," try tapping gently on one corner to free the heads or mount the drive upside down. Back up data and replace drive as soon as possible.
Drive makes scratching or "boinging" noise internally; won't boot.	Severe head damage, probably caused by impact (fall or drop).	Replace drive.
Drive spins normally but can't be recognized.	If cable and jumpering okay, probably failed logic board.	Replace logic board or replace drive.
Drive has repetitive errors detected by SCANDISK or other disk-testing utility.	If system rebooted or turned off without proper shutdown, these are temporary files that weren't closed. This does not indicate a hardware problem.	Remind user to shut down computer normally.

Symptom	Cause	Solution
	If normal shutdown procedure followed, might indicate marginal disk surface.	If normal shutdown procedure followed, get manufacturer utility to detect and remap sectors and retest drive frequently. If drive doesn't improve, replace as soon as possible.

If replacing the logic assembly does not solve the problem, contact the manufacturer or a specialized repair shop that has clean-room facilities for hard disk repair.

Chapter 5

Floppy, Removable, Optical, and Tape Storage

Floppy Drives

A 3 1/2-inch 1.44MB floppy drive, the most common type of floppy drive in use today, isn't very expensive to replace. However, when it stops working, you might *not* need to replace it right away, if you have the "inside story." Figure 5.1 shows an exploded view of a typical 3 1/2-inch 1.44MB floppy drive.

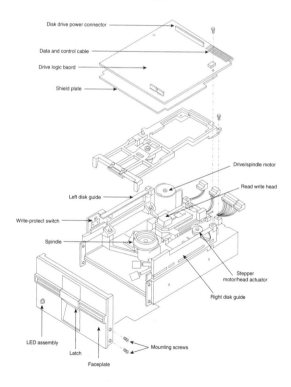

Disk drive power connector

Data and control cable

Drive logic baord

Shield plate

Drive/spindle motor

Read write head

Left disk guide

Write-protect switch

Spindle

Stepper motor/head actuator

Right disk guide

LED assembly

Latch

Faceplate

Mounting screws

Figure 5.1 A typical 3 1/2 floppy disk drive.

Where Floppy Drives Fail—and Simple Fixes

I spent several years on the road carrying around disassembled PCs for use in computer-troubleshooting classes. Typically, I had more floppy-drive failures than about anything else, due to the combination of inexperienced students, rough handling by airline baggage carousels, and the simple fact that a floppy drive is designed to be used within the confines of a computer case. I learned how to fix drives the hard way—when the only spare I had wasn't working, either.

The Drive Cover

The drive cover acts as a dust cover, which is obviously a good idea for a drive that uses exposed, relatively soft flexible magnetic media. However, a damaged or bent drive cover can bind the disk ejector, preventing it from moving. The drive cover can easily be removed and bent back into shape.

The Stepper Motor

The stepper motor moves the head actuator across the surface of the floppy disk media, reading or writing data (see Figure 5.2).

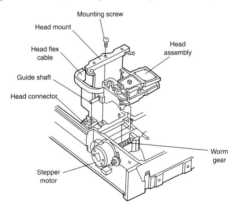

Figure 5.2 An expanded view of a stepper motor and head actuator.

On a 3 1/2-inch drive, the stepper motor is often a worm-gear arrangement rather than the band drive that was used on the older 5 1/4-inch drives. The worm gear is very compact, but can be jammed by shock. To free it up, carefully unscrew the stepper motor from the rear of the drive frame and move the head actuator back and forth gently until the worm gear moves freely again.

Reassemble the drive and test it outside the case by running the data and power cable to it before you secure it into its normal position.

Interface Circuit Boards

A drive's *interface circuit board* (a.k.a. *logic board*) can be damaged by shock, by static electricity, or by a power surge. It can usually be easily removed from the bottom of the drive and replaced by a spare circuit board from an identical drive with a bad read/write head or stepper motor. Keep such failures around for spare parts.

Read/Write Heads

Because of the contact between the heads and disk, a buildup of the magnetic material from the disk eventually forms on the heads. The buildup should periodically be cleaned off the heads as part of a preventive-maintenance or normal service program.

The best method for cleaning the heads involves the use of a commercial wet-method diskette head cleaner and a program that will spin the cleaning diskette and move the heads around the cleaning media. MicroSystems Development (www.msd.com) offers the TestDrive floppy drive testing program, which contains such a cleaning utility. Depending on the drive usage and the amount of contaminants (smoke, dust, soot) in the air, you should clean the read/write heads on a floppy drive only about once every six months to a year.

Do *not* use standard 3 1/2-inch floppy head cleaners with LS-120 SuperDisk floppy drives; although these drives can read and write to standard diskettes as well as the 120MB SuperDisk media, a conventional cleaner will damage their special read/write heads. Check www.superdisk.com for a SuperDisk-compatible cleaning kit.

Floppy Drive Hardware Resources

Whether it is built-in or not, all primary floppy controllers use a standard set of system resources as follows:

- IRQ 6 (Interrupt Request)
- DMA 2 (Direct Memory Address)
- I/O ports 3F0-3F5, 3F7 (Input/Output)

These system resources are standardized and generally not changeable. This normally does not present a problem because no other devices will try to use these resources (which would result in a conflict).

Don't Use a Floppy Drive While Running a Tape Backup

About the only circumstance that would cause a hardware conflict would be the use of a floppy drive while a tape backup is running. While most high-capacity tape backup drives today no longer use the floppy interface, they still often use DMA 2 for fast data transfers. Because DMA transfers are not checked by the CPU or any other part of the system, simultaneous use of DMA 2 by a tape backup and a floppy drive could easily result in data loss on either or both media types.

Disk Drive Power and Data Connectors

There are two sizes used for disk drive power connectors. The following figure shows the original "Molex" power connector used on 5 1/4-inch floppy drives. Most 3 1/2-inch floppy drives and tape backups use a smaller connector, but either size normally has the same four-wire pinout shown in Figure 5.3.

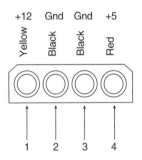

Figure 5.3 A disk drive female power supply cable connector.

Some 3 1/2-inch tape drives may come with an extension cable with only two wires: a ground wire (black) and a +5v wire (red), because their motors use the same +5v power as the logic board does.

Figure 5.4 shows a typical 5-connector floppy data cable. Typically, the 5 1/4-inch edge connectors are seldom used today, unless a 3 1/2-inch drive has a pin-to-edge connector adapter attached.

Table 5.1 compares floppy and hard disk ribbon cables.

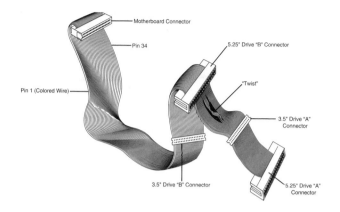

Figure 5.4 Standard five-connector floppy interface cable.

Table 5.1	Comparing Ribbon Cables—Floppy Versus Hard Disk			
Interface Type	**Floppy**	**ST-506 ESDI**	**IDE**	**SCSI**
Cable Width	34-pin	34-pin	40-pin or 80-strand	50-pin or 68-pin
Notes	Almost all have twist between A: drive connectors and B: drive connectors; twist toward pin 1 (colored edge of cable)	May be straight or twisted; twist away from pin 1; obsolete and seldom seen today; used with 20-pin ribbon cable	80-strand cable has 40 pins; designed for use with UDMA/66 motherboards and drives	

Table 5.2 lists the parameters for current and obsolete disk drives used on PCs. If you are preparing a drive with FORMAT that is smaller than the drive's capacity, you will need to set the FORMAT parameter's manually.

A damaged media descriptor byte will prevent programs from properly accessing the disk; this problem can be fixed with Norton Utilities.

Table 5.2   Floppy Disk Logical Formatted Parameters

	Current Formats					Obsolete Formats		
Disk Size (inches)	3 1/2	3 1/2	3 1/2	5 1/4	5 1/4	5 1/4	5 1/4	51/4
Disk Capacity (KB)	2,880	1,440	720	1,200	360	320	180	160
Media Descriptor Byte	F0h	F0h	F9h	F9h	FDh	FFh	FCh	Feh
Sides (Heads)	2	2	2	2	2	2	1	1
Tracks per Side	80	80	80	80	40	40	40	40
Sectors per Track	36	18	9	15	9	8	9	8
Bytes per Sector	512	512	512	512	512	512	512	512
Sectors per Cluster	2	1	2	1	2	2	1	1
FAT Length (Sectors)	9	9	3	7	2	1	2	1
Number of FATs	2	2	2	2	2	2	2	2
Root Dir. Length (Sectors)	15	14	7	14	7	7	4	4
Maximum Root Entries	240	224	112	224	112	112	64	64
Total Sectors per Disk	5,760	2,880	1,440	2,400	720	640	360	320
Total Available Sectors	5,726	2,847	1,426	2,371	708	630	351	313
Total Available Clusters	2,863	2,847	713	2,371	354	315	351	313

Floppy Drive Troubleshooting

Table 5.3   Floppy Drive Troubleshooting Tips

Problem	Cause	Solution
Dead drive— the drive does not spin and the LED never comes on.	Bad power supply or power cable.	Measure the power at the cable with a voltmeter, ensure that 12v and 5v are available to the drive.

Problem	Cause	Solution
	Drive or controller not properly configured in BIOS Setup.	Check BIOS setup for proper drive type and make sure the controller is enabled if built-in to the motherboard; if an add-on card contains a floppy controller and the motherboard also has one, disable one or the other.
	Bad data cable.	Replace the cable and retest.
	Defective drive.	Replace the drive and retest.
	Defective controller.	Replace the controller and retest. If the controller is built into the motherboard, disable it via the BIOS Setup, install a ard-based controller, and retest, or replace the entire motherboard and retest.
Drive LED remains on continuously.	Data cable is on backward at either the drive or controller connection.	Reinstall the cable properly and retest.
	The data cable could be offset on the connector by one or more pins.	Reinstall the cable properly and retest; replace cable if this doesn't work.
Phantom directories— you have exchanged disks in the drive, but the system still believes the previous disk is inserted, and even shows directories of the previous disk.	Defective cable.	Replace the cable and retest.
	Improper drive configuration.	Older drives must have their DC jumper (for Drive Changeline support) enabled.
	Defective drive or interface.	Replace the drive and retest.

Note

Windows users: Windows does *not* automatically refresh the display with File Manager, Explorer, etc. by default. Use the F5 key or click Refresh to re-read diskette.

Common Floppy Drive Error Messages—Causes and Solutions

Table 5.4   Handling Floppy Drive Error Messages

Error Message	Cause	Solution
Invalid Media or Track Zero Bad, Disk Unusable	You are formatting the disk and the disk media type does not match the format parameters.	Make sure you are using the right type of disk for your drive and formatting the disk to its correct capacity.
	Defective or damaged disk.	Replace the disk and retest.
	Dirty read/ write heads.	Clean drive, allow heads to dry, and retest.
CRC Error or Disk Error 23	The data read from the diskette does not match the data that was originally written. (CRC stands for Cyclic Redundancy Check.)	Replace the disk and retest. Clean the drive heads, allow to dry and retest. Use Norton Utilities or SpinRite to recover data from diskette.
General Failure Reading Drive A, Abort, Retry, Fail or Disk Error 31	The disk is not formatted or has been formatted for a different operating system (Macintosh, for example).	Reformat the disk and retest.
	Damaged areas on the disk medium.	Replace the disk and retest. Use Norton Utilities or SpinRite to recover data from diskette.
	Diskette not seated properly in drive.	Remove and reinsert in drive. Try holding diskette in place with your hand. If you can read the data, copy it to a reliable diskette.
Access Denied	You are trying to write to a write-protected disk or file.	Move the write-protect switch to allow writing on the disk, or remove t he read-only file attribute from the file(s). File attributes can be changed by the ATTRIB command or through the file properties in Windows.
Insufficient Disk Space or Disk Full	The disk is filled, or the root directory is filled.	Check to see if sufficient free space is available on the disk for your intended operation Use folders on the. diskette to store files, or change to a new diskette.
Bytes in Bad Sectors (greater than 0)	Displayed after FORMAT, CHKDSK, or SCANDISK if allocation units (clusters) have been marked bad.	Operating system will not use bad sectors, but this is a sign of a marginal diskette; reformat or discard and use a new diskette with no bad sectors.

Error Message	Cause	Solution
Disk Type or Drive Type Incompatible or Bad	You are attempting to DISKCOPY between two incompatible drive or disk types.	Disks can only be copied between drives using the same disk density and size. Use COPY or XCOPY instead, unless you are trying to create an exact copy.

Removable Storage Drives

For backup or alternative main storage, many users today are de-emphasizing floppy diskettes in favor of alternative storage media. Use Table 5.5 to select the media and drives with the best characteristics for your needs. Of the drives listed, only the LS120/SuperDisk drives are also read/write compatible with standard 3 1/2-inch floppy media.

Table 5.5	Removable Drive Specifications		
Drive Type Mfr.	**Disk/Cartridge Capacity/Type**	**Average Seek Time**	**Data Transfer Rate**
Iomega Clik Parallel	40MB Clik	not listed	620KB/sec
Iomega Zip Parallel1	100MB Zip	29ms	1.4MB/sec
Iomega Zip IDE/ATAPI	100MB Zip	29ms	1.4Mb/sec
Iomega Zip SCSI1	100MB Zip	29ms	1.4MB/sec
Iomega Zip USB	100MB Zip	29ms	1.2MB/sec
Iomega Zip 250 SCSI2	250MB Zip	29ms	2.4MB/sec
Iomega Zip 250 Parallel2	250MB Zip	29ms	0.8MB/sec
Iomega Zip 250 ATAPI/IDE2	250MB Zip	29ms	2.4MB/sec
Imation LS-120 IDE Internal3	120MB SuperDisk	70ms	1.1MB/sec
Imation LS-120 Parallel4	120MB SuperDisk	70ms	750KB/sec
Imation LS-120 USB5	120MB SuperDisk	70ms	700KB/sec
Imation LS-120 PCMCIA	120MB SuperDisk	70ms	440KB/sec
SyQuest 230 Parallel6	230MB EzFlyer	13.5ms	1.25MB/sec

(continues)

Table 5.5	Removable Drive Specifications Continued		
Drive Type Mfr.	**Disk/Cartridge Capacity/Type**	**Average Seek Time**	**Data Transfer Rate**
SyQuest 230 SCSI/IDE6	230MB EzFlyer	13.5ms	2.4MB/sec
Avatar Shark 250 Parallel7	250MB Shark	12ms	1.2MB/sec
Avatar Shark PCMCIA7	250MB Shark	12ms	2.0MB/sec
Avatar Shark IDE7	250MB Shark	12ms	2.5MB/sec
Iomega Jaz (SCSI)8	2GB Jaz	12ms	7.35MB/sec
SyQuest SyJet SCSI6	1.5GB SyJet	12ms	5.3MB/sec
SyQuest SyJet IDE6	1.5GB SyJet	12ms	5.3MB/sec
SyQuest SparQ IDE6	1GB SparQ	12ms	6.9MB/sec
SyQuest SparQ Parallel6	1GB SparQ	12ms	1.25MB/sec
CD-R/CD-RW Drives	650MB CD-R/CD-RW	<150ms	150K/sec –2.4MB/sec9
Castlewood ORB IDE	2GB ORB	12ms	12.2MB/sec
Castlewood ORB SCSI	2GB ORB	12ms	12.2MB/sec
Castlewood ORB Parallel	2GB ORB	12ms	2MB/sec

1 While Iomega rates ZIP 100 parallel and SCSI versions as having same transfer rates, SCSI versions are as much as 8x faster in actual use.

2 Zip 250 drives can also read/write ZIP 100 drives.

3 New version; original version maximum transfer rate was 660KB/second.

4 New version; original version maximum transfer rate was 290KB/second.

5 New version; original version maximum transfer rate was 400KB/second.

6 SyQuest is now known as SYQT; company declared bankruptcy in November 1998 but still offers products, drivers, repairs and support at www.syqt.com; SyQuest 230 can also use EzFlyer 135MB cartridges; SyQuest was purchased by Iomega.

7 Avatar is out of business; drivers and user forum Q&A are available at www.windrivers.com.

8 Jaz 2GB drive can also read/write Jaz 1GB cartridge.

9 Transfer rate varies with interface and drive X-rating.

Emergency Access to Iomega Zip Drive Files in Case of Disaster

Most removable-media drives are optimized for use with Windows 9x/NT/2000, but in the event that the operating system fails, you want to be able to get access to your files, even if you must boot the machine to a command prompt.

The Iomega Zip drive is the most popular removable-media drive, and files stored on the PC version can be accessed from an MS-DOS prompt using its real-mode Guest.exe driver, even if the drive was originally used with Windows 9x/NT/2000. All long filenames and folder names will be displayed using their short MS-DOS alias names.

Because the Iomega parallel-port Zip drive can be used on virtually any system, I recommend that organizations which use Zip media have a parallel-port version, even though it's slower than other versions.

Table 5.6 indicates what's needed to access the parallel-port Zip drive. You can get the files needed from the IomegaWARE CD-ROM supplied with recent versions of the Zip drive, or from www.iomega.com.

Table 5.6 Accessing Parallel Port Zip Drives		
Drive	**Interface**	**Files**
Iomega Zip 100, Zip 250	Parallel	Guest.exe, guest.ini, Aspippm1.sys, Aspippm2.sys, Nibble.ilm,
Nibble2.ilm, Guesthlp.txt, Manual.exe	Set parallel port to EPP or bidirectional modes, not ECP	

Parallel-port versions of the SyQuest SparQ and EzFlyer 230 drives are also available from SYQT (formerly SyQuest).

Troubleshooting Removable Media Drives

Table 5.7 Troubleshooting Removable Media Drives		
Drive/Interface	**Problem**	**Solution**
Any parallel-port model	Can't detect drive with install program	Check for IRQ conflicts; IRQ for parallel port must not be used by sound cards or other devices; verify that install diskette has correct drivers.
Any SCSI interface model	Drive not available	Check SCSI IDs; each SCSI device must have a unique ID number; check termination; verify correct drivers installed; ASPI drivers must be installed for both SCSI interface and each device on interface.

(continues)

Table 5.7	Troubleshooting Removable Media Drives Continued	
Drive/Interface	**Problem**	**Solution**
Iomega Zip— any interface	Drive makes "clicking" sound; can't access files	Drive might have "click of death" problem; physically examine media for damage; use Iomega Diagnostics to check media; download Trouble in Paradise (TIP) from Gibson Research www.grc.com for more thorough testing.
Any drive, any interface	Drive letter interferes with network, CD-ROM, etc.	Under Windows 9x/NT/2000, check drive properties and select an available drive letter not used by CD-ROM or network.

MS-DOS Command-Line Access to CD-ROM Drives for Reloading Windows

CD-ROM drives are normally controlled in Windows 9x by 32-bit drivers, but these drivers *will not work* if the operating system becomes corrupted or if Windows will only work in Safe mode. In those cases, having access to the CD-ROM drive becomes critical to allow you to reload the operating system.

In Windows 98, the Emergency Diskette you can create during initial installation or later contains drivers that work for most IDE/ATAPI and SCSI-based CD-ROM drives, and the diskette will try each driver until it finds one that works.

In Windows 9x, the Emergency Diskette does *not* contain drivers for the CD-ROM. Follow these general guidelines to create a working boot disk with CD-ROM support. This same process will work for MS-DOS/Windows 3.1 users.

1. Create the Windows 95 Emergency Diskette (it's bootable) from the Control Panel's Add/Remove Programs icon— Windows Setup tab. Or, use FORMAT A:/s to create a bootable diskette manually. Either process *destroys* all previous contents on the diskette.

2. Copy the following files to your bootable diskette in A: drive:

   • *MYCDROM*.SYS

     Use the actual driver name for your CD-ROM drive and copy it from the file's actual location. If you don't have an MS-DOS driver, you can download one from the drive's manufacturer, or download an ATAPI driver called AOATAPI.SYS available from several Web sites.

- MSCDEX.EXE

  Copy from C:\WINDOWS\COMMAND or your CD-ROM drive's folder; the same file for any CD-ROM drive.

Then you'll need to create a CONFIG.SYS file that will load the CD-ROM device driver and an AUTOEXEC.BAT that will load the MSCDEX.EXE CD-ROM extensions for MS-DOS program. Use a text editor such as the Windows notepad.

- Contents of CONFIG.SYS

  DEVICE=*MYCDROM.SYS* /D:mscd001

  Lastdrive=M

- Contents of AUTOEXEC.BAT

  MSCDEX.EXE /d:mscd001 /m:10 /L:M

Note

Note that the /d: switch refers to the same device name, which could be "Charlie" or "Kumquat" or anything that matches! A mismatch will cause the loading process to fail.

Check your computer's BIOS setup and verify that the floppy drive is the first bootable device, restart the computer with this floppy in drive A: and you should see the CD-ROM driver initialize, and then MSCDEX should assign the CD-ROM the drive letter listed after the /L: option (M:).

Bus-Mastering Chipsets for IDE

Most late-model Pentium-class and higher motherboards can support bus-mastering drivers for their IDE interfaces. The benefits of bus-mastering include faster IDE data transfer for CD-ROM, CD-R/CD-RW and hard drives, and lower CPU utilization rates (the percentage of total time the CPU spends handling a particular task). Table 5.8 lists the major chipsets providing bus-mastering features, and where to get the driver. Make sure you install the correct driver for your chipset.

Table 5.8   Bus-Mastering Chipsets by Vendor and Operating System

Vendor	Chipsets	Driver Source by Operating System
Intel	430FX 430HX 430VX 440FX 430TX 440LX 440BX 440EX 440GX 440ZX 440ZX-66 450NX	(Same driver for all Intel chipsets) Windows 95 original and OSR1 (95a): Download from the Intel Web site Windows 95B, 95C (OSR 2.x), Windows 98: included on Windows CD-ROM
VIA	MVP3 VP3 VP2 VPX VP1	For Windows 95 (any version) and NT 3.51 and higher: Download the drivers from the VIA Web site. For Windows 98: included on CD-ROM
SiS	611 85c496 5513, 5571, 5581/5582, 5591, 5597/5598, 5600 IDE Driver* SiS530/5595 & SiS620/5595 IDE Driver	Download the drivers from the SiS Web site. *(For SiS chipsets 5511/5512/5513, 5596/5513, 5571, 5581/5582, 5598/5597, 5591/5595, 600 /5595)
ETEQ	Various motherboard models	See www.soyo.com.tw to look up models and drivers; download there or from related FTP site.
PCChips	TXPRO HXPRO VXPRO	Download DOS, Windows 3.1, Windows 95, and Windows NT 4 drivers from the PCChips FTP site Download DOS, Windows 3.1, Windows 95, Windows NT 3.51 and 4.0 drivers from the PCChips FTP site. Download DOS, Windows 3.1, Windows 95, UNIX, OS/2, Windows NT 3.5, or NetWare drivers from the PCChips FTP site
Ali	See note	Drivers are available from the motherboard maker using ALi chipsets.

All Intel chipsets that contain a PIIXn device (PIIX, PIIX3, PIIX4, PIIX4E, and so on) are bus-mastering chipsets.

Although PCChips chipset names are similar to certain Intel Pentium chipsets (Triton series TX, HX, and VX), the drivers listed are strictly for PCChips chipsets, not Intel's.

Troubleshooting Optical Drives

Failure Reading a CD

If your CD-ROM drive fails to read a CD, try the following solutions:

- Check for scratches on CD data surface.

- Check drive for dust, dirt; use cleaning CD.

- Make sure drive shows up as working device in System Properties.

- Try a CD that you know to work.

- Restart computer (the magic cure-all).

- Remove drive from Device Manager in Windows 9x, allow system to redetect drive and reinstall drivers (if PnP-based system).

Failure Reading CD-R, CD-RW Disks in CD-ROM or DVD Drive

If your CD-ROM or DVD drive fails to read CD-R and CD-RW disks, try the following solutions:

- Check compatibility; some very old 1x CD-ROM drives can't read CD-R media. Replace drive with newer, faster, cheaper model.

- Many early-model DVD drives can't read CD-R, CD-RW media; check compatibility.

- CD-ROM drive must be multi-read compatible to read CD-RW because of lower reflectivity of media; replace drive.

- If some CD-Rs but not others can be read, check media color combination to see whether some color combinations work better than others; change brand of media.

- Packet-written CD-Rs (from Adaptec DirectCD and backup programs) can't be read on MS-DOS/Windows 3.1 CD-ROM drives because of limitations of operating system.

IDE/ATAPI CD-ROM Drive Runs Slowly

If your IDE/ATAPI CD-ROM drive performs poorly, check the following items:

- Check cache size in the Performance tab of the System Properties Control Panel. Select the quad-speed setting (largest cache size)

- Check to see whether the CD-ROM drive is set as the slave to your hard disk; move CD-ROM to the secondary controller if possible.

- Your PIO or UDMA mode might not be set correctly for your drive in the BIOS; check drive specs and use autodetect in BIOS for best results (see Chapter 4, "Hard Drives").

- Check to see that you are using bus-mastering drivers on compatible systems; install appropriate drivers for motherboard's chipset and operating system in use. See "DMA (Direct Memory Access)" earlier in this chapter.

- Check to see whether you are using the CD-ROM interface on your sound card instead of IDE connection on motherboard. Move the drive connection to the IDE interface on motherboard and disable sound card IDE if possible to free up IRQ and I/O port address ranges.

- Open the System Properties Control Panel and select the Performance tab to see whether system is using MS-DOS Compatibility mode for CD-ROM drive. If all IDE drives are running in this mode, see www.microsoft.com and query on "MS-DOS Compatibility Mode" for a troubleshooter. If only the CD-ROM drive is in this mode, see whether you're using CD-ROM drivers in CONFIG.SYS and AUTOEXEC.BAT. Remove the lines containing references to the CD-ROM drivers (don't actually delete the lines—REM them), reboot the system and verify that your CD-ROM drive still works and that it's running in 32-bit mode. Some older drives require at least the CONFIG.SYS driver to operate.

Trouble Reading CD-RW Disks on CD-ROM

If you cannot read CD-RW disks in your CD-ROM, check the vendor specifications to see whether your drive is multi-read compliant. Some drives are not compliant.

If your drive is multi-read compliant, try the CD-RW disk on known-compliant CD-ROM drive (drive with multi-read feature).

Trouble Reading CD-R Disks on DVD Drive

If your DVD drive cannot read a CD-R disk, check drive compliance—original DVDs cannot read CD-R media. Newer, faster DVD drives support CD-R media.

Trouble Using Bootable CDs

If you are having problems using a bootable CD, try these possible solutions:

- Check the contents of bootable floppy disk from which you copied the boot image during the creation of the bootable CD. To access entire contents of a CD-R, a bootable disk must contain CD-ROM drivers, AUTOEXEC.BAT, and CONFIG.SYS. Test the bootable diskette by starting the system with it and seeing if you can access the CD-ROM drive afterward.

- Use ISO 9660 format. Don't use Joliet format because it is for long-filename CDs and can't boot.

- Check your system's BIOS for boot compliance and boot order; CD-ROM should be listed first.

- Check drive for boot compliance.

- SCSI CD-ROMs need SCSI card with BIOS and bootable capability as well as special motherboard BIOS settings.

Tape Backup Drives and Media

Despite the recent rise of high-capacity drives such as Zip, Jaz, CD-R/CD-RW and others, most backups are still stored on tape. The most common and longest-lived series of standards for tape drives are those established by QIC (the Quarter Inch Committee). Because QIC has created many standards over the years, you might have tape cartridges from several older QIC drives in storage. Table 5.9 will help you to determine what newer drives may be capable of reading your older tapes.

Table 5.9 Tape Drive and Media Compatibility			
QIC Standard	**Compatible With**	**Example Drive**	**Capacity/at 2:1 compression**
QIC-40	—	Colorado Jumbo 120	60MB/120MB
QIC-80	QIC-40*	Colorado Jumbo 250	125MB/250MB
QIC-3010	QIC-40 and QIC-80*	Exabyte Eagle 96	340MB/680MB
QIC-3020	QIC-40, QIC-80, and QIC-3010*	Iomega Ditto 3200	680MB/1.4GB
QIC-3095	QIC-3010 and QIC-3020*	AIWA TD-8000 series	4GB/8GB
QIC-3220	QIC-3095*	HP SureStore T20	10GB/20GB

Read-only compatibility

QIC-Wide Tape Formats

QIC-Wide tape cartridges, developed by Sony, are a physically wider variant of QIC. While relatively few drives are designed specifically for QIC-Wide, they can be read and written by many Travan-class drives (see Table 5.10).

Table 5.10 QIC-Wide Formats		
QIC-Wide Format	**Based on QIC Format (Read/ Write Compatible)**	**Capacity 2:1 Compression**
QW5122	QIC-80	210MB/420MB
QW3010XLF	QIC-3010	425MB/850MB
QW3020XLF	QIC-3020	850MB/1.7GB
QW3080XLF	QIC-3080	2.0GB/4.0GB
QW2GB	Ditto 2GB	1.0GB/2.0GB

Travan and QIC Compatibility

Travan-based tape backup drives, using a modified QIC-type technology originated by Imation, have largely replaced QIC-only tape backups in workstation and small network use. Travan 1, Travan 3, and Travan 4 drives are backward compatible with specified QIC and QIC-Wide tape formats. See Table 5.11.

Table 5.11 Travan and QIC Compatibility				
Travan Standard	**Read- Compatible**	**Read & Write- Compatible**	**Capacity/ with 2:1 Compression**	**Example Drive**
Travan 1 (TR-1)	QIC-40	QIC-80, QW5122	400MB/800MB	Iomega Ditto 800
Travan 2 (TR-2)	QIC-80	QIC-3010, QW3010XL	800MB/1.6GB	Teac Tape 1600
Travan 3 (TR-3)	QIC-3010	QIC-3020, QW3020XL	1.6GB/3.2GB	Exabyte Eagle TR-3
Travan 8GB (was Travan 4/TR-4)	QIC-3020	—	4GB/8GB	AIWA TD-8000 series
Travan NS-8* Hornet NS8	—	—	4GB/8GB	Seagate
Travan NS-20*	Travan NS-8, QIC-3095	—	10GB/20GB	Tecmar NS20

Has read-while-write for faster backup and compare.

Successful Tape Backup and Restore Procedures

A backup tape might be the only thing separating you from a complete loss of data. To assure that every backup can be restored, follow the guidelines shown in Tables 5.12 and 5.13 when you create a backup or restore one.

Table 5.12	Tape Backup Tips	
Tip	**Benefit**	**Notes**
Perform the confidence test during tape backup software installation	Tests DMA channels in computer for safe data transfer; sets default transfer rate for backup	Keep a spare blank tape at all times to allow you to perform this test whenever new hardware is installed or before running a new backup for safety
Select the correct backup type	"Full" backup backs up contents of system but operating system must be restored first before restoring backup. "Disaster Recovery" backup creates special boot diskettes and allows entire system recovery straight from tape to an empty hard drive. Other backup types are designed primarily for data backup.	Make a disaster recovery backup and test your ability to restore your backup to an empty hard drive. Use other backup types for periodic backups.
Choose speed and safety	Maximum data compression uses the least amount of tape and is often about as fast as other backup types. Use Compare after toassure readability.	
Don't use multiple tapes for a single backup	Tape backups are typically rated with 2:1 compression assumed; this ratio is seldom achieved. Using multiple tapes for a single backup can cause loss of data if first tape is lost, because it contains tape catalog. Back up a large drive with a small tape drive by backing up sections.	Use actual compression ratio reported during your initial full backup to determine your nominal tape size. If your tape drive is a Travan 3 or smaller, get extra capacity per tape by using Verbatim QIC-EX series tapes (see the following chart).

(continues)

Table 5.12	Tape Backup Tips Continued	
Tip	**Benefit**	**Notes**
Avoid multitasking during the tape backup.	Let the tape backup run without interruptions, due to DMA transfers. Turn off screensavers and power management. Turn off your monitor.	Don't use floppy drives, since floppy DMA 2 is often used during backups.

Table 5.13	Tape Restore Tips
Tip	**Benefit**
Restore full backups to an empty drive if possible.	Avoids overwriting drive with junk data if your backup has failed.
If your full backup is not a disaster recovery type, install the smallest possible operating system image first.	You'll wait less time before you can install your backup software and restore your backup.
Run the confidence test again before you start the restore process	Verifies that DMA transfers will be successful; this requires a blank tape or one that can be overwritten, so keep one handy.

Getting Extra Capacity with Verbatim QIC-EX Tape Media

Many older model, small-capacity tape backups are still in use on older workstations and small networks. The rapid increase in hard disk capacity is causing many problems in creating tape backups that are as safe as possible. The "1 backup = 1 tape" rule is harder to live by when Travan 3 (3.2MB compressed capacity) or smaller tape drives are used with 4GB or larger hard drives.

If you use any of the tape standards shown in Table 5.14, you can use the listed Verbatim QIC-Extra cartridges as a replacement. Note that the same QIC-Extra series cartridge can be interchanged between a particular QIC, QIC-Wide, and Travan drive type. This is because QIC-EX tapes are the same width as normal QIC cartridges, but are much longer. Since some tape backup drives can't handle the extra capacity with their own backup software, some models of QIC-EX cartridges come with replacement backup software that will use the full capacity.

Table 5.14   QIC-EX Tape Media

Original Tape	Capacity/ Compressed 2:1	Verbatim QIC-Extra	Capacity/ Compressed 2:1
QIC-80 normal length (DC-2120)	125MB/250MB	DC2120EX	400MB/800MB
QIC-80 longer length (DC-2120XL)	170MB/340MB		
QW5122	210MB/420MB		
Travan 1 (TR-1)	400MB/800MB		
Travan 1 (TR-1)	400MB/800MB	TR-1EX	500MB/1.0GB
QIC-3020	680MB/1.4GB	MC3020EX	1.6GB/3.2GB
QW3020	850MB/1.7GB		
Travan 3 (TR-3)	1.6GB/3.2GB		
Travan 3 (TR-3)	1.6GB/3.2GB	TR-3EX	2.2MB/4.4GB

Chapter 6

Serial, USB, and IEEE-1394 Ports and Devices

Understanding Serial Ports

The asynchronous serial interface was designed as a system-to-system communications port. *Asynchronous* means that no synchronization or clocking signal is present, so characters can be sent with any arbitrary time spacing.

Each character that is sent over a serial connection is framed by a standard start-and-stop signal. A single 0 bit, called the start bit, precedes each character to tell the receiving system that the next eight bits constitute a byte of data. One or two stop bits follow the character to signal that the character has been sent. At the receiving end of the communication, characters are recognized by the start-and-stop signals instead of by the timing of their arrival. *Serial* refers to data that is sent over a single wire, with each bit lining up in a series as the bits are sent. This type of communication is used over the phone system because this system provides one wire for data in each direction. Compared to parallel ports, serial ports are very slow, but their signals can be transmitted a greater distance.

Serial ports are also referred to as COM ports, because they are used to COMmunicate between devices.

Physically, serial ports come in two forms, although through adapters or specially-wired cable, they have no problems communicating with each other. The following figures show the standard 9-pin (see Figure 6.1) and 25-pin (see Figure 6.2) serial ports. The 25-pin serial port has pins sticking out, as opposed to the 25-parallel port, which has holes for pins.

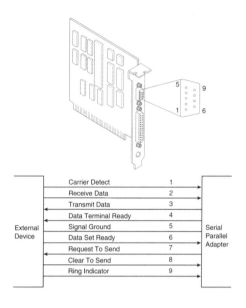

Figure 6.1 AT-style 9-pin serial-port connector specifications.

Pinouts for Serial Ports

Tables 6.1, 6.2, and 6.3 show the pinouts of the 9-pin (AT-style), 25-pin, and 9-pin-to-25-pin serial connectors.

Table 6.1	9-Pin (AT) Serial Port Connector		
Pin	**Signal**	**Description**	**I/O**
1	CD	Carrier detect	In
2	RD	Receive data	In
3	TD	Transmit data	Out
4	DTR	Data terminal ready	Out
5	SG	Signal ground	—
6	DSR	Data set ready	In
7	RTS	Request to send	Out
8	CTS	Clear to send	In
9	RI	Ring indicator	In

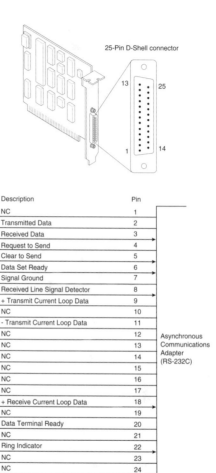

25-Pin D-Shell connector

Description	Pin
NC	1
Transmitted Data	2
Received Data	3
Request to Send	4
Clear to Send	5
Data Set Ready	6
Signal Ground	7
Received Line Signal Detector	8
+ Transmit Current Loop Data	9
NC	10
- Transmit Current Loop Data	11
NC	12
NC	13
NC	14
NC	15
NC	16
NC	17
+ Receive Current Loop Data	18
NC	19
Data Terminal Ready	20
NC	21
Ring Indicator	22
NC	23
NC	24
- Receive Current Loop Return	25

External Device

Asynchronous Communications Adapter (RS-232C)

Figure 6.2 Standard 25-pin serial-port connector specifications.

Table 6.2   25-Pin (PC, XT, and PS/2) Serial Port Connector

Pin	Signal	Description	I/O
1	—	Chassis ground	—
2	TD	Transmit data	Out
3	RD	Receive data	In
4	RTS	Request to send	Out

(continues)

Table 6.2   25-Pin (PC. XT. and PS/2) Serial Port Connector Continued

Pin	Signal	Description	I/O
6	DSR	Data set ready	In
7	SG	Signal ground	—
8	CD	Carrier detect	In
9	—	+Transmit current loop return	Out
11	—	-Transmit current loop data	Out
18	—	+Receive current loop data	In
20	DTR	Data terminal ready	Out
22	RI	Ring indicator	In
25	—	-Receive current loop return	In

Table 6.3   9-Pin to 25-Pin Serial Cable Adapter Connections

9-Pin	25-Pin		Signal
1	8	CD	Carrier detect
2	3	RD	Receive data
3	2	TD	Transmit data
4	20	DTR	Data terminal ready
5	7	SG	Signal ground
6	6	DSR	Data set ready
7	4	RTS	Request to send
8	5	CTS	Clear to send
9	22	RI	Ring indicator

Note

Macintosh systems use a similar serial interface, defined as RS-422. Most external modems that are in use today can interface with either RS-232 or RS-422, but it is safest to make sure that the external modem you get for your PC is designed for a PC, not a Macintosh.

UARTs

The heart of any serial port is the Universal Asynchronous Receiver/Transmitter (UART) chip. This chip completely controls the process of breaking the native parallel data within the PC into serial format, and later converting serial data back into the parallel format.

A few modem models lack a true UART, and use the resources of the computer and operating system for communications in place of a UART. These so-called *Winmodems* are less expensive than ordinary modems, but are slower and not compatible with non-Windows operating systems such as Linux.

UART Types

UART chips have been improved many times over the years, and it's important to know what UART your serial port(s) use, especially under the following circumstances:

- You want to attach a modem to the serial port

- You plan to transfer data between machines via the serial port

- You want to assure reliable multitasking while using Windows with your modem.

Table 6.4 summarizes the characteristics of the major UART chips (and equivalents) found in PCs. For more information about UARTs, be sure to see Chapter 16 of *Upgrading and Repairing PCs, Eleventh Edition*, from Que.

Table 6.4   Overview of UART Chip Types

UART Type	Maximum Speed	Buffer	Typical System	Notes
8250	Up to9600bps	No	8088	Original UART; replaced by 8250B
8250A	Up to 9600bps	No	8088	Not recommended because it's incompatible with 8250
8250B	Up to 9600bps	No	8088/286	Debugged version of 8250
16450	Up to 19200 bps (19.2Kbps)	No	386/486	Minimum UART for OS/2
16550A -> D	Up to 115000bps (115Kbps)	16-byte FIFO	386/486 Pentium	First chip suit able for multitasking; can be used as pin-compatible replacement for socketed 16450

(continues)

Table 6.4	Overview of UART Chip Types Continued			
UART Type	Maximum Speed	Buffer	Typical System	Notes
16650	Up to 230000 bps (230Kbps)	32-byte	Specialized I/O cards, ISDN terminal adapters	Faster throughput than 16650 series
16750	Up to 460000 bps (460Kbps)	64-byte	Specialized I/O cards, ISDN terminal adapters	Faster throughput than 16650, 16650 series

Determining What UART Chips Your System Has

The minimum desirable UART chip is the 16550A series or above, but older systems and inexpensive multi-I/O cards might use the bufferless 8250 or 16450 series UARTs instead. There are two major methods you can use to determine which UARTs you have in a system.

MS-DOS Method (also for Windows NT)

Use a diagnostic program such as Microsoft MSD, CheckIt, AMIDiag, or others to examine the serial ports. These programs will also list the IRQ and I/O port addresses in use for each serial port. Because ports are virtualized under Windows, the reports from a DOS-based utility will not be accurate unless you boot straight to a DOS prompt and run the diagnostic from there.

OS/2 Method

Use the MODE COMx command from the OS/2 prompt to view serial port information. Look for an entry called "Buffer" in the list of serial port characteristics. If "Buffer" is set to "Auto", the chip is a true 16650A or better. If "Buffer" is set to "N/A", it's an older 16450 chip.

Windows 9x Method

Open the Start menu, and then choose Settings, Control Panel. Next, double-click Modems, and then click the Diagnostics tab. The Diagnostics tab shows a list of all COM ports in the system, even if they don't have a modem attached to them. Select the port you want to check in the list and click More Info. Windows 95 or 98 communicates with the port to determine the UART type, and that information is listed in the Port Information portion of the More Info box. If a modem is attached, additional information about the modem is displayed.

High-Speed Serial Ports (ESP and Super ESP)

Some modem manufacturers have gone a step further in improving serial data transfer by introducing Enhanced Serial Ports (ESP) or Super High-Speed Serial Ports. These ports enable a 28.8Kbps or faster modem to communicate with the computer at data rates up to 921.6Kbps. The extra speed on these ports is generated by increasing the buffer size. These ports are usually based on a 16550, 16650, or 16750 UART, and some even include more buffer memory on the card.

Lava Computer Mfg. is one company that offers a complete line of high-speed serial and parallel port cards.

Upgrading the UART Chip

Use Table 6.5 to determine where any UART chip may be located and what you would need to do to replace it.

Table 6.5 Upgrading UARTs		
Device Type	**UART Location**	**Upgrade Method**
Internal modem	Modem chipset	Replace modem
Multi-I/O card with 8250	Socketed or soldered chips	Replace card; 16550 not pin-compatible
Multi-I/O card with 16450	Socketed or soldered chips	Remove 16450 if socketed; replace card if soldered
Multi-I/O card with Super I/O	Equivalent to normal UART inside of a highly integrated surface-mounted chip	Replace card
Motherboard-based I/O	Older systems socketed chip	
Newer systems— UART equivalent inside Super I/O	See the section "UARTs" earlier in this chapter	

Serial Port Configuration

Each time a character is received by a serial port, it has to get the attention of the computer by raising an *interrupt request line (IRQ)*. Eight-bit ISA bus systems have eight of these lines, and systems with a 16-bit ISA bus have 16 lines. The 8259 interrupt controller chip usually handles these requests for attention. In a standard configuration, COM 1 uses IRQ 4, and COM 2 uses IRQ 3.

When a serial port is installed in a system, it must be configured to use specific I/O addresses (called *ports*), and *interrupts*. The best plan is to follow the existing standards for how these devices are to be set up. For configuring serial ports, use the addresses and interrupts indicated in Table 6.6.

Table 6.6	Standard Serial I/O Port Addresses and Interrupts	
COM x	**I/O Ports**	**IRQ**
COM 1	3F8-3FFh	IRQ 4
COM 2	2F8-2FFh	IRQ 3
COM 3	3E8-3EFh	IRQ 4*
COM 4	2E8-2EFh	IRQ 3*

Although many serial ports can be set up to share IRQ 3 and 4 with COM 1 and COM 2, it is not recommended. The best recommendation is setting COM 3 to IRQ 10 and COM 4 to IRQ 11 (if available). If ports above COM 3 are required, it is recommended that you purchase a special multiport serial board.

Avoiding Conflicts with Serial Ports

Use Table 6.7 to understand possible conflicts with serial ports and avoid them.

Table 6.7	Troubleshooting Serial Port Conflicts	
Problem	**Reason**	**Solution**
DOS-based program can't find COM 3 or 4 on modem or other device	DOS and PC BIOS support COM 1 and 2 only	Disable COM 2 and set new device to use COM 2; use Windows program instead
Device using COM 3 or 4 conflicts with COM 1 and 2 (see earlier)	Shared IRQs don't work for ISA devices	Relocate IRQ for device to a different port. If device is external, connect to multiport board. (Windows 95/98/NT can handle up to 128 serial ports!)

For modem troubleshooting, see "Modems" later in this chapter.

Troubleshooting I/O Ports in Windows

Windows 95/98 can tell you whether your ports are functioning. First, you need to verify that the required communications files are present to support the serial ports in your system:

1. Verify the file sizes and dates of both COMM.DRV (16-bit serial driver) and SERIAL.VXD (32-bit serial driver) in the SYSTEM directory, compared to the original versions of these files from the Windows 9x CD-ROM. They should be the same date or *later*, not older.

2. Confirm that the following lines are present in SYSTEM.INI:

```
[boot]

comm.drv=comm.drv

[386enh]

device=*vcd
```

The SERIAL.VXD driver is not loaded in SYSTEM.INI; instead, it is loaded through the Registry. If both drivers are present and accounted for, you can determine if a particular serial port's I/O address and IRQ settings are properly defined by following these steps:

1. Right-click the "My Computer" icon and select Properties, or open Control Panel, double-left-click the "System" icon.

   Then, click on the Device Manager tab, Ports entry, and then select a specific port (such as COM 1).

2. Click the Properties button, and then click the Resources tab to display the current resource settings (IRQ, I/O) for that port.

3. Check the Conflicting Devices List to see if the port is using resources that conflict with other devices. If the port is in conflict with other devices, click the Change Setting button, and then select a configuration that does not cause resource conflicts. You might need to experiment with these settings until you find the right one.

4. If the resource settings cannot be changed, most likely they must be changed via the BIOS Setup. Shut down and restart the system, enter the BIOS setup, and change the port configurations there.

In addition to the COM 1/COM 3 and COM 2/COM 4 IRQ conflicts noted earlier, some video adapters have an automatic address conflict with COM 4's I/O port address (not IRQ).

Advanced Diagnostics Using Loopback Testing

One of the most useful types of diagnostic test is the *loopback test*, which can be used to ensure the correct function of the serial port and any attached cables. Loopback tests are basically internal (digital) or external (analog). You can run internal tests by unplugging any cables from the port and executing the test via a diagnostics program.

The external loopback test is more effective. This test requires that a special loopback connector or wrap plug be attached to the port in question. When the test is run, the port is used to send data out to the loopback plug, which routes the data back into the port's receive pins so that the port is transmitting and receiving at the same time. A *loopback* or *wrap plug* is nothing more than a cable that is doubled back on itself.

Following is a list of the wiring needed to construct your own loopback or wrap plugs. Check with the vendor of your testing software to determine which loopback plug design you need to use or purchase pre-built ones from the vendor.

Loopback Plug Pinouts—Serial Ports

- Standard IBM type 25-Pin Serial (Female DB25S) Loopback Connector (Wrap Plug). Connect the following pins:

  1 to 7

  2 to 3

  4 to 5 to 8

  6 to 11 to 20 to 22

  15 to 17 to 23

  18 to 25

- Norton Utilities (Symantec) 25-Pin Serial (Female DB25S) Loopback Connector (Wrap Plug). Connect the following pins:

  2 to 3

  4 to 5

  6 to 8 to 20 to 22

- Standard IBM type 9-Pin Serial (Female DB9S) Loopback Connector (Wrap Plug). Connect the following pins:

  1 to 7 to 8

  2 to 3

  4 to 6 to 9

- Norton Utilities (Symantec) 9-Pin Serial (Female DB9S) Loopback Connector (Wrap Plug). Connect the following pins:

2 to 3

7 to 8

1 to 4 to 6 to 9

To make these loopback plugs, you need a connector shell with the required pins installed. Then wire wrap or solder wires, interconnecting the appropriate pins inside the connector shell as specified in the preceding list.

One advantage of using loopback connectors is that you can plug them into the ends of a cable that is included in the test. This can verify that both the cable and the port are working properly.

Modems

Modems provide a vital communications link between millions of small to medium-sized businesses and homes and the Internet, electronic banking, and other services. The following information will help you get the most out of your modem.

Modems and Serial Ports

External modems connect to existing serial ports and don't contain a UART chip. Most internal modems contain their own serial port, and do contain a UART chip.

Any external modem that will be used at speeds of 28Kbps or above must be connected to a 16550A-type UART or better to run at top speeds.

Modem Modulation Standards

Modems are frequently identified by their protocols. Use Table 6.8 to determine the speed and other characteristics of a particular protocol. Most modems support multiple protocols.

Table 6.8	Modem Modulation Standards and Transmission Rates	
Protocol	Maximum Transmission Rate (bps)	Duplex Mode
Bell 103	300bps	Full
CCITT V.21	300bps	Full
Bell 212A	1200bps	Full
ITU V.22	1200bps	Half
ITU V.22bis	2400bps	Full
ITU V.23	1,200/75bps	Pseudo-Full

(continues)

Table 6.8   Modem Modulation Standards and Transmission Rates Continued

Protocol	Maximum Transmission Rate (bps)	Duplex Mode
ITU V.29	9,600bps	Half
ITU V.32	9,600bps	Full
ITU V.32bis	14,400bps (14.4Kbps)	Full
ITU V.32fast	28,800bps (28.8Kbps)	Full
ITU V.34	28,800bps (28.8Kbps)	Full
ITU V.34bis	33,600bps (33.6Kbps)	Full
ITU V.90	56,000bps (56Kbps)*	Full

While the ITU V.90 (successor to the proprietary 56Kflex and X2 standards) allows for this speed of transmission, the U.S. FCC (Federal Communications Commission) allows only 53,000bps (53Kbps) at this time.

56Kbps Standards

Virtually every modem sold today corresponds to one or more of the so-called *56Kbps* standards for faster downloading from an Internet service provider (ISP). Uploading to a remote computer must run at the slower V.34bis speeds.

Table 6.9 lists the original and final 56Kbps standards.

Table 6.9   56Kbps Modem Standards

Standard	Modem Chipsets Supported *Major Brand Example*	Notes
x2	Texas Instruments *US Robotics*	First 56Kbps standard in use; not compatible with K56flex
K56flex	Rockwell *Hayes, Zoom*	Second 56Kbps standard in use; not compatible with x2
V.90	All 56Kbps modems with updated firmware	Official ITU standard has replaced previous proprietary standards listed earlier

Because 56Kbps was originally a proprietary standard that was chipset dependent, many "early adopters" have had problems getting high-speed access as more and more ISPs have switched their x2- or K56flex-specific modem pools to V.90. Table 6.10 provides guidelines for upgrading your non-V.90 modem to the V.90 standard.

Table 6.10	Upgrade Options to V.90	
Original Modem Model	**Firmware in Modem**	**Upgrade Method**
x2 or K56flex	Flash-upgradable	Check manufacturer's Web site for download to upgrade firmware
x2 or K56flex	Not upgradable	Check manufacturer's Web site for details about a physical modem swap; might cost money
V.34bis or earlier	Any	A firmware download or physical modem swap will be involved; will cost money
Hayes, Practical Peripherals, and Cardinal Technologies (all defunct)	Any	Contact Modem Express at 612-553-2075 or on the Web at www.hayes.com for upgrades and drivers (costs and availability will vary by brand and model)

Upgrading from x2 or K56flex to V.90 with Flash Upgrades

The flash upgrades to V.90 work like a BIOS upgrade for a PC: You download the appropriate software from the modem vendor, run the flash software, wait a few minutes, and your modem is ready to dial in to V.90-based ISPs at top speeds. One major problem is what happens *inside* the modem to the existing firmware.

- *X2 Modems to V.90.* x2 and V.90 firmware can coexist in modem

- *K56flex to V.90.* Most K56flex modems don't have room for both sets of firmware, so the V.90 firmware *replaces* the K56flex. The lack of a "fallback" standard has caused problems for some users of V.90 modems that were upgraded from K56flex models. Table 6.11 will help you find a solution if your V.90 connections aren't reliable.

Table 6.11	Troubleshooting the V.90 (ex-K56flex) Modems	
Problem	**Solution**	**Method**
Can't get reliable connection with V.90.	Download and install the latest firmware revisions from the vendor's Web site, even if you have a "brand new" modem.	If you're having problems making the connection, dial in with your modem on a 33.6Kbps line, or "pretend" that your modem is an older model by installing it as a 33.6Kbps model from the same vendor.

(continues)

Table 6.11   Troubleshooting the V.90 (ex-K56flex) Modems Continued

Problem	Solution	Method
Your ISP supports both V.90 and K56flex, and you'd like a choice.	If your modem is a so-called "Dualmode" modem, install both K56flex and V.90 firmware.	The modem needs to have a 2MB ROM chip to have sufficient room for both firmware types.
	If your modem won't permit both firmware types, download both V.90 and K56flex firmware, try both and see which one works better.	
You're not sure the latest firmware upgrade was really an "improvement"	If your vendor has several versions of firmware available for download, try some of the earlier versions, as well as the latest version. An earlier version might actually work better for you.	
Your modem is a non-U.S./Canada model.	Download the country-specific upgrade for your modem.	Check the Web site for your country; contact tech support if your country isn't listed.
The firmware upgrade was installed, and the modem only works at 33.6Kbps or less.	Make sure you are using a V.90 dial-up number.	
	Make sure you downloaded updated INF files or other drivers for your operating system.	

Note

The problems with moving from K56flex to V.90 do not apply to users who have updated their V.34/V.34bis modems directly to the V.90 standard, whether by a downloadable firmware update or physical modem or chip swap. Even if your V.34/V.34bis modem was made by a company that later made K56flex modems, you don't need to worry about this unless you updated to K56flex before going to V.90. Then, the troubleshooting advice given earlier applies to you as well.

External Versus Internal Modems

Both external and internal modems are available for desktop systems. Table 6.12 helps you determine which type is better suited to your needs.

Table 6.12 External Versus Internal Modems		
Features	**External**	**Internal**
Built-in 16550 UART or higher	No (uses computer's serial port UART or may use USB)	Yes (if 14.4Kbps or faster)
Price comparison	Higher	Lower
Extras to buy	RS-232 Modem Interface cable or USB cable	Nothing
Ease of moving to another computer	Easy—unplug the cables and go! (USB modems require a functioning USB port on the other computer)	Difficult—must open case and remove card, open other PC's case and insert card
Power supply	Plugs into wall ("brick" type)	None—powered by host PC
Reset if modem hangs	Turn modem off, and then on again	Restart computer
Monitoring operation	Easy—External signal lights	Difficult—unless your communication software simulates the signal lights
Interface type	Almost always via the RS-232 port although , USB modems are now on the market Parallel-port modems were made a few years ago, but never proved popular	Traditionally ISA, but many models now available in PCI, which should work better in new machines, allow mapping of COM 3 and 4 away from COM 1 and 2 to avoid IRQ sharing, and be usable in machines of the future that will lack ISA slots

Modem Troubleshooting

Table 6.13 will help you troubleshoot modem problems and get you back online.

Table 6.13 Modem Troubleshooting (all Types)		
Modem Type	**Problem**	**Solution**
Any	Modem fails to dial	Check line and phone jacks on modem. Line jack—modem to telco service
		Phone jack—modem to telephone receiver

(continues)

Table 6.13	Modem Troubleshooting (all Types) Continued	
Modem Type	**Problem**	**Solution**
		If you've reversed these cables, you'll get no dial tone.
		Check the cable for cuts or breaks. If the cable looks bad, replace it.
		Make sure your modem has been properly configured by your OS. With Windows 9x, use the Modems icon in Control Panel to view and test your modem configuration. From the General tab, click the Diagnostics tab, click on your modem on the serial port it's installed on, and then click More Info. This sends test signals to your modem. A properly working modem responds with information about the port and the modem.
External	Modem fails to dial	Make sure the RS-232 modem cable is running from the modem to a working serial port on your computer and that it is switched on. Signal lights on the front of the modem can be used to determine if the modem is on and if it is responding to dialing commands.
PCMCIA/PC Card	Modem fails to dial	Make sure it is fully plugged into the PCMCIA/PC slot. With Windows 9x, you should see a small PCMCIA/PC card icon on the toolbar. Double-click it to view the cards that are currently connected. If your modem is properly attached, it should be visible. Otherwise, remove it, reinsert it into the PCMCIA/PC card slot, and see if the computer detects it.
		Check dongle used to attach modem PCMCIA/PC card modems to jack; carry a spare. If your dongle doesn't have a connector to a standard phone line, use a line coupler to attach the short dongle cable to a longer standard RJ-11 cable for easier use. Carry at least a 10 RJ-11 phone cable with you for easier use in hotel rooms.
Any	Couldn't Open Port error message	Modem may be in use already, or IRQ I/O port–address conflict. Use Device Manager to check settings, and reinstall drivers.
	System can't dial from wall jack	Never use a wall jack unless it is clearly marked as a "data jack" or you check with the staff. A digital phone system's jack looks identical to the safe analog jack your modem is made for, but its higher voltage will fry your phone. You can get phone-line voltage testers from sources such as http://warrior.com. If your hotel telephone has a "data jack" built-in, use it. Some hotels now offer built-in Ethernet in some rooms, so carry your NIC with you as well for faster Web access.

Modem Type	Problem	Solution
Internal	System locks up when trying to boot up or dial modem	Modem trying to share a non-sharable IRQ with another port, probably a mouse. Move a serial mouse that uses the same IRQ as the modem to a different COM port with a different IRQ (from COM 1/IRQ 4 to COM 2/IRQ 3), or use a PS/2 mouse (IRQ 12). If your Pentium-class system lacks a visible PS/2 port, check with your system vendor for the (optional) header cable you need.
		Disable your system's COM 2, set the modem to COM 2 using IRQ 3.
External	Computer can't detect modem	Check cable type Must be RS-232 modem (not null modem or straight-through) cable (see the following pinouts)
		Check power switch and supply
		COM port might not be working
		Check BIOS and enable COM port; test port with CheckIt, Windows 9x Modem diagnostics, others; use loopback plug with CheckIt, AMIDiag, Norton, etc. for most thorough check
		Check for IRQ conflicts
USB	Computer can't detect modem	Check USB ports; enable if necessary Check USB cables and hubs

Pinouts for External Modem Cable (9-pin at PC)

For most external modems, you need an RS-232 modem cable, which will have a 9-pin connector on one end and a 25-pin connector on the other end. Because RS-232 is a flexible standard encompassing many different pinouts, make sure the cable is constructed according to the following diagram:

1. PC (with 9-pin COM port - male)
   Modem (25-pin port - female)

3	TX data	2
2	RX data	3
7	RTS	4

8	CTS	5
6	DSR	6
5	SIG GND	7
1	CXR	8
4	DTR	20
9	RI	22

2. If you purchase an RS-232 modem cable prebuilt at a store, you'll have a cable that works with your PC and your modem. However, you can use the preceding chart to build your own cable or, by using a cable tester, determine whether an existing RS-232 cable in your office is actually made for modems or some other device.

Universal Serial Bus (USB)

The USB port will eventually be used to replace the current serial, parallel, and PS/2 ports on systems in the early twenty-first century, but it is already being used for a wide variety of devices. Use this section to help you detect and configure USB ports effectively.

USB Port Identification

Figures 6.3 and 6.4 help you identify USB devices and ports.

Figure 6.3 This icon is used to identify USB cables, connectors, and peripherals.

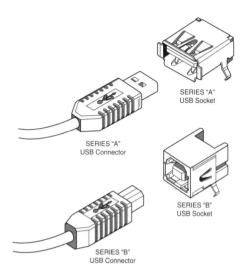

Figure 6.4 USB Series A and Series B plugs and receptacles.

Pinout for the USB Connector

Table 6.14 shows the pinout for the USB connector.

Table 6.14   USB Connector Pinout

Pin	Signal Name	Comment
1	VCC	Cable power
2	- Data	
3	+ Data	
4	Ground	Cable ground

Prerequisites for Using USB Ports and Peripherals

Before you buy or try to install a USB peripheral, make sure your system meets the requirements shown in Table 6.15. Some adjustments or updates to the system configuration might be necessary.

Table 6.15   Prerequisites for Use of USB Ports/Peripherals

Requirement	Reason	Notes
Windows 98	Built-in support for USB peripherals require Win98	Windows 95B OSR 2.1 and above has USB support but many peripherals
Working USB ports	Many systems shipped with disabled USB ports	Check BIOS and enable there if necessary; some systems may require header cables to bring the USB connector to the rear of the system

IEEE-1394

The so-called *FireWire* or *iLINK* interface pioneered by Apple is also available for Windows-Intel type computers. While IEEE-1394 ports are seldom standard equipment at present, the performance features they offer suggest that they will become a part of the "twenty-first century PC" for many users.

Figure 6.5 shows you how to recognize an IEEE-1394 connector plug, cable, and socket.

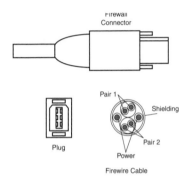

Figure 6.5 IEEE-1394 cable, socket, and connector plug.

Comparing USB and IEEE-1394

Because of the similarity in both the form and function of USB and 1394, there has been some confusion about the two. Table 6.16 summarizes the differences between the two technologies:

Table 6.16 Comparing IEEE-1394 and USB Technologies		
	IEEE-1394 (i.LINK) (FireWire)	**USB**
PC-Host Required	No	Yes
Maximum Number of Devices	63	127
Hot-Swappable	Yes	Yes
Maximum Cable Length Between Devices	4.5 meters	5 meters
Current Transfer Rate	200Mbps (25MB/sec)	12Mbps (1.5MB/sec)
Future Transfer Rates	400Mbps (50MB/sec) 800Mbps (100MB/sec) 1Gbps+ (125MB/sec+)	None

	IEEE-1394 (i.LINK) (FireWire)	**USB**
Typical Devices	-DV Camcorders	-Keyboards
	-High-Res. Digital Cameras	-Mice
		-Joysticks
	-HDTV	-Low-Resolution Digital Cameras
	-Set-Top Boxes	
	-High-Speed Drives	-Low-Speed Drives
	-High-Res. Scanners	-Modems
		-Printers
		-Low-Res. Scanners

The main difference is speed. Currently, 1394 offers a data transfer rate that is more than 16 times faster than that of USB. This speed differential may change in the future as higher speed versions of 1394 debut, and faster versions of USB might be introduced. In the future, PCs will likely include both USB and 1394 interfaces. Together, these two buses can replace most of the standard connections found on the back of a typical PC. Because of the performance differences, USB is clearly designed for low-speed peripherals such as keyboards, mice, modems, and printers, whereas 1394 will be used to connect high-performance computer and digital video electronics products.

Another important benefit of 1394 is that a PC host connection is not required. As such, 1394 can be used to directly connect a Digital Video (DV) camcorder and a DV-VCR for dubbing tapes or editing.

Chapter 7

Parallel Ports, Printers, and Scanners

Parallel Port Connectors

There are actually three different types of parallel port connectors defined by the IEEE-1284 parallel port standard. In Figure 7.1, the DB-25 connector used on PCs for parallel cables (also called "Type A") is on the left. The Centronics 36 connector (also called "Type B") is in the middle. Virtually every parallel-interface printer, from the oldest dot-matrix to the newest laser printer, uses the Type B connector. Hewlett-Packard introduced the "Type C" connector and has added it to most of its recent laser printers, although it still uses the Type B connector as well. Type C is a high-density connector that uses a cable with an integral clip, as opposed to the clumsy, easy-to-lose wire clips used on the Type B port.

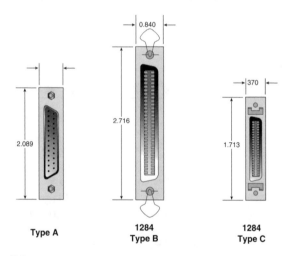

Figure 7.1 The three different types of IEEE-1284 parallel port connectors.

Parallel Port Performance

As printers have gotten faster and more devices besides printers are attached to parallel ports, the need for increasing parallel port speed has become more and more apparent. Use the following tables to help determine if your parallel ports are set to the fastest standard supported by your printers or other parallel port devices.

Table 7.1 summarizes the different types of parallel ports, their input and output modes, speed, and hardware settings:

Table 7.1 Parallel Port Types as Defined by IEEE-1284				
Parallel Port Type	**Input Mode**	**Output Mode**	**Input/ Output Speed**	**Comments**
SPP Standard Parallel Port	Nibble (4 bits)	Compatible	Input – 50KB/ second Output – 150KB/second	4-bit input, 8-bit output
	Compatible (8 bits)	Input/Output	Bidirectional 8-bit I/O – 150KB/second	Byte
EPP (Enhanced Parallel Port)	EPP	EPP	Input/Output –500KB– 2MB/sec	8-bit I/O, uses IRQ
ECP (Enhanced Capabilities Port)	ECP	ECP	Input/Output –500KB– 2MB/sec	8-bit I/O, uses IRQ and DMA

EPP Versus ECP Modes

Both EPP and ECP ports are part of the IEEE-1284 bidirectional parallel port standard, but they are not identical. Use the following table to understand how they differ, and consult your parallel port device manuals to see which mode is best for your system.

Port Type	IRQ Usage	DMA Usage	Designed For	Notes
EPP	Yes (see chart)	No	Tape drives, CD-ROM, LAN adapters	Version 1.7 predates IEEE-1284 standard; IEEE-1284 version often called "EPP 1.9"
ECP	Yes (see chart)	DMA 3 (Standard) DMA 1 (Optional; default on some Packard-Bell models)	High-speed printers, scanners	Many systems offer an "EPP/ECP" port setting for best results with all types of parallel port devices

Some older parallel printers don't recommend either mode. To use these advanced modes, you must use an IEEE-1284 printer cable. This cable carries all signal lines to the printer, is heavily shielded, and produces very reliable printing with old and new printers alike in any parallel port mode. IEEE-1284 cables can also be purchased in a "straight-through" version for use with printer-sharing devices.

Parallel Port Configurations

Table 7.2 lists the standard parallel port settings. While add-on multi-I/O or parallel port cards may offer additional settings, other settings will work only if software can be configured to use them.

Table 7.2	Parallel Interface I/O Port Addresses and Interrupts		
Standard LPTx	**Alternate LPTx**	**I/O Ports**	**IRQ**
LPT1	—	3BC-3BFh	IRQ 7
LPT1	LPT2	378-37Ah	IRQ 5
LPT2	LPT3	278h-27Ah	IRQ 5

Testing Parallel Ports

The most reliable way to test printer ports is to use a parallel port testing program along with the appropriate loopback plug. This method isolates the port and allows the system to "capture" output back as input. Parallel port testing programs are included in major diagnostic programs such as Norton Utilities, CheckIt, AMIDiag, QA+ family, MicroScope 2000, and many others.

Building a Parallel Loopback Plug

There are several different loopback plugs used for parallel ports, because of the different testing procedures performed by the various diagnostic programs. If you have the correct pinouts, you can build your own, or you can purchase them directly from the diagnostic software company, either with the software or separately.

Most use the IBM style loopback, but some use the style that originated in the Norton Utilities diagnostics. *Check with your diagnostic software vendor to see which of these loopback designs is the correct one for your system, or if a different design is needed.*

The following wiring is needed to construct your own loopback or wrap plugs to test a parallel port:

- IBM 25-Pin Parallel (Male DB25P) Loopback Connector (Wrap Plug). Connect the following pins:

    1 to 13

    2 to 15

    10 to 16

    11 to 17

- Norton Utilities 25-Pin Parallel (Male DB25P) Loopback Connector (Wrap Plug). Connect the following pins:

    2 to 15

    3 to 13

    4 to 12

    5 to 10

    6 to 11

Troubleshooting Parallel Ports

Table 7.3   Resolving Parallel Port Problems

Symptoms	Cause(s)	Solution
Device on port not recognized; can't configure printer; printer won't print	Wrong parallel-port setting	Check device manual; probably need to change port to EPP, ECP, or EPP/ECP mode
	Wrong cable	If you're using EPP or ECP, you must use an IEEE-1284 cable.
	Switchbox between device and computer	All cables and switchbox must be IEEE-1284 compliant; remove switchbox and connect directly to device. If it works, replace non-compliant switchbox or cables.
	IRQ or I/O port address conflict	EPP and ECP require a non-shared IRQ; use Windows 9x Device Manager to see if IRQ for LPT (parallel) port is conflicting with another device; also check I/O port address and DMA.
	Device not powered on	Power on device before starting computer.
	Port defective	Use loopback and test software to verify data going out port is readable.

Printers

While some printers can be attached to serial or USB ports, parallel ports are the dominant means of connecting printers to computers.

Use Tables 7.4 and 7.5 to help you keep your printer running reliably.

Hewlett-Packard PCL Versions

Use the following table to determine what Printer Control Language (PCL) features a printer offers based on the version of HP-PCL it supports. You can also use this table to choose "compatible" printers in case you don't have exactly the right driver for a given HP-PCL printer or compatible.

Table 7.4   Hewlett-Packard Printer Control Language (PCL) Versions

Version	Date	Models	Benefits
PCL 3	May 1984	LaserJet LaserJet Plus	Full page formatting; vector graphics
PCL 4	Nov 1985	LaserJet Series II	Added typefaces; downloadable macros; support for larger bitmapped fonts and graphics
PCL 4e	Sep 1989 IIP Plus	LaserJet IIP, fonts; images raster	Compressed bitmap
PCL 5	Mar 1990	LaserJet III, IIID, IIIP, IIIsi, HP-GL/2	Scalable typefaces; outline fonts; (vector) graphics
PCL 5e	Oct 1992	LaserJet 4, 4M, 4L, 4ML, 4P, 4MP, 4 Plus, 4M Plus, 5P, 5MP, 5L, 5L-FS, 5Lxtra, 6L, 6Lxi, 6Lse, 6P, 6MP, 6Psi, 6Pse	600dpi support; bidirectional communication between printer and PC; additional fonts for Microsoft Windows
PCL 5c	Oct 1994	Color LaserJet Color LaserJet 5, 5M	Color extensions
PCL 6	Apr 1996	LaserJet 5, 5se, LaserJet 6, 6Pse, 6Psi, 6MP	Faster graphics printing and return to application
PCL XL	1996	LaserJet 6P, 6MP	Enhanced graphics commands, multipage printing on one sheet, watermark, smaller file sizes

Comparing Host-based to PDL-based Printers

Most printers use a Page Description Language (PDL). PDL-based printers receive commands from applications or the operating system that describes the page to the printer, which then renders it before printing. More and more low-cost printers are using a host-based printing system in which the computer renders the page instead of the printer.

Use Table 7.5 to determine which type of printer is suitable for your users.

Table 7.5   PDL Versus Host-based Printers

Printer Type	Feature	Benefit	Drawback
PDL (includes HP-PCL and compatibles, PostScript)	Page rendered in printer	Printer can be used independent of a PC or particular operating system; MS-DOS support	Higher cost because "brains" inside printer
Host-based	Page rendered by computer	Lower cost because "brains" inside the PC, not the printer	Printer must be "married" to a computer witha compatible operating system and minimum performance requirements; non-Windows support chancy; often can't be networked

Use Table 7.6 to determine the simplest way to test a printer. Note that host-based printers *must* have their drivers installed before they can print.

Table 7.6   Testing Printers

Printer Type	Test Method
Non-PostScript printer using PDL or escape sequences (HP-PCL, compatibles, dot-matrix, inkjet)	Enter DIR>LPT1 From a command prompt (MS-DOS or Windows 9x); printer will print directory listing
PostScript printer	You must send PostScript commands to the printer directly to test it without drivers. You can use PostScript printer test in Microsoft MSD or Install correct drivers and use test print (Windows 9x/NT/2000 offer a printer test at the end of the driver install process. This test can also be performed at any time through the printer's icon in the Printer's folder)
Host-based printer	Install correct drivers, and then use test print as earlier

Printer Hardware Problems

Use Table 7.7 to track down problems and solutions with printers (any interface type).

Table 7.7   Troubleshooting Printer Problems

Symptom	Printer Type	Cause(s)	Solutions
Fuzzy printing	Laser	Damp paper	Use paper stored at proper temperature and humidity

Symptom	Printer Type	Cause(s)	Solutions
	Inkjet	Wrong paper type or printer settings	Use inkjet-rated paper; check print setting and match settings and resolution to paper type; make sure you're using correct side of paper (look for a "print this side first" marking on the package)
	Inkjet	Cartridge clogged or not seated correctly	Reseat cartridge; run cleaning utility; remove Canon cartridge from unit and clean printhead
Variable print density	Laser	Toner unevenly distributed in drum or toner cartridge	Remove toner cartridge and shake from side to side; check printer position and assure it's level; check for light leaks; replace toner cartridge or refill toner
Fuzzy white lines on pages	Laser	Dirty corotrons (corona wires)	Clean corotrons per mfr. recommendation
Pages print solid black	Laser	Broken charger corotron	Replace toner cartridge if it contains corotron, or repair printer
Pages print solid white	Laser	Broken transfer corotron	Repair transfer corotron
Sharp vertical white lines	Laser	Dirty developer unit	Clean developer if separate; replace toner cartridge if it contains developer unit
Regularly spaced spots	Laser	Spots less than 3 inches apart indicates dirty fusing roller	Clean fusing roller
		Widely spaced spots, or one per page indicates scratched or flawed drum	Replace drum and fuser cleaning pad
Gray print or gray background	Laser	Worn out drum	Replace drum (most common with separate drum and toner supply)
Loose toner	Laser	Fusing roller not hot enough	Service fusing roller
Solid vertical black line	Laser	Toner cartridge nearly empty	Shake toner cartridge to redistribute toner
		Scratched drum	Replace drum or toner cartridge

(continues)

Table 7.7   Troubleshooting Printer Problems Continued

Symptom	Printer Type	Cause(s)	Solutions
Paper jams and misfeeds	Laser and inkjet	Incorrect paper loading; paper too damp; paper wrinkled; paper too heavy/thick for printer	Use paper that is in proper condition for printing; don't overfill paper tray; don't dog-ear paper when loading it
Envelope jams	Laser and inkjet	Incorrect paper loading; failure to set laser printer to use rear paper exit tray; printer can't handle envelopes	Check correct envelope handling procedures; consider using labels to avoid envelopes
Blank pages between printed pages	Laser and inkjet	Paper stuck together; paper is damp or wrinkled	Riffle paper before loading paper tray; make sure all paper is the same size
Blank page between print jobs	Laser and inkjet	Print spooler set to produce a blank divider page	Change print spooler setting
Error light on printer flashes; printer ejects partial page	Laser	Memory overflow or printer overrun error	Reduce graphics resolution; simplify a PostScript page; reduce number of fonts; check printer memory size is accurately set; run printer self-test to determine amount of RAM onboard; add RAM to printer

Printer Connection Problems

Use Table 7.8 to determine the cause and cure for problems with your printer connection.

Table 7.8   Troubleshooting Printer Connections

Symptom	Printer Type	Cause(s)	Solutions
Gibberish printing	Any	PDL used for print job doesn't match printer	Make sure print job sent to correct printer; check default printer value; check port used for printer; check switchbox for proper printer selection; replace switchbox with LPT2 card or with USB-parallel cable

Symptom	Printer Type	Cause(s)	Solutions
	PostScript laser	PostScript preamble not properly received	Check cable; check serial port configuration; reload drivers
Printer not available	Any	Print job has timed out; computer is using offline mode to spool jobs	Check for paper out; reload paper. Check printer cable or serial port settings; look for IRQ conflicts and correct them; set switchbox to automatic mode, or "lock" it to computer you want to print from
Printer doesn't notify Windows of paper out, jams, out of toner or ink, etc.	Laser and Inkjet	IEEE-1284 connection not working	Make sure port and cable(s) and switchbox are all IEEE-1284 (EPP or ECP or EPP/ECP); check cable connection
Intermittent or failed communications with printer	Any	Bad switchbox or cables	Use direct connection to printer; check cables; replace rotary-dial manual switchbox with autosensing switchbox
		Device daisy-chain with printer	Use printer only; change order of daisy-chain; avoid use of Zip, scanner and printer on single LPT port
Port busy; printer goes offline	Laser and Inkjet	ECP port prints too fast for printer	Use Windows 9x Control Panel to load standard LPT driver in place of ECP driver; change setting in BIOS to EPP or bidirectional

Printer Driver and Application Problems

Printers use driver software to communicate with operating systems and applications. Use Table 7.9 to solve problems with drivers and applications.

Table 7.9   Troubleshooting Printer Drivers and Applications

Symptom	Printer Type	Cause(s)	Solutions
Prints okay from command prompt (DIR>LPT1), but not from applications	Any	Printer driver damaged or buggy	Reload printer driver and test; reinstall printer driver; switch to compatible new version can be downloaded

(continues)

Table 7.9   Troubleshooting Printer Drivers and Applications Continued

Symptom	Printer Type	Cause(s)	Solutions
Form-feed light comes on, but nothing prints	Laser	Incomplete page sent to printer	Normal behavior for Print-Screen or envelope printing; eject paper manually; otherwise, reinstall driver
Incorrect fonts printing	Laser or Inkjet	Printer using internal fonts instead of TrueType	Check driver setting to determine which fonts will be used
Incorrect page breaks	Any	Printer changed between document composition and printing	If you change printers or plan to use a fax modem to "print" your document, select the printer and scroll through your document first to check page breaks due to differences in font rendering, etc; correct as needed
Page cut off on left, right, top or bottom edges	Laser or Inkjet	Margins set beyond printable area of printer	Reset document margins; use "print tofit" to scale page or document to usable paper size; check for proper paper size set in printer properties

Troubleshooting Scanners

Scanners are among the most popular add-ons to computers, but they can cause plenty of problems for users. Use Table 7.10 to help make scanning trouble-free.

Table 7.10   Scanner Troubleshooting

Interface Type	Problem	Causes	Solution
Parallel	Slow scanning speed	Wrong port setting	Use ECP or EPP mode per scanner
	Scanner not recognized	Problems with daisy-chain when scanner used with non-printer devices or as third item (printer, scanner, and anything else)	Shuffle order of scanner and non-printing device; check port settings; try scanner by itself; install second parallel port; make sure SCSI/Parallel scanner set for parallel mode; check device driver setup during boot; and set SCSI/Parallel scanner for SCSI mode; check cable

Interface Type	Problem	Causes	Solution
SCSI	Scanner not recognized	Termination set wrong; wrong SCSI ID; no drivers installed	Terminate scanner only if last device inSCSI daisy-chain; look for switch or terminating plug and check operation; check SCSI IDs already in use and select an unused number; install TWAIN or ISIS drivers as well as SCSI drivers; check cable
USB	Scanner not recognized	USB port not working or not present	Enable USB port in BIOS or install card; check port for IRQ conflict; use Windows 98 or Windows 2000 to avoid support problems with Windows 95B; get updated drivers; check cable
All	Scanner worked with Windows 95, but not after Windows 98 upgrade	TWAIN.DLL file was replaced by Windows 98	Use Windows 98's Version Conflict Manager to determine if TWAIN.DLL was replaced; use the original version (backed up by VCM)
All	Scanner not recognized	Scanner turned off when system booted	Turn on scanner, open Windows9x/2000's Device Manager and "refresh" devices; if this doesn't work, leave the scanner on and reboot the system
All	"Acquire" command in Photoshop or other programs won't launch scanner	TWAIN or ISIS drivers not properly installed or registered in system Registry; scanner turned off	Verify scanner detected by system; if scanner works with its own software (not launched from another app.), reinstall drivers and verify Acquire command works
All	Graphics look distorted during scan	Wrong scanning mode set for document	Use the following table to determine best scanning mode by document type

Use Table 7.11 as a quick reference to help determine the best scanning mode for your documents.

Table 7.11	Recommended Scanning Modes for Document Types			
Document Type	**Color photo**	**Drawing**	**Text**	**B&W Photo Scanning Mode**
Line Art	No	Yes	Yes	No
OCR	No	No	Yes	No
Grayscale	No	Yes1	No	Yes
Color Photo	Yes	No	No	Yes2
Color Halftone	Yes3	No	No	No
Color Drawing	No	Yes	No	No
256-color	No	Yes	No	No
Copy/Fax	Yes4	Yes4	Yes4	Yes4

1 Recommended only for drawings containing pencil shading and ink wash effects

2 Use to convert color to black and white if photo-editing software conversion is unavailable or produces inferior results

3 Adjust halftone options to match output device's requirements

4 Use to prepare scanned image for sending as fax or when image will be photocopied; converts all tones to digital halftones

Chapter 8

Keyboards and Input Devices

Keyboard Designs

The primary keyboard types are as follows:

- 101-key Enhanced keyboard
- 104-key Windows keyboard
- 83-key PC and XT keyboard (obsolete)
- 84-key AT keyboard (obsolete)

> **Note**
>
> If you need information about the 83-key PC and XT keyboard or 84-key AT keyboard, see Chapter 7 of *Upgrading and Repairing PCs, Tenth Anniversary Edition*—included in PDF format on the Eleventh Edition CD-ROM.

The 101-Key Enhanced Keyboard

This keyboard design serves as the basis for virtually all current-model keyboards.

101- Versus 102-key Keyboards

Foreign language versions of the Enhanced keyboard include 102 keys and a slightly different layout from the 101-key U.S. versions.

The 104-key Windows Keyboard

The Microsoft Windows keyboard specification outlines a set of new keys and key combinations. The familiar 101-key layout has now grown to 104 keys, with the addition of left and right Windows keys and an Application key. These keys are used for operating-system and application-level keyboard combinations, similar to today's Ctrl and Alt combinations.

(Figure 8.2 shows the standard Windows keyboard layout, including the three new keys.)

Using Windows Keys

Table 8.1 shows a list of all the Windows 95 and Windows 98 key combinations that can be performed with the 104-key Windows keyboards. These keyboard shortcuts can be useful, especially if your mouse stops working or you want to work more quickly with the Windows desktop.

Table 8.1 Windows Key Combinations	
Key Combination	**Resulting Action**
WIN+R	Run dialog box
WIN+M	Minimize All
Shift+WIN+M	Undo Minimize All
WIN+F1	Help
WIN+E	Windows Explorer
WIN+F	Find Files or Folders
Ctrl+WIN+F	Find Computer
WIN+Tab	Cycle through taskbar buttons
WIN+Break	System Properties dialog box
Application key	Displays a context menu for the selected item

When a 104-key Windows keyboard is used with Microsoft IntelliType Software installed, the additional key combinations shown in Table 8.2 can be used:

Table 8.2 Additional Key Combinations	
Key Combination	**Resulting Action**
WIN+L	Log off Windows
WIN+P	Opens Print Manager
WIN+C	Opens the Control Panel
WIN+V	Opens Clipboard
WIN+K	Opens Keyboard Properties dialog box
WIN+I	Opens Mouse Properties dialog box
WIN+A	Opens Accessibility Options (if installed)
WIN+spacebar	Displays the list of IntelliType hotkeys
WIN+S	Toggles the Caps Lock key on and off

Keyboard-Only Commands for Windows 9x with Any Keyboard

If your mouse stops working, or if you want to work faster, use the keys shown in Table 8.3 to perform common Windows 9x actions.

Table 8.3   Keyboard Commands

Key Combination	Resulting Action
F1	Starts Windows Help.
F10	Activates menu bar options.
Shift+F10	Opens a context menu (shortcut menu) for the selected item.
Ctrl+Esc	Opens the Start menu. Use the arrow keys to select an item.
Ctrl+Esc, Esc	Selects the Start button. Press Tab to select the taskbar, or press Shift+F10 for a context menu.
Alt+Tab	Switch to another running application. Hold down the Alt key, and then press the Tab key to view the task-switching window.
Shift	Press down and hold the Shift key while you insert a CD-ROM to bypass the AutoPlay feature.
Alt+spacebar	Displays the main window's System menu. From the System menu, you can restore, move, resize, minimize, maximize, or close the window.
Alt+- (Alt+hyphen)	Displays the Multiple Document Interface (MDI) child window's System menu. From the MDI child window's System menu, you can restore, move, resize, minimize, maximize, or close the child window.
Ctrl+Tab	Switch to the next child window of a MDI application.
Alt+<underlined letter in menu>	Opens the corresponding menu.
Alt+F4	Closes the current window.
Ctrl+F4	Closes the current MDI window.
Alt+F6	Switch between multiple windows in the same program. For example, when Notepad's Find dialog box is displayed, Alt+F6 switches between the Find dialog box and the main Notepad window.

Here are the Windows dialog box keyboard commands:

Key Combination	Resulting Action
Tab	Move to the next control in the dialog box.
Shift+Tab	Move to the previous control in the dialog box.
Spacebar	If the current control is a button, this keyboard command clicks the button. If the current control is a check box, it toggles the check box. If the current control is an option button, it selects the option button.
Enter	Equivalent to clicking the selected button (the button with the outline).
Esc	Equivalent to clicking the Cancel button.
Alt+<underlined letter in dialog box item>	Move to the corresponding item.
Ctrl+Tab/ Ctrl+Shift+Tab	Move through the property tabs.

These are the keyboard combinations for Windows Explorer tree controls:

Key Combination	Resulting Action
Numeric Keypad *	Expands everything under the current selection.
Numeric Keypad +	Expands the current selection.
Numeric Keypad -	Collapses the current selection.
Right arrow	Expands the current selection if it is not expanded; otherwise, goes to the first child.
Left arrow	Collapses the current selection if it is expanded; otherwise, goes to the parent.

Here are the general Windows folder/shortcut controls:

Key Combination	Resulting Action
F4	Selects the Go To a Different Folder box and moves down the entries in the box (if the toolbar is active in Windows Explorer).
F5	Refreshes the current window.
F6	Moves among panes in Windows Explorer.
Ctrl+G	Opens the Go To Folder tool (in Windows 95 Windows Explorer only).
Ctrl+Z	Undoes the last command.
Ctrl+A	Selects all the items in the current window.
Backspace	Switches to the parent folder.
Shift+click	Selects the Close button. (For folders, closes the current folder plus all parent folders.)

These are general folder and Windows Explorer shortcuts for a selected object:

Key Combination	Resulting Action
F2	Renames object.
F3	Finds all files.
Ctrl+X	Cuts.
Ctrl+C	Copies.
Ctrl+V	Pastes.
Shift+Del	Deletes selection immediately, without moving the item to the Recycle Bin.
Alt+Enter	Opens the property sheet for the selected object.
To copy a file	Press down and hold the Ctrl key while you drag the file to another folder.
To create a shortcut	Press down and hold Ctrl+Shift while you drag a file to the desktop or a folder.

Standard Versus Portable Keyboards

Table 8.4 lists the differences in configuration and system setup for standard versus portable keyboards.

Table 8.4 Standard and Portable Keyboards Compared		
Feature	**Standard**	**Portable**
Key size	Full-sized keys on entire keyboard	Full-sized keys on typing keys only; directional and function keys usually smaller
Cursor keys	Inverted-T layout standard	Inverted-T layout seldom used; makes "blind" cursor movements difficult
Numeric keypad	Separate keys at right of directional keys	Embedded into right-hand alphanumerics; should disable numlock in BIOS to avoid keying errors; might require use of *Fn* key to use
Add-on keypad	Not needed	Popular option for number-intensive uses; must plug into external port

Keyswitch Types

The most common type of keyswitch is the mechanical type, available in the following variations:

- Pure mechanical
- Foam element
- Rubber dome
- Membrane

Table 8.5 compares user feel, repair, and servicing issues for these keyswitch types.

Table 8.5 Mechanical Keyswitch Types Compared				
Keyswitch Type				
Feature	**Pure Mechanical**	**Foam**	**Rubber-Dome**	**Membrane**
Tactile feedback	Usually a "click"	Minimal feedback	"Soft click"	No click
Durability and Servicability	High: 20-million keystroke rating	Variable: Contacts can corrode; easy to clean	High: Rubber dome protects contacts from corrosion	Extreme: No moving parts, sealed unit for harsh industrial environments

The pure mechanical type of keyboard, often using Alps keyswitches, is second only to the keyboards using capacitive switches in terms of tactile feedback and durability. Capacitive keyswitches are rated for up to 25 million keystrokes. Traditionally, the only vendors of capacitive keyswitch keyboards have been IBM and the inheritors of its keyboard technology, Lexmark and Unicomp.

Cleaning a Foam-Element Keyswitch

Figure 8.1 shows a foam-element keyswitch, often found in keyboards sold by Compaq and keyboards manufactured by Keytronics.

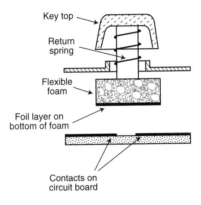

Figure 8.1 A typical foam element mechanical keyswitch.

The foil contacts at the bottom of the key and the contacts on the circuit board often become dirty or corroded, causing erratic key operation. Disassemble the keyboard to gain access to the foil pads, clean them, and treat them with Stabilant 22a from DW Electrochemicals to improve the switch-contact quality.

If you need to clean or repair a keyboard, you'll find much more information in Chapter 17 of *Upgrading and Repairing PCs, Eleventh Edition*, from Que.

Adjusting Keyboard Parameters in Windows

To modify the default values for the typematic repeat rate and delay parameters in any version of Windows, open the Keyboard Control Panel. In Windows 95, 98, and NT, the controls are located on the Speed page. The Repeat Delay slider controls the amount of times a key must be pressed before the character begins to repeat, and the Repeat Rate slider controls how fast the character repeats after the delay has elapsed.

> **Note**
>
> The increments on the Repeat Delay and Repeat Rate sliders in the Keyboard Control Panel correspond to the timings given for the MODE command's RATE and DELAY values. Each mark in the Repeat Delay slider adds about 0.25 seconds to the delay, and the marks in the Repeat Rate slider are worth about one character per second each.

Keyboard Layouts and Scan Codes

Figure 8.2 shows the keyboard numbering and character locations for the 101-key Enhanced keyboard. Table 8.6 shows each of the three scan code sets for each key in relation to the key number and character. Scan Code Set 1 is the default; the other two are rarely used. Figure 8.3 shows the layout of a typical foreign language 102-key version of the Enhanced keyboard—in this case, a U.K. version.

Knowing these key number figures and scan codes are useful when you are troubleshooting stuck or failed keys on a keyboard. Diagnostics can report the defective keyswitch by the scan code, which varies from keyboard to keyboard on the character it represents and its location.

Figure 8.2 101-key Enhanced keyboard key number and character locations (U.S. version).

Figure 8.3 102-key Enhanced keyboard key number and character locations (U.K. English version).

Table 8.6	101-/102-Key (Enhanced) Keyboard Key Numbers and Scan Codes			
Key Number	Key/Character	Scan Code Set 1	Scan Code Set 2	Scan Code Set 3
1	'	29	0E	0E
2	1	2	16	16
3	2	3	1E	1E
4	3	4	26	26
5	4	5	25	25
6	5	6	2E	2E
7	6	7	36	36
8	7	8	3D	3D
9	8	9	3E	3E
10	9	0A	46	46
11	0	0B	45	45
12	-	0C	4E	4E
13	=	0D	55	55
15	Backspace	0E	66	66

Key Number	Key/Character	Scan Code Set 1	Scan Code Set 2	Scan Code Set 3
16	Tab	0F	0D	0D
17	Q	10	15	15
18	W	11	1D	1D
19	E	12	24	24
20	R	13	2D	2D
21	T	14	2C	2C
22	Y	15	35	35
23	U	16	3C	3C
24	I	17	43	43
25	O	18	44	44
26	P	19	4D	4D
27	[	1A	54	54
28	]	1B	5B	5B
29	\ (101-key only)	2B	5D	5C
30	Caps Lock	3A	58	14
31	A	1E	1C	1C
32	S	1F	1B	1B
33	D	20	23	23
34	F	21	2B	2B
35	G	22	34	34
36	H	23	33	33
37	J	24	3B	3B
38	K	25	42	42
39	L	26	4B	4B
40	;	27	4C	4C
41	'	28	52	52
42	# (102-key only)	2B	5D	53
43	Enter	1C	5A	5A
44	Left Shift	2A	12	12
45	\ (102-key only)	56	61	13
46	Z	2C	1A	1A
47	X	2D	22	22
48	C	2E	21	21
49	V	2F	2A	2A
50	B	30	32	32
51	N	31	31	31

(continues)

Key Number	Key/Character	Scan Code Set 1	Scan Code Set 2	Scan Code Set 3
	Table 8.6 101-/102-Key (Enhanced) Keyboard Key Numbers and Scan Codes Continued			
52	M	32	3A	3A
53	,	33	41	41
54	.	34	49	49
55	/	35	4A	4A
57	Right Shift	36	59	59
58	Left Ctrl	1D	14	11
60	Left Alt	38	11	19
61	Spacebar	39	29	29
62	Right Alt	E0, 38	E0, 11	39
64	Right Ctrl	E0, 1D	E0, 14	58
75	Insert	E0, 52	E0, 70	67
76	Delete	E0, 53	E0, 71	64
79	Left arrow	E0, 4B	E0, 6B	61
80	Home	E0, 47	E0, 6C	6E
81	End	E0, 4F	E0, 69	65
83	Up arrow	E0, 48	E0, 75	63
84	Down arrow	E0, 50	E0, 72	60
85	Page Up	E0, 49	E0, 7D	6F
86	Page Down	E0, 51	E0, 7A	6D
89	Right arrow	E0, 4D	E0, 74	6A
90	Num Lock	45	77	76
91	Keypad 7 (Home)	47	6C	6C
92	Keypad 4 (Left arrow)	4B	6B	6B
93	Keypad 1 (End)	4F	69	69
95	Keypad /	E0, 35	E0, 4A	77
96	Keypad 8 (Up arrow)	48	75	75
97	Keypad 5	4C	73	73
98	Keypad 2 (Down arrow)	50	72	72
99	Keypad 0 (Ins)	52	70	70
100	Keypad *	37	7C	7E
101	Keypad 9 (PgUp)	49	7D	7D
102	Keypad 6 (Left arrow)	4D	74	74
103	Keypad 3 (PgDn)	51	7A	7A

Key Number	Key/Character	Scan Code Set 1	Scan Code Set 2	Scan Code Set 3
104	Keypad . (Del)	53	71	71
105	Keypad -	4A	7B	84
106	Keypad +	4E	E0, 5A	7C
108	Keypad Enter	E0, 1C	E0, 5A	79
110	Escape	1	76	8
112	F1	3B	5	7
113	F2	3C	6	0F
114	F3	3D	4	17
115	F4	3E	0C	1F
116	F5	3F	3	27
117	F6	40	0B	2F
118	F7	41	83	37
119	F8	42	0A	3F
120	F9	43	1	47
121	F10	44	9	4F
122	F11	57	78	56
123	F12	58	7	5E
124	Print Screen	E0, 2A, E0, 37	E0, 12, E0, 7C	57
125	Scroll Lock	46	7E	5F
126	Pause	E1, 1D, 45, E1, 9D, C5	E1, 14, 77, E1, F0, 14, F0, 77	62

The new keys on a 104-key Windows keyboard have their own unique scan codes. Table 8.7 shows the scan codes for the new keys.

Table 8.7   104-Key Windows Keyboard New Key Scan Codes

New Key	Scan Code Set 1	Scan Code Set 2	Scan Code Set 3
Left Windows	E0,5B	E0, 1F	8B
Right Windows	E0,5C	E0, 27	8C
Application	E0,5D	E0, 2F	8D

Keyboard Connectors

While some of the newest systems offer color-code keyboard connectors and cables, the best way to recognize the keyboard connector is still to know what it looks like. There are two common standards, and low cost adapters are available to switch a device using one standard to a connector using the other standard. The keyboard connector standards are

- *5-pin DIN connector.* Used on most PC systems with Baby-AT form factor motherboards.

- *6-pin mini-DIN connector.* Used on PS/2 systems and most PCs with LPX, ATX, and NLX motherboards.

Figure 8.4 and Table 8.8 show the physical layout and pinouts of all the respective keyboard connector plugs and sockets.

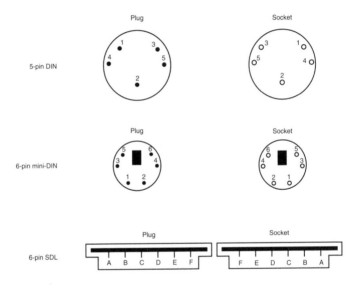

Figure 8.4 Keyboard and mouse connectors.

Keyboard Connector Signals

Table 8.8 lists the keyboard connector signals for three common keyboard connectors.

Table 8.8 Keyboard Connector Signals			
Signal Name	5-Pin DIN	6-Pin Mini-DIN	6-Pin SDL
Keyboard Data	2	1	B
Ground	4	3	C
+5v	5	4	E
Keyboard Clock	1	5	D

Signal Name	5-Pin DIN	6-Pin Mini-DIN	6-Pin SDL
Not Connected	—	2	A
Not Connected	—	6	F
Not Connected	3	—	—

DIN = German Industrial Norm (Deutsche Industrie Norm), a committee that sets German dimensional standards.

SDL = Shielded Data Link, a type of shielded connector created by AMP and used by IBM and others for keyboard cables. It is used inside the keyboard housing to attach the cable to the keyboard's electronics, and the other end of the cable will have the DIN or mini-DIN connector to attach to the computer.

USB Keyboard Requirements

USB (Universal Serial Bus) devices are becoming increasingly popular, and over the next few years are expected to replace serial, parallel, keyboard, and mouse port connectors with this single, versatile, sharable port (see Chapter 6, "Serial UBS, Optical, and Tape Storage," for more information about USB).

To use a keyboard connected via the USB port, you must meet three requirements:

- Have a USB port in the system

- Run either Microsoft Windows 98 or Microsoft Windows 2000 (which include USB keyboard drivers)

- Have what is referred to as USB Legacy support in your BIOS

USB Legacy support means your motherboard ROM BIOS includes drivers to recognize a USB keyboard. Without USB Legacy support in the BIOS, you can't use a USB keyboard when in MS-DOS or when installing Windows on the system for the first time. Also, if the Windows installation fails and requires manipulation outside of Windows, the USB keyboard will not function unless it is supported in the BIOS. Virtually all 1998 and newer systems with USB ports include a BIOS with USB Legacy (meaning USB Keyboard) support.

Keyboard Troubleshooting and Repair

Keyboard errors are usually caused by two simple problems. Other more difficult, intermittent problems can arise, but they are much less common. The most frequent problems are as follows:

- Defective cables

- Stuck keys

Use Table 8.9 to help you troubleshoot a defective keyboard.

Table 8.9   Keyboard Troubleshooting

Problem	Symptoms	Solution
Defective cable	No keyboard operation; all keys produce errors or wrong characters	Swap keyboard with known, working spare. If problem isn't repeated, original keyboard is problem.
		Replace cable with spare (if available, check "scrap" keyboards or vendor spare parts lists) or replace keyboard.
		Test cable with Digital Multimeter (DMM) with continuity tester; each wire (see pinouts earlier) should make a connection, even when you wriggle the cable. Replace failed cable.
Stuck key	"Stuck key error" or 3xx error onscreen during POST	Look up scancode from table in this chapter to determine which key is stuck. Clean keyswitch.
Damaged motherboard keyboard connector	Known-working keyboards don't work when plugged in.	For a simple test of the motherboard keyboard connector, you can check voltages on some of the pins. Measure the voltages on various pins of the keyboard connector. To prevent possible damage to the system or keyboard, turn off the power before disconnecting the keyboard. Then unplug the keyboard and turn the power back on. Make measurements between the ground pin and the other pins according to the following table.
		Repair or replace motherboard if voltage fails specifications.

Keyboard Connector Voltage and Signal Specifications

Use Table 8.10 along with a DMM to determine if your keyboard connector is working correctly.

Table 8.10   Keyboard Connector Specifications

DIN Connector Pin	Mini-DIN ConnectorPin	Signal	Voltage
1	5	Keyboard Clock	+2.0v to +5.5v
2	1	Keyboard Data	+4.8v to +5.5v
3	—	Reserved	—
4	3	Ground	—
5	4	+5v Power	+2.0v to +5.5v

If your measurements do not match these voltages, the motherboard might be defective. Otherwise, the keyboard cable or keyboard might be defective. If you suspect that the cable is the problem, the easiest thing to do is replace the keyboard cable with a known good one. If the system still does not work normally, you might have to replace the entire keyboard or the motherboard.

Keyboard Error Codes

Some BIOSes use the following 3xx-series numbers to report keyboard errors. Look up the error code and fix the problem.

Table 8.11 lists some standard POST and diagnostics keyboard error codes.

Table 8.11	Keyboard POST Codes
Error Code	**Description**
3xx	Keyboard errors
301	Keyboard reset or stuck-key failure (XX 301; XX = scan code in hex)
302	System unit keylock switch is locked
302	User-indicated keyboard test error
303	Keyboard or system-board error; keyboard controller failure
304	Keyboard or system-board error; keyboard clock high
305	Keyboard +5v error; PS/2 keyboard fuse (on motherboard) blown
341	Keyboard error
342	Keyboard cable error
343	Keyboard LED card or cable failure
365	Keyboard LED card or cable failure
366	Keyboard interface cable failure
367	Keyboard LED card or cable failure

Mice and Pointing Devices

The most common type of mouse mechanism is the opto-mechanical, used by Logitech and many other vendors. The following figure shows what the mechanism looks like inside. Dirt on the mouse ball, rollers, or fuzz in the light paths will cause skipping and erratic mouse cursor operation.

Pointing Device Interface Types

The connector used to attach your mouse to the system depends on the type of interface you are using. Mice are most commonly connected to your computer through the following three interfaces:

- Serial interface

- Dedicated motherboard mouse port (PS/2 port)

- Bus-card interface

Some mice are now shipping with USB interfaces, although they can normally be adapted to another type as well. Many serial mice are shipped with a PS/2 adapter, also.

The serial interface can be seen in Chapter 6, while the PS/2 mouse port is the same connector as the keyboard 6-pin mini-DIN shown earlier in this chapter—they are not interchangable.

The bus-mouse connector is found on the back of a dedicated bus-mouse interface card or on some old ATI video cards.

Note

Microsoft sometimes calls a bus mouse an *Inport mouse*, which is its proprietary name for a bus mouse connection.

Software Drivers for the Mouse

Depending on the operating system you're using or the operating mode, you might need to manually load a driver, or it may be loaded automatically for you. Use Table 8.12 to determine what's needed for your mouse.

Table 8.12   Mouse Drive Type and Location by Operating System

Operating System	Driver Type	Loading Method	Notes
Windows 9x, NT, 2000	32-bit .DRV and .VXD	Automatically detected and installed	Most mice with PS/2 ports can PS/2 ports standard Microsoft driver, although third-party drivers provide support for scroll wheels, third buttons, etc.
MS-DOS mode under Windows 9x	Uses Windows 9x 32-bit driver	Automatically supported in windowed and full-screen modes	In window, can use mouse to mark text for the Windows Clipboard
MS-DOS, including Windows 9x command prompt (not MS-DOS mode)	Mouse.com Device= mouse.sys	Run MOUSE from command-line or Autoexec.bat or Add device= mouse.sys to Config.sys	New versions of Mouse.com from Microsoft and Logitech can load into UMB RAM above 640KB with little conventional memory used

Notebook Computer Pointing Devices

Table 8.13 provides an overview of pointing devices used with notebook computers.

Table 8.13	Notebook Computer Pointing Devices		
Device	**Where located**	**How Operated**	**Tips & Notes**
Glidepoint Developed by Alps Electric (a.k.a. touchpad)	Flat surface below spacebar on notebook PCs; might be separate device or on right-hand side of keyboard on desktop PCs	Move finger across surface; use left and right buttons beneath spacebar, or tap/ double-tap with finger in place of click/double-click	Most commonly used built-in mouse alternative; also available for desktop PCs Requires you move hand from keyboard; depends on skin moisture and resistance Accuracy can be a problem If you prefer to use a "real" mouse, disable the touchpad in the BIOS, because it may still be active on some machines, even when a mouse is installed
Trackpoint Developed by IBM	Small "eraserhead" pointing stick located in middle of keyboard	Gently press surface of "eraser" in the direction you want to go	Very fast operation because it's on the keyboard Licensed by Toshiba as "Accupoint" and also found on some IBM/ Lexmark/Unicomp keyboards and on some other notebook computer brands

Keep in mind that many notebook computer users use "real" mice or trackballs when they have room.

Mouse Troubleshooting

If you are experiencing problems with your mouse, you need to look in only two general places—hardware or software. Because mice are basically simple devices, looking at the hardware takes very little time. Detecting and correcting software problems can take a bit longer, however.

Use Table 8.14 to keep your mouse in top condition.

Table 8.14 Troubleshooting Mouse Problems

Symptom	Problem	Solution
Jerky mouse pointer	Dirt and dust on rollers and ball	Remove retainer plate on bottom of mouse, remove ball, clean ball and rollers with non-abrasive solvents such as contact lens cleaner. Blow dust away from wheels and sensor. Reassemble and test.
Mouse pointer freezes when another device (modem, etc.) is used	IRQ conflict	If mouse is PS/2, make sure no other device is using IRQ 12. If mouse is serial, check for modem on same IRQ as mouse. COM 1/3 share IRQ 4; COM 2/4 share IRQ 3 by default. See Chapter 6 for information on avoiding mouse/modem conflicts. If mouse is bus, check its IRQ usage and try to find an unused IRQ. Use Windows 9x Device Manager if available to find IRQ information.
Mouse won't work at all	Defective mouse	Replace the original mouse with a known-working similar spare. If it works, replace the original mouse for good.
	Defective port	Any mouse plugged into the port won't work. First, check to see if port's disabled. If the port is not disabled, use add-on port card or replace motherboard.
	Disabled COM, USB or PS/2 port	Check BIOS or motherboard jumpers and enable if IRQ used by port isn't already in use.
Mouse works as PS/2, but not as serial	Mouse designed for PS/2 port only	Most "bundled" mice are designed for the PS/2 port only. Retail mice are designed to be used with adapters. Get a mouse built for the serial port.
Mouse locks up when accessed by Microsoft MSD or other diagnostic	Bad mouse	To verify mouse is the problem, run MSD /I to bypass initial detection. Detect computer and other information; then detect mouse. If the mouse is at fault, you'll lock up your system. Turn off system, replace with known-working mouse, and repeat. If replacement mouse works okay, you've solved the problem.

Chapter 9

Video and Audio

Selecting a Monitor Size

As monitor prices fall and tube sizes increase, you'll want to upgrade
existing systems with larger monitors. Keep in mind that CRT (glass-
tube) monitors' screen sizes are rated by the diagonal measurement of
the tube. Thus, some actual viewable area is lost because of the plastic
case surrounding the tube. This is not an issue for the rapidly growing
family of LCD displays.

Table 9.1 shows the monitor's advertised diagonal screen size, along
with the approximate diagonal measure of the actual active viewing
area for the most common display sizes.

Table 9.1 Advertised Screen Size Versus Actual Viewing Area	
Monitor Size (in Inches)	**Viewing Area (in Inches)**
12	10 1/2
14	12 1/2
15	13 1/2
16	14 1/2
17	15 1/2
18	16 1/2
19	17 1/2
20	18 1/2
21	19 1/2

The size of the actual viewable area varies from manufacturer to
manufacturer but tends to be approximately 1 1/2 inches less than
the actual screen size. However, you can adjust some monitors—such
as some models made by NEC, for example—to display a high-quality
image that completely fills the tube from edge to edge. Other makes
can fill the screen also, but some of them do so only by pushing the
monitor beyond its comfortable limits. The result is a distorted image
that is worse than the monitor's smaller, properly adjusted picture.

This phenomenon is a well-known monitor-purchasing issue, and as a
result, most manufacturers and vendors have begun advertising the size
of the active viewing area of their monitors along with the screen size.
This makes it easier for consumers to compare what they are paying for.

Monitor Resolution

Resolution is the amount of detail a monitor can render. This quantity is expressed in the number of horizontal and vertical picture elements, or pixels, contained in the screen. The greater the number of pixels, the more detailed the images. Pixels are also referred to *pels*, which is short for "picture elements". The resolution required depends on the application. Character-based applications (such as DOS command-line programs) require little resolution, whereas graphics-intensive applications (such as desktop publishing and Windows software) require a great deal.

It's important to realize that CRTs are designed to handle a range of resolutions natively, but LCD panels (both desktop and notebook) are built to run a single native resolution and must scale to other choices.

As PC video technology developed, the screen resolutions supported by video adapters grew at a steady pace. Table 9.2 shows standard resolutions used in PC video adapters and the terms commonly used to describe them:

Table 9.2 Monitor Resolutions		
Resolution	**Acronym**	**Standard Designation**
640×480	VGA	Video Graphics Array
800×600	SVGA	Super VGA
1,024×768	XGA	eXtended Graphics Array
1,280×1,024	UVGA	Ultra VGA

Today, the term VGA is still in common use as a reference to the standard 640×480 16-color display that the Windows operating systems use as their default. The 15-pin connector to which you connect the monitor on most video adapters is also often called a VGA plug.

However, the terms SVGA, XGA, and UVGA have fallen into disuse. The industry now describes screen resolutions by citing the number of pixels. Nearly all the video adapters sold today support the 640×480, 800×600, and 1,024×768 pixel resolutions at several color depths, and many support 1,280×1,024 and higher as well.

What resolution do you want for your display? Generally, the higher the resolution, the larger the display you will want.

Note

To understand this issue, you might want to try different resolutions on your system. As you change from 640×480 to 800×600 and 1024×768, you'll notice several changes to the appearance of your screen.

At 640×480, text and onscreen icons are very large. Because the screen elements used for the Windows 9x desktop and software menus are at a fixed pixel width and height, you'll notice that they shrink in size onscreen as you change to the higher resolutions. You'll be able to see more of your document or Web page onscreen at the higher resolutions because each object requires less of the screen.

Table 9.3 shows the minimum-size monitors I recommend to properly display the resolutions that users typically select:

Table 9.3 Resolution and Monitor Size Recommendations	
Resolution	**Minimum Recommended Monitor**
640×480	13-inch
800×600	15-inch
1,024×768	17-inch
1,280×1,024	21-inch

These minimum recommended display sizes are the advertised diagonal display dimensions of the monitor. Note that these are not necessarily the limits of the given monitors' capabilities, but they are what I recommend because of the eyestrain resulting from too-small icons and text and the flicker that can result from running many monitors at their maximum resolution.

LCD Versus CRT Display Size

LCD panels, especially all-digital units, provide high-quality displays that are always crisp and perfectly focused. Plus, their dimensions are fully usable and can comfortably display higher resolutions than comparably-sized CRTs. Table 9.4 provides common CRTs screen sizes and the comparable LCD display panels size.

Table 9.4 CRT Versus LCD Usable Screen Size Comparison		
CRT Monitor Size Display (in Inches)	**CRT Viewing Area (in Inches)**	**Comparable LCD (Also Viewing Area In Inches)**
14	12.5	12.1
15	13.5	13.3, 13.7
16	14.5	14.1, 14.5
17	15.5	15, 15.1
19	17.5	17, 17.1
20	18.5	18.1

As you can see, a 15" LCD actually provides a usable viewing area similar to a 17" CRT. This allows you to use smaller LCD panels to replace larger, bulkier CRTs when space is at a premium.

Monitor Power Management Modes

CRT monitors that are left on continuously without any type of power management represent a substantial waste of power. To reduce this waste and enhance monitor life, several power-management standards have been developed for monitors and for PCs.

One of the first energy-saving standards for monitors was VESA's Display Power Management Signaling (DPMS) spec, which defines the signals that a computer sends to a monitor to indicate idle times. The computer or video card decides when to send these signals.

In Windows 9x, you need to enable this feature if you want to use it because it's turned off by default. To enable it, open the Display properties in the Control Panel, switch to the Screen Saver tab and make sure the Energy Star low-power settings and Monitor shutdown settings are checked. You can adjust how long the system remains idle before the monitor picture is blanked or the monitor shuts down completely.

Table 9.5 summarizes the DPMS modes.

Table 9.5	Display Power Management Signaling				
State	**Horizontal**	**Vertical**	**Video**	**Power Savings**	**Recovery Time**
On	Pulses	Pulses	Active	None	Not Applicable
Stand-By	No Pulses	Pulses	Blanked	Minimal	Short
Suspend	Pulses	No Pulses	Blanked	Substantial	Longer
Off	No Pulses	No Pulses	Blanked	Maximum	System Dependent

Microsoft and Intel developed a more broadly-based power management specification called APM (Advanced Power Management), and Microsoft developed an even more advanced power management specification called ACPI (Advanced Configuration and Power Interface for use with Windows 98 and beyond. Table 9.6 summarizes the differences between DPMS, APM, and ACPI.

Table 9.6	Power Management Standards Compared		
Standard	**Devices Controlled**	**How Implemented**	**Notes**
DPMS	Monitor and video card	Drivers for display and video card; must be enabled by operating system such as Windows 9x via Control Panel	DPMS will work alongside APM or ACPI; user defines timer intervals for various modes listed

Standard	Devices Controlled	How Implemented	Notes
APM	Monitor, hard disks, other peripherals	Implemented in BIOS; enable in BIOS and in operating system (Windows 9x via Control Panel)	User defines timer intervals for various devices in BIOS or operating system
ACPI	All APM peripherals plus other PC and consumer devices	Implemented in BIOS; support must be present in BIOS and devices; supports automatic power-up and power-off for PC and consumer devices including printers, stereos, CDs and others	If ACPI support is present in the BIOSwhen Windows 98 is first installed, Windows 98 ACPI drivers are installed; update BIOS before installing Windows 98 if ACPI support is not present in BIOS

VGA Video Connector Pinout

Virtually all displays in use today are descended from the 1987-vintage IBM VGA display introduced with the IBM PS/2s. The connector pinout is shown in Table 9.7.

Table 9.7   Standard 15-pin VGA Connector Pinout

Pin	Function	Direction	Pin	Function	Direction
1	Red Video	Out	8	Blue Analog Ground	-_
2	Green Video	Out	9	Key (Plugged Hole)	-_
3	Blue Video	Out	10	Sync Ground	-_
4	Monitor ID 2	In	11	Monitor ID 0	In
5	TTL Ground	-_ (monitor self-test)	12	Monitor ID 1	In
6	Red Analog Ground	-_	13	Horizontal Sync	Out
7	Green Analog Ground	-_	14	Vertical Sync	Out
			15	Monitor ID 3	In

On the VGA cable connector that plugs into your video adapter, pin 9 is often pinless. Pin 5 is used only for testing purposes, and pin 15 is rarely used; these are often pinless as well. To identify the type of monitor connected to the system, some manufacturers use the presence or absence of the monitor ID pins in various combinations.

VGA Video Display Modes

The original IBM VGA display card offered only a few video modes compared to more recent "Super VGA" and above graphics accelerators. Depending on the application, you might need to identify a desired mode by the BIOS mode numbers listed here.

Table 9.8 lists the video modes of the Chips and Technologies 65554 SVGA graphics accelerator, a typical chipset used today.

BIOS Mode	Mode Type	Resolution	Character	Colors (displayed from pallet)	Scan Freq. (hor./vert.)
0, 1	VGA Text	40×25 char	9×16	16/256KB	31.5KHz/70Hz
2, 3	VGA Text	80×25 char	9×16	16/256KB	31.5KHz/70Hz
4, 5	VGA Graph	320×200 pels	8×8	4KB/256KB	31.5KHz/70Hz
6	VGA Graph	640×200 pels	8×8	2KB/256KB	31.5KHz/70Hz
7	VGA Text	80×25 char	9×16	Mono	31.5KHz/70Hz
D	VGA Graph	320×200 pels	8×8	16KB/256KB	31.5KHz/70Hz
E	VGA Graph	640×200 pels	8×8	16KB/256KB	31.5KHz/70Hz
F	VGA Graph	640×350 pels	8×14	Mono	31.5KHz/70Hz
10	VGA Graph	640×350 pels	8×14	16KB/256KB	31.5KHz/70Hz
11	VGA Graph	640×480 pels	8×16	2KB/256KB	31.5KHz/60Hz
12	VGA Graph	640×480 pels	8×16	16KB/256KB	31.5KHz/60Hz
13	VGA Graph	320×200 pels	8×8	256KB/256KB	31.5KHz/70Hz
20	SVGA Graph	640×480 pels	8×16	16KB/256KB	31.5KHz/60Hz
					37.6KHz/75Hz
					43.2KHz/85Hz
22	SVGA Graph	800×600 pels	8×8	16KB/256KB	37.9KHz/60Hz
					46.9KHz/75Hz
					53.7KHz/85Hz
24	SVGA Graph	1024×768 pels	8×16	16KB/256KB	35.5KHz/87Hz*
					48.5KHz/60Hz
					60.0KHz/75Hz
					68.8KHz/85Hz
28	SVGA Graph	1280×1024 pels	8×16	16KB/256KB	35.5KHz/87Hz*
					35.5KHz/60Hz
30	SVGA Graph	640×480 pels	8×16	256KB/256KB	31.5KHz/60Hz
					37.6KHz/75Hz
					43.2KHz/85Hz
32	SVGA Graph	800×600 pels	8×16	256KB/256KB	37.9KHz/60Hz
					46.9KHz/75Hz
					53.7KHz/85Hz
34	SVGA Graph	1024×768 pels	8×16	256KB/256KB	35.5KHz/87Hz*
					48.5KHz/60Hz
					60.0KHz/75Hz
					68.8KHz/85Hz

Table 9.8   Chips and Technologies 65554 Graphics Accelerator Chipset Video Modes

BIOS Mode	Mode Type	Resolution	Character	Colors (displayed/ from pallet)	Scan Freq. (hor./vert.)
38	SVGA Graph	1280×1024 pels	8×16	256KB/256KB	35.5KHz/87Hz*
					35.5KHz/60Hz
40	SVGA Graph	640×480 pels	8×16	32KB/32KB	31.5KHz/60Hz
					37.6KHz/75Hz
					43.2KHz/85Hz
41	SVGA Graph	640×480 pels	8×16	64KB/64KB	31.5KHz/60Hz
					37.6KHz/75Hz
					43.2KHz/85Hz
42	SVGA Graph	800×600 pels	8×16	32KB/32KB	37.9KHz/60Hz
					46.9KHz/75Hz
					53.7KHz/85Hz
43	SVGA Graph	800×600 pels	8×16	64KB/64KB	37.9KHz/60Hz
					46.9KHz/75Hz
					53.7KHz/85Hz
44	SVGA Graph	1024×768 pels	8×16	32KB/32KB	48.5KHz/60Hz
45	SVGA Graph	1024×768 pels	8×16	64KB/64KB	48.5KHz/60Hz
50	SVGA Graph	640×480 pels	8×16	16MB/16MB	31.5KHz/60Hz
52	SVGA Graph	800×600 pels	8×16	16MB/16MB	37.9KHz/60Hz

*Interlaced displays draw half the screen lines in a single pass. Lines 1-3-5-7 and so forth are drawn in one pass of the electron gun. The second pass draws lines 2-4-6-8 and so on. Interlacing was once common, but is now rare because of improvements in monitor design. Any interlaced display will be prone to eye-straining flicker. Flicker can be minimized by using a dark-glass glare screen.

From the standpoint of user comfort, you should use this type of information, supplied with both graphics cards and monitors, to select the most comfortable viewing settings. Comfortable viewing comes from the optimal combination of resolution, color depth, and vertical refresh rates.

In deciding whether a video card is suitable for a particular task, or whether it's obsolete and should be replaced, the amount of video RAM on the card is a critical factor.

Video RAM

Video adapters rely on their own onboard memory that they use to store video images while processing them. The amount of memory on the adapter determines the maximum screen resolution and color depth that the device can support.

Most cards today come with at least 4MB, and many have 8MB or more. Although adding more memory is not guaranteed to speed up your video adapter, it can increase the speed if it enables a wider bus (from 64-bits wide to 128-bits wide) or provides nondisplay memory as a cache for commonly displayed objects. It also enables the card to generate more colors and higher resolutions.

Many different types of memory are used on video adapters today. These memory types are summarized in Table 9.9.

Table 9.9	Memory Types Used in Video Display Adapters		
Memory Type	**Definition**	**Relative Speed**	**Usage**
FPM DRAM	Fast Page-Mode RAM	Slow	Low-end ISA cards; obsolete
VRAM*	Video RAM	Very fast	Expensive; rare today
WRAM*	Window RAM	Very fast	Expensive; rare today
EDO DRAM	Extended Data Out DRAM	Moderate	Low-end PCI-bus
SDRAM	Synchronous DRAM	Fast	Midrange PCI/AGP
MDRAM	Multibank DRAM	Fast	Little used; rare
SGRAM	Synchronous Graphics DRAM	Very fast	High-end PCI/AGP

VRAM and WRAM are dual-ported memory types that can read from one port and write data through the other port. This improves performance by reducing wait times for accessing the video RAM.

Memory, Resolution, and Color Depth

The amount of video memory on the graphics card, combined with the selected display resolution, affects how many colors can be displayed onscreen. For maximum realism in such tasks as full-motion video playback, videoconferencing, or photo-editing, a color depth of 24-bits (over 16 million colors) is desirable at the highest comfortable display resolution possible with your monitor.

Use Table 9.10 to determine if your video card has the required memory to display some of the most commonly used screen resolutions and color depths.

Table 9.10	Video Display Adapter Minimum Memory Requirements			
Resolution	**Color Depth**	**No. Colors**	**RAM on Video Card**	**Memory Required**
640×480	4-bit	16	256KB	153,600 bytes
640×480	8-bit	256	512KB	307,200 bytes
640×480	16-bit	65,536	1MB	614,400 bytes
640×480	24-bit	16,777,216	1MB	921,600 bytes
800×600	4-bit	16	256KB	240,000 bytes

Resolution	Color Depth	No. Colors	RAM on Video Card	Memory Required
800×600	8-bit	256	512KB	480,000 bytes
800×600	16-bit	65,536	1MB	960,000 bytes
800×600	24-bit	16,777,216	2MB	1,440,000 bytes
1,024×768	4-bit	16	512KB	393,216 bytes
1,024×768	8-bit	256	1MB	786,432 bytes
1,024×768	16-bit	65,536	2MB	1,572,864 bytes
1,024×768	24-bit	16,777,216	4MB	2,359,296 bytes
1,280×1,024	4-bit	16	1MB	655,360 bytes
1,280×1,024	8-bit	256	2MB	1,310,720 bytes
1,280×1,024	16-bit	65,536	4MB	2,621,440 bytes
1,280×1,024	24-bit	16,777,216	4MB	3,932,160 bytes

From this table, you can see that a video adapter with 2MB can display 65,536 colors in 1,024×768 resolution mode, but for a true color (16.8M colors) display, you would need to upgrade to 4MB.

Although many of the newest video cards on the market today have memory sizes of 8MB, 16MB, or even 32MB, this additional memory will not be used for 24-bit color in high resolutions for 2D graphics unless the display resolution exceeds 1,280×1,024 at 24-bit color. The additional RAM is used for 3D texture mapping and display caching.

Determining the Amount of RAM on Your Display Card

Because the size of video memory is increasingly important to most computer users, it's useful to know how much memory your display card has onboard.

Table 9.11 summarizes some methods you can use.

Table 9.11 Methods for Determining the Amount of RAM on a Video Card		
Method	**Benefits**	**Cautions**
Use memory/resolution table earlier and adjust video settings to options requiring 1MB, 2MB, and 4MB.	If the settings work (a reboot is often required), you have at least that much RAM on your video card.	Method assumes that video card is set correctly by system; often can't be used to detect memory above 4MB because of driver limitations.

(continues)

Table 9.11 Methods for Determining the Amount of RAM on a Video Card Continued		
Method	**Benefits**	**Cautions**
Use third-party system diagnostics to probe video card.	"Universal" solution for organizations with mixed display card standards.	Must use up-to-date diagnostics; may be confused by "shared memory" technologies found on low-cost systems.
Use diagnostics provided by video-card or video-chipset maker to probe video card.	Best source for technical information.	Must use different programs for different chipsets.

Given the low cost and high performance of today's video cards, you should seriously consider replacing any video card with less than 4MB of display memory onboard, because even the least-powerful cards in use today far outstrip top-end models of just a couple of years ago.

Local-Bus Video Standards

If you are in the market for a new video card, you need to consider your upgrade options. All video cards worth considering use a so-called "local-bus" technology, which uses a high-speed connection to the CPU that bypasses the slow ISA standard in use for many years. The major standards are VL-Bus (VESA Local-Bus), PCI (Peripheral Component Interconnect), and AGP (Advanced Graphics Port).

VL-Bus, PCI, and AGP have some important differences, as Table 9.12 shows.

Table 9.12 Local Bus Specifications			
Feature	**VL-Bus**	**PCI**	**AGP**
Theoretical maximum	132MB/sec	132MB/sec*	533MB/sec throughput (2X) 1.06GB/sec throughput (4X)
Slots**	3 (typical)	4/5 (typical)	1
Plug and Play support	No	Yes	Yes
Cost	Inexpensive	Slightly higher	Slightly higher than PCI
Ideal use	Low-cost 486	High-end 486, Pentium, P6	Pentium II, III, Celeron, AMD K6, K7

*At the 66MHz bus speed and 32 bits. Throughput will be higher on the 100MHz system bus.

**More slots are possible through the use of PCI bridge chips.

Obviously, of the three local-bus standards, AGP is the fastest, but only very recent systems offer AGP video. Use Table 9.13 to determine what your best video upgrade is, depending on your system.

Table 9.13	Best Video Upgrades by CPU and Slot Type		
CPU	**Slot Type**	**Best Option**	**Notes**
486	VL-Bus	No current video cards available in VL-Bus; obsolete	Buy used or surplus; replace motherboard; retire system
486	PCI	Buy any low-cost PCI card with at least 4MB of RAM	Verify that card will work with 486; some require Pentium
Pentium, K6	PCI	Buy PCI card with at least 8MB of RAM; look for DVD playback, TV out as desirable features	Choose a card with a chipset that can be used as secondary video in case you move to AGP later by upgrading to a new motherboard or by moving the card to a system with AGP
Pentium II/ III/Celeron K6/Athlon	AGP	Buy AGP card with 16MB or more RAM; should support AGP 2X or faster speed; look for DVD playback, TV out as desirable features	AGP upgrade only available on systems with AGP slot Many low-cost systems have AGP video on mother board only; must use PCI for upgrade (see previous table entry)

RAMDAC

In addition to choosing the fastest expansion slot design possible and a large amount of video RAM (8–16MB or more), you should also examine the speed of the RAMDAC (the digital-to-analog converter) chip on the video card. The speed of the RAMDAC is measured in MHz; the faster the conversion process, the higher the adapter's vertical refresh rate. Table 9.14 shows the effect of faster RAMDAC chips on typical video card chipsets. As RAMDAC speed increases, higher resolutions with higher vertical refresh rates are supported.

Table 9.14	Typical Chipset and RAMDAC Speed Pairings and Their Effects on Resolution and Refresh Rates		
Chipset	**RAMDAC speed**	**Maximum Resolution**	**Refresh Rate**
Matrox G200	250MHz	1920×1200 (2D) 1920×1080 (3D)	70Hz (2D)
Matrox G400MAX	360MHz	2048×1536 (2D/3D)	85Hz 75Hz (3D)

> **Note**
>
> In some cases, the maximum resolutions and refresh rates listed for any video card may require a RAM upgrade or the purchase of a video card with more RAM.

Refresh Rates

The speed of the RAMDAC affects the vertical refresh rate. The refresh rate (also called the *vertical scan frequency*) is the rate at which the screen display is rewritten. This is measured in hertz (Hz). A refresh rate of 72Hz means that the screen is refreshed 72 times per second. A refresh rate that is too low causes the screen to flicker, contributing to eyestrain. The higher the refresh rate, the better for your eyes and your comfort during long sessions at the computer.

A *flicker-free refresh rate* is a refresh rate high enough to prevent you from seeing any flicker. The flicker-free refresh rate varies with the resolution of your monitor setting (higher resolutions require a higher refresh rate) and must be matched by both your monitor and your display card.

One factor that is important to consider when you purchase a monitor is the refresh rate, especially if you are planning to use the monitor at 1,024×768 or higher resolutions. Low-cost monitors often have refresh rates that are too low to achieve flicker-free performance for most users, and thus can lead to eyestrain.

Table 9.15 compares two typical 17-inch CRT monitors and a typical midrange graphics card.

Although the ATI All-in-Wonder Pro video card supports higher refresh rates than either monitor, rates higher than the monitor can support cannot be used safely because rates in excess of the monitor's maximum refresh rate may damage the monitor and will certainly result in a distorted, unusable screen image.

Table 9.15	Refresh Rates Comparison		
Resolution	**ATI Video Card Vertical Refresh**	**LG 760SC (17") Monitor Vertical Refresh (Maximum)**	**LG 790SC (17") Monitor Vertical Refresh (Maximum)**
1,024×768	43–150Hz*	87Hz*	124Hz*
1,280×1024	43–100Hz*	65Hz	93Hz*
1,600×1200	52–85Hz*	Not supported	80Hz*

Rates above 72Hz will be flicker-free for many users; VESA standard for flicker-free refresh is 85Hz or above.

For a user who wants to run at resolutions above 1,024×768, the monitor with the higher refresh rate is preferable.

Adjusting the Refresh Rate of the Video Card

The refresh rate of the video card can be adjusted in several ways:

- With older cards, a command-line program or separate Windows program was often provided.

- With recent and new cards, the standard display properties sheet offers a selection of refresh rates.

In any case, you need to know the allowable refresh rates for the monitor before you can make an appropriate selection. If your Windows 9x installation uses an "unknown" or "Super VGA..." display type, rather than a particular brand and model of monitor, you will be prevented from selecting the higher, flicker-free refresh rates. Install the display manufacturer's driver for your monitor model to get highest refresh rates.

Comparing Video Cards with the Same Chipset

Many manufacturers create a line of video cards with the same chipset to sell at different pricing points. Why not save some dollars and get the cheapest model? Why not say "price is no object" and get the most expensive one? When you're faced with various cards in the "chipsetX" family, look for differences such as those shown in Table 9.16.

Table 9.16 Comparing Video Cards with the Features You Need	
Feature	**Effect on You**
RAMDAC speed	Less-expensive cards in a family often use a slower RAMDAC. As you saw earlier, this reduces maximum and flicker-free resolutions. If you use a 17-inch or larger monitor, this could be an eye-straining problem. Buy the card with the fastest RAMDAC, especially for use with 17-inch or larger monitors. Faster RAMDACs are often paired with SGRAM or WRAM, which are the fastest types of RAM currently found on video cards.
Amount of RAM	The former standard of 4MB as the practical maximum on a video card has been shattered by the rise of 3D games and applications and low memory prices. Although AGP video cards can use "AGP memory" (a section of main memory borrowed for texturing), it's still faster to perform as much work as possible on the card's own memory. PCI cards must perform all functions within their own memory. Less-expensive cards in a chipset family often have lower amounts of memory onboard, and most current-model cards aren't expandable. Buy a card with enough memory for your games or applications—today and tomorrow.
Memory type	High-end video cards frequently use the new SGRAM (Synchronous Graphics RAM), with SDRAM (Synchronous DRAM) as a popular choice for midrange video cards. The once-popular EDO (Extended Data Out) RAM is fading from view in both main memory and video memory applications. Choose SGRAM, and then SDRAM, in order of preference when possible.)
Memory and core clock speed	Many suppliers adjust the recommended speed of graphics controllers in an effort to provide users with maximum performance. Sometimes the supplier may choose to exceed the rated specification of the graphics chip. Be cautious. Current controller chips are large and they can overheat. An overclocked device in an open system with great airflow may work—or it may fail in a period of months from overstress of the circuitry. If you have questions about the rated speed of a controller, check the chip suppliers' Web site. Many reputable companies do use overclocked parts, but the best vendors supply large heat sinks or even powered fans to avoid overheating.
TV tuner	You can save some money by having it built in, but it's not as important as the other issues listed earlier.

Setting Up Multiple Monitor Support in Windows 98

Windows 98 includes a video display feature that Macintosh systems have had for years: the capability to use multiple monitors on one system. Windows 98 supports up to nine monitors (and video adapters), each of which can provide a different view of the desktop. You can display a separate program on each monitor, use different resolutions and color depths, and enjoy other features.

On a multimonitor Windows 98 system, one display is always considered to be the primary display. The primary display can use any PCI or AGP VGA video adapter that uses a Windows 98 minidriver with a linear frame buffer and a packed (non-planar) format, meaning that most of the brand name adapters sold today are eligible. Additional monitors are called secondaries and are much more limited in their hardware support.

Video cards with the Permedia chipset (not the later Permedia NT and Permedia 2) cannot be used in a multiple-monitor configuration.

The following list of video card chipsets with the specified Microsoft Windows 98 drivers can be used in any combination of primary or secondary adapters. Unlisted chipsets may also work as primary adapters. This list is condensed from Microsoft's Knowledge Base article # Q182/7/08. Check it for updates.

- *ATI.* Mach 64 GX and beyond, including 3D cards, Rage Pro series, Xpert series, and others using the ATIM64.drv or ATIR3.drv

- *S3.* 765 (Trio64V+)S3MM.drv

Note

Only certain updates work. These are 40, 42, 43, 44, 52, 53, and 54. Note that if the card is at one of these updates, Windows 98 recognizes the card as a Trio 64V+, provided the Microsoft driver is used. If the card is not at one of these updates, it is recognized as a Trio 32/64. Some OEM drivers don't care which update is present; be sure to note carefully which Microsoft driver Windows 98 selects when you use this card.

Other S3 chipsets include the Trio64V2, various Diamond, STB, Hercules, Number Nine, and other cards using the Virge or newer chipsets.

- *Cirrus.* 5436, Alpine, 5446, and other cards using the CIRRUSMM.drv

- *Tseng.* Cards with the ET6000 chipset

- *Trident.* 9685/9680/9682/9385/9382/9385 chipsets

It's important that the computer correctly identifies which one of the video adapters is the primary one. This is a function of the system BIOS, and if the BIOS on your computer does not let you select which device should be the primary VGA display, it decides based on the order of the PCI slots in the machine. You should, therefore, install the primary adapter in the highest priority PCI slot. Because many systems do not list the slot priority in their documentation, you might need to experiment by switching the cards around between different PCI expansion slots.

After the hardware is in place, you can configure the display for each monitor from the Display Control Panel's Settings page. The primary display is always fixed in the upper-left corner of the virtual desktop, but you can move the secondary displays to view any area of the desktop you like. You can also set the screen resolution and color depth for each display individually.

Video Card and Chipset Makers Model Reference
3D Chipsets

As with standard 2D video adapters, there are several manufacturers of popular 3D video chipsets and many more manufacturers of video adapters that use them.

> **Note**
>
> See Chapter 15 of *Upgrading and Repairing PCs, Eleventh Edition,* for an exhaustive listing of current 3D chipsets and the boards on which they are found.

Multimedia Devices

More and more users are using their business or home PCs for multimedia purposes. When choosing TV, video-out, or video capture options for your PC, use Table 9.17 to help you decide which solution may be best for you. Consider what ports you have, your operating system, and the speed of the multimedia input or output you need.

Table 9.17 Multimedia Device Comparison

Device Type	Pros	Cons
Graphics card w/ built-in TV tuner	Convenience, single-slot solution	Upgrading requires card replacement
TV-tuner attachment	Allows upgrade to existing graphics cards; may be movable to newer models	Can't be used with all graphics cards
Parallel-port attachment	Universal usage on desktop or notebook computer; inexpensive	Frame rate limited by speed of port
USB-port attachment	Easy installation on late-model USB-equipped computers with Windows 98	May not work on Windows 95B OSR 2.x with USB; requires active USB port
Dedicated ISA or PCI interface card	Fast frame rate for realistic video; doesn't require disconnecting parallel printer; works with any graphics card	High resource requirements (IRQ, and so on) on some models; ISA nearly obsolete; requires internal installation
SCSI interface	SCSI card can be used with wide range of other peripherals; fast frame rate for realistic video; external control box for cabling	Requires internal installation
IEEE-1394 (FireWire, iLINK) connection to digital video	No conversion from analog to digital needed; all-digital image is very high quality without compression artifacts (blocky areas) in video; fast throughput	Requires IEEE-1394 interface card and IEEE-1394 digital video source; new and expensive; card requires internal installation

Troubleshooting Video Capture Devices

Table 9.18 provides some advice for troubleshooting problems with video capture devices.

Table 9.18 Troubleshooting Video Capture Devices

Device Type	Problem	Solutions
Parallel-port attachment	Can't detect device, but printers work okay	Check port settings; device may require IEEE-1284 settings (EPP and ECP); change in BIOS; make sure device is connected directly to port; avoid daisy-chaining devices unless device specifically allows it; check Windows 9x Device Manager for IRQ conflicts.
TV tuners (built-in graphics card or add-on)	No picture	Check cabling; set signal source correctly in software.

Device Type	Problem	Solutions
All devices	Video capture is jerky	Frame rate is too low; increasing it may require capturing video in a smaller window; use fastest parallel-port setting you can.
All devices	Video playback has pauses, dropped frames	Hard disk may be pausing for thermal recalibration; use AV-rated SCSI hard drives or new UDMA EIDE drives; install correct bus-mastering EIDE drivers for motherboard chipset to speed things up.
USB devices	Device can't be detected or doesn't work properly	Use Windows 98; late versions of Windows 95 have USB drivers, but they often don't work; if you use a USB hub, make sure it's powered.
Interface cards (all types)	Card can't be detected or doesn't work	Check for IRQ conflicts in Windows 9x Device Manager; consider setting card manually if possible.
All devices	Capture or installation problems	Use the newest drivers available; check manufacturer's Web site for updates, FAQs, and so on.

Testing a Monitor with Common Applications

Even without dedicated test and diagnostics software, you can use the software accessories (WordPad, Paint, etc.) that come with Microsoft Windows to test a monitor for picture quality.

One good series of tasks is as follows:

- Draw a perfect circle with a graphics program. If the displayed result is an oval, not a circle, this monitor will not serve you well with graphics or design software.

- Using a word processor, type some words in 8- or 10-point type (1 point equals 1/72 inch). If the words are fuzzy or if the black characters are fringed with color, select another monitor.

- Turn the brightness up and down while examining the corner of the screen's image. If the image blooms or swells, it is likely to lose focus at high brightness levels.

- Display a screen with as much white space as possible and look for areas of color variance. This might indicate a problem only with that individual unit or its location, but if you see it on more than one monitor of the same make, it may be indicative of a manufacturing problem; or it could indicate problems with the signal coming from the graphics card. Move the monitor to another system equipped with a different graphics card model and retry this test to see for certain whether it's the monitor or video card.

- Load Microsoft Windows to check for uniform focus. Are the corner icons as sharp as the rest of the screen? Are the lines in the title bar curved or wavy? Monitors usually are sharply focused at the center, but seriously blurred corners indicate a poor design. Bowed lines may be the result of a poor video adapter, so don't dismiss a monitor that shows those lines without using another adapter to double-check the effect.

- A good monitor will be calibrated so that rays of red, green, and blue light hit their targets (individual phosphor dots) precisely. If they don't, you have bad convergence. This is apparent when edges of lines appear to illuminate with a specific color. If you have good convergence, the colors will be crisp, clear, and true, provided there isn't a predominant tint in the phosphor.

- If the monitor has built-in diagnostics (a recommended feature), try them as well to test the display independent of the graphics card and system to which it's attached.

Use Table 9.19 to troubleshoot specified problems.

Table 9.19   Troubleshooting Display Problems

Symptom	Cause	Solution
No Picture	LED indicates power-saving mode (flashing green or yellow by power switch)	Move the mouse or press Alt+Tab on the keyboard and wait up to one minute to wake up the system if the system is turned on.
	LED indicates normal mode	Check monitor and video data cables; replace with known, working spare
		Turn off monitor; reset mode switch to correct setting (analog for VGA)
		Check brightness and contrast control; adjust as needed
No picture; no power lights on monitor	No power flowing to monitor	Cycle monitor off and on in case power management has kicked in; check power cable and replace; check surge protector and replace; replace monitor and retest
Jittery Picture Quality	LCD monitors display not adjusted	Use display-adjustment software to reduce or eliminate pixel jitter and pixel swim.
	Cables loose	Check cables for tightness at the video card and the monitor (if removable).
	Defective main or extender cable	Remove the extender cable and retest with the monitor plugged directly into the video card; if the extended cable is bad, replace it; if the main cable is bad, replace it.

Symptom	Cause	Solution
	Jitter is intermittent	Check for interference; microwave ovens near monitors can cause severe picture distortion when turned on.
	CRT monitor—Wrong refresh rate	Check settings; reduce refresh rate until acceptable picture quality is achieved.
		Use onscreen picture adjustments until an acceptable picture quality is achieved.
	Intermittent—not due to external interference	If the problem can be "fixed" by waiting or gently tapping the side of the monitor, the monitor power supply is probably bad or has loose connections internally; service or replace the monitor.

Audio I/O Connectors

Sound cards, or built-in audio chips, provide another significant part of modern PC's multimedia capabilities. Learning the correct uses for the basic input/output connectors will help you as you set up typical sound-equipped computers.

- *Stereo line or audio out connector.* The line out connector is used to send sound signals from the audio adapter to a device outside the computer. You can hook up the cables from the line out connector to stereo speakers, a headphone set, or your stereo system. If you hook up the PC to your stereo system, you can have amplified sound. Some adapters , such as the Microsoft Windows Sound System, provide two jacks for line out. One is for the left channel of the stereo signal; the other is for the right channel.

- *Stereo line or audio in connector.* With the line in connector, you can record or mix sound signals from an external source, such as a stereo system or VCR, to the computer's hard disk.

- *Speaker/headphone connector.* The speaker/headphone connector is provided on most audio adapters, but not necessarily all of them. Instead, the line out doubles as a way to send stereo signals from the adapter to your stereo system or speakers. When the adapter provides both a speaker/headphone and a line out connector, the speaker/headphone connector provides an amplified signal that can power your headphones or small bookshelf speakers. Most adapters can provide up to four watts of power to drive your speakers. The signals that the adapter sends through the line out connector are not amplified. The line out connector generally provides better sound reproduction because it relies on the external amplifier built-in to your stereo system or speakers, which is typically more powerful than the small amplifier on the audio adapter.

- *Microphone or mono in connector.* The mono in connector is used to connect a microphone for recording your voice or other sounds to disk. This microphone jack records in mono not in stereo and is therefore not suitable for high-quality music recordings. Many audio adapters cards use Automatic Gain Control (AGC) to improve recordings. This feature adjusts the recording levels on-the-fly. A 600ohm to 10KB ohm dynamic or condenser microphone works best with this jack. Some inexpensive audio adapters use the line in connector instead of a separate microphone jack.

- *Joystick connector.* The joystick connector is a 15-pin, D-shaped connector that can connect to any standard joystick or game controller. Sometimes the joystick port can accommodate two joysticks if you purchase an optional Y-adapter. Many computers already contain a joystick port as part of a multi-function I/O circuit on the motherboard or an expansion card. If this is the case, you must take note of which port your operating system or application is configured to use when connecting the game controller.

- *MIDI connector.* Audio adapters typically use the same joystick port as their MIDI connector. Two of the pins in the connector are designed to carry signals to and from a MIDI device, such as an electronic keyboard. In most cases, you must purchase a separate MIDI connector from the audio adapter manufacturer that plugs into the joystick port and contains the two round, 5-pin DIN connectors used by MIDI devices, plus a connector for a joystick. Because their signals use separate pins, you can connect the joystick and a MIDI device at the same time. You need only this connector if you plan to connect your PC to external MIDI devices. You can still play the MIDI files found on many Web sites by using the audio adapter's internal synthesizer.

- *Internal pin-type connector.* Most audio adapters have an internal pin-type connector that you can use to plug an internal CD-ROM drive directly into the adapter, using a ribbon cable. This connection enables you to channel audio signals from the CD-ROM directly to the audio adapter, so you can play the sound through the computer's speakers. Note that this connector is different from the CD-ROM controller connector found on some audio adapters. This connector does not carry data from the CD-ROM to the system bus; it only provides the CD-ROM drive with direct audio access to the speakers. If your adapter lacks this connector, you can still play CD audio through the computer speakers by connecting the CD-ROM drive's headphone jack to the audio adapter's line in jack with an external cable.

> **Tip**
>
> The line in, line out, and speaker connectors on an audio adapter all use the same 1/8-inch minijack socket. The three jacks are usually labeled, but when setting up a computer on or under a desk, these labels on the back of the PC can be difficult to read. One of the most common reasons why a PC fails to produce any sound is that the speakers are plugged into the wrong socket.
>
> If your sound card, microphone, and speakers aren't color-coded, do it yourself.

Sound Quality Standards

Many sound-card owners never record anything, but if you like the idea of adding sound to a Web site or presentation, you should know the quality and file size impact that typical sound settings will have. The Windows 9x standard sound quality settings are shown in Table 9.20:

Table 9.20 Windows 9x Sound File Resolutions

Resolution	Frequency	Bandwidth	File Size
Telephone quality	11,025Hz	8-bit mono	11KB/sec
Radio quality	22,050Hz	8-bit mono	22KB/sec
CD quality	44,100Hz	16-bit stereo	172KB/sec

Note that the higher the sound quality, the larger the file size. The file sizes are for WAV files saved with the Windows Sound Recorder's default settings. If you want to add your sound effects or speech to a Web site, you should get a program such as Real Networks' RealProducer, which is capable of compressing sound as much as 100:1 and still maintaining reasonable quality.

Configuring Sound Cards

Traditionally, sound cards have been one of the toughest single installation tasks because they use three of the four settings possible for an add-on card: IRQ, DMA, and I/O port addressing. The rule of thumb is: "The sound card first!", no matter what else you need to install.

PCI Versus ISA Sound Cards

PCI cards have become the best choice recently for all types of upgrades, including sound cards. Compared to ISA cards, PCI cards are faster, have a lower CPU utilization rate, and use fewer hardware resources (see Table 9.21). Compare the configuration of the Sound Blaster 16 card with the native configuration for an Ensoniq-chipset PCI sound card.

Table 9.21 Default Resource Assignments for ISA and PCI Sound Card in Native and Emulation Modes				
Card Onboard Device	IRQ	I/O	DMA (16 bit)	DMA (8 bit)
Sound Blaster 16—ISA Bus				
Audio	5	220h-233h	5	1
MIDI Port	—	330h-331h	—	—
FM Synthesizer	—	388h-38Bh	—	—
Game Port	—	200h-207h	—	—
Ensoniq Audio PCI—PCI Bus Native Mode				
Audio	11	DC80-DCBFh	—	—
Game Port	—	200h-207h	—	—
Ensoniq Audio PCI—PCI Bus Legacy (SB Pro) Mode				
Audio	7*	DC80-DCBFh	—	—
MIDI Port	—	330h-331h	—	—
FM Synthesizer	—	388h-38Bh	—	—
(Ensoniq SoundScape)	—	0530-0537h	—	—
Game Port	—	200h-207h	—	—

Shared IRQ with printer port; allowed by Ensoniq driver

While the Ensoniq Audio PCI card uses only one IRQ and one I/O port address in its native mode, if you have software (mostly older Windows and DOS game/educational titles) that requires Sound Blaster Pro compatibility, the "Legacy" settings must also be used. However, if you are *not* running Sound Blaster-specific software (all your software is native Windows 9x, for example), you may be able to disable the Legacy mode for a PCI-based sound card.

Troubleshooting Audio Hardware
Hardware (Resource) Conflicts

The most common problem for audio adapters is that they conflict with other devices installed in your PC. You may notice that your audio adapter doesn't work (no sound effects or music), repeats the same sounds over and over, or causes your PC to freeze. This situation is called a device, or hardware conflict, centering around IRQ, DMA, and I/O port address settings in your computer (see Chapter 2, "System Components and Configuration").

Detecting Resource Conflicts

Use the Table 9.22 to help you determine resource conflicts caused by your sound card.

Table 9.22   Resolving Sound Card Resource Conflicts

Problem	Symptom	How to Detect	Solution
Sound card using same IRQ as another device	Skipping, jerky sound, or system lockups	Use Windows 9x Device Manager. For other systems: Use IRQ and DMA card as described in Chapter 2	For PnP device: Disable automatic configuration for conflicting device and try to set card manually through direct alteration of settings or by choosing alternative configurations
Sound card and device another using the same DMA channel	No sound at all from sound card		For non-PnP device: Move conflicting device to another setting to allow sound card to use defaults
PCI-slot sound card works okay with Windows, but not MS-DOS apps.	Windows software plays; DOS software doesn't play card; can't detect card	Check for "Legacy" or "SB"settings in the Windows 9x Device Manager	If no Legacy support installed, install it. Follow instructions carefully for using card with older software. May need to run Setup programor TSR before starting DOS program. Might need software patch from game developer. In extreme cases, you may need to use an actual SB Pro/16 card alongside your PCI sound card
Some DOS and Windows software works, some can't use card	Error messages abou incorrect card settings	Check card or Legacy software settings; alternative settings work okay for some programs, but not others	Software expects SB default settings; use settings in preceding table for Sound Blaster 16 (all but DMA 5 apply to SB Pro)
DSP-equipped card like IBM Mwave not installed properly or out of resources	Multifunction sound and modem card doesn't work	Check Windows 9x Device Manager for DSP host configuration	Mwave and similar cards require basic SB settings as above, plus serial (COM) port settings resources for the DSP! Reinstall card with all drivers
PnP card on a non-PnP system was working, but has now stopped	PnP enumerator program in startup process probably removed or damaged	Check CONFIG.SYS or AUTOEXEC.BAT for driver; use REM to create labels before and after driver commands in these files	Reinstall software and test; upgrade BIOS to PnP mode if possible

Most Common Causes of Hardware Conflicts with Sound Card

The most common causes of system resource conflicts are the following:

- SCSI host adapters

- Network interface cards

- Bus mouse adapter cards

- Serial port adapter cards for COM 3: or COM 4:

- Parallel port adapter cards for LPT2:

- Internal modems

- Scanner interface cards

All these cards use IRQ, DMA, and I/O port addresses, which in some cases can overlap with default or alternative sound card settings.

Freeing Up IRQ 5 for Sound Card Use and Still Print

If you are using an LPT2 port card for a slow-speed device such as a dot-matrix or low-end inkjet printer, you can often free up its default IRQ 5 by disabling EPP/ECP/IEEE-1284 modes. These modes require use of an IRQ (ECP also uses a DMA channel). Reverting to standard printing will cause most LPT ports to use only I/O port addresses. This will permit you to use the port for printing and its IRQ 5 for a sound card.

Other Sound Card Problems

Like the common cold, audio adapter problems have common symptoms. Table 9.23 will help you diagnose sound card problems.

Table 9.23	Diagnosing Sound Card Problems	
Symptom	**Cause**	**Solution**
No sound	Incorrect or missing speaker wires	Plug speakers into the correct jack (Stereo Line out/speaker out)
	No power to amplified speakers	Turn on; attach to AC adapter or use fresh batteries
	Mono speaker attached to stereo plug	Use stereo speaker or headset
	Mixer settings too low	Adjust master volume setting; turn off "mute" option
	Sound card may not be working	Test with diagnostic software and sounds provided
	Sound card hardware needs to be reset	Power down, then on again or use reset button to restart PC
	Some games play, but others don't	Check hardware defaults as above; verify correct version of Windows DirectX or other game API's installed

Symptom	Cause	Solution
Mono Sound	Mono plug in stereo jack	Use stereo speaker jack
	Incorrectly wired speakers	Check color coding
	Audio card in left-channel mono "fail safe" mode because of driver problem	Reload drivers and test stereo sound
	Speakers with independent volume controls may be set differently	Adjust volume to match on both
Low volume	Speakers plugged into headphone jack	Use higher powered speaker jack if separate jacks provided
	Mixer settings too low	Boost volume in mixer
	Hardware volume control (thumbwheel) on sound card turned too low	Adjust volume on card
	Speakers not powered or require more power	Power speakers, add amplifier or replace speakers
Scratchy Sound	Audio card picking up interference from other cards	Move away from other cards
	ISA sound card may be dropping signals during hard disk access	Normal problem due to high CPU utilization of ISA card; use PCI sound card instead
	Interference from monitor causing interference	Move speakers them farther away. Put subwoofers on the floor to maximize low-frequency transmission and to keep their big magnets away from the monitor
	Poor quality FM-synthesis music from sound card	Change to wavetable sound card; check wavetable settings
Computer won't start after card installation	Card not seated tightly in expansion slot	Remove card; reinsert; restart PC
"IOS Error" displayed during Windows 95 startup; system locked up	Sound card software clashes with Windows Input/Output System (IOS)	Check with sound card vendor for an IOS fix program; may be supplied on install disk; start Windows 9x in Safe mode to locate and install
Joystick doesn't work	Duplicate joystick ports on sound card and another card causing I/O port address conflict	Disable sound card joystick port
	Computer too fast for inexpensive joystick port	Buy high-speed joystick port; disable port on sound card; install replacement joystick port card
		Slow down computer with "de-turbo" button or BIOS routine

Chapter 10

Networking

Client Server Versus Peer-to-Peer Networking

The following table compares the features of client/server networking (such as with Novell NetWare, Windows NT Server and Windows 2000) with peer-to-peer networking (such as with Windows for Workgroups, Windows 9x, and Windows NT Workstation). Table 10.1 will help you decide which type of network is appropriate for your situation.

> **Note**
>
> Networking is an enormous topic. The following content serves as a reference for field technicians and other professionals. If you need more in-depth information about networking, see Chapter 19 of *Upgrading and Repairing PCs, Eleventh Edition,* or pick up a copy of *Upgrading and Repairing Networks, Second Edition.*

Table 10.1 Comparing Client/Server and Peer-to-Peer Networking

Item	Client/Server	Peer-to-Peer
Access control	Via user/group lists of permissions; single password provides user access to only the resources on his/her list; users can be given several different levels of access	Via password lists by resource; each resource requires a separate password; all-or-nothing access; no centralized user list
Security	High, because access is controlled by user or by group identity	Low, because knowing the password gives anybody access to a shared resource
Performance	High, because server doesn't waste time or resources handling workstation tasks	Low, because servers often act as workstations.

(continues)

Table 10.1 Comparing Client/Server and Peer-to-Peer Networking Continued

Item	Client/Server	Peer-to-Peer
Hardware Cost	High, because of specialized design of server, high-performance nature of hardware, redundancy features	Low, because any workstation can become a server by sharing resources
Software Cost	License fees per workstation user are part of the cost of the Network Operating System server software (Windows NT and Windows 2000 Server, Novell NetWare)	Free; all client software is included with any release of Windows 9x and Windows NT Workstation and Windows 2000 Professional
Backup	Centralized when data is stored on server; allows use of high-speed, high-capacity tape backups with advanced cataloging	Left to user decision; usually mixture of backup devices and practices at each workstation
Redundancy	Duplicate power supplies, hot-swappable drive arrays, and even redundant servers are common; network OS normally capable of using redundant devices automatically	No true redundancy among either peer "servers" or clients; failures require manual intervention to correct with high possibility of data loss

RAID Levels Summary

If you decide that a client/server network is desirable because of its higher performance, consider taking advantage of the benefits a RAID (Redundant Array of Inexpensive Drives) can provide your network. Network servers can use RAID to boost disk access performance and enhance data safety. Use Table10.2 to choose the RAID level appropriate for your network.

Table 10.2	RAID Levels Summary	
RAID Level	**Features**	**Notes**
0	Data transferred in parallel across several drives; no redundancy	Creates a single logical drive from several drives without any failure recovery capabilities; useful for high band-width data handling such as video and image editing
1	Disk mirroring; data written to one drive is duplicated on another	Has been implemented on EIDE as well as SCSI-based drive pairs; requires only two identical drives and special interface card; can be implemented on client PCs as well as servers; hardware imple mentation more reliable and faster than software implementations
2	Bit interleaving across 32 drives with parity information created on 7 drives	Very expensive in hardware costs, but offers fast performance; suitable for enterprise-level servers
3	Data striping across multiple drives; parity information stored on a dedicated drive; implemented at byte level	Popular choice for data integrity at a relatively low hardware cost; three drive minimum
4	Data striping across multiple drives; parity information stored on a dedicated drive; implemented at block level	Not widely supported on PC servers; difficult to rebuilt lost data in case of drive replacement; poor performance
5	Error-correction data striped across all drives in the array; concurrent read/write	Most powerful form of RAID; allows easy "hot swapping" of any failed drive with appropriate server hardware; three drive minimum

Selecting a Network Protocol

Regardless of the type of network (client/server or peer-to-peer) you select, you can choose from a wide variety of network protocols. The most common ones in use for PCs are listed here. Use Table 10.3 to understand the requirements, limitations, and performance characteristics of the major types of network protocols.

Table 10.3		Network Protocol Summary		
Network Type	**Speed**	**Max number of Stations**	**Cable types**	**Notes**
ARCnet	2.5Mbps	255 stations	RG-62 coax UTP[1]/Type 1 STP[2]	Obsolete for new installations; was used to replace IBM 3270 terminals (which used the same coax cable)
Ethernet	10Mbps	Per segment: 10BaseT- 2 10Base2- 30 10Base5-100 10BaseFL-2	UTP[1] Cat 3 (10BaseT), Thicknet (coax; 10Base5), Thinnet (RG-58 coax; 10Base2), Fiber optic (10BaseF)	Being replaced by Fast Ethernet; can be interconnected with Fast Ethernet by use of dual-speed hubs and switches; use switches and routers to overcome "5-4-3" rule in building very large networks
Fast Ethernet	100Mbps	Per segment: 2	Cat 5 UTP[1]	Fast Ethernet can be interconnected with standard Ethernet through use of dual-speed hubs, switches, and routers
Token Ring	4Mbps or 16Mbps	72 on UTP[1] 250-260 on type 1 STP[2]	UTP[1], Type 1 STP[2], and Fiber Optic	High price for NICs[3] and MAUs[4] to interconnect clients; primarily used with IBM mid-size and mainframe systems

1 UTP = Unshielded Twisted Pair
2 STP = Shielded Twisted Pair
3 NIC = Network Interface Card
4 MAU = Multiple Access Unit

Network Cable Connectors

There are three types of network cable connectors. Table 10.4 summarizes these and indicates which ones are in current use.

Table 10.4   Network Cable Connectors

Connector Type	Used By	Notes
DB-15	Thick Ethernet	Used a "vampire tap" cable from the connector to attach to the main cable; obsolete.
DB-9	Token Ring	Obsolete.
BNC	RG-62 ARCnet (obsolete) RG-58 Thin Ethernet	Thin Ethernet uses T-connector to allow pass-through to another station or a terminating resistor to indicate end of network segment. Obsolescent in most installations; BNC still used in small networks or to connect hubs.
RJ-45	Newer Token-Ring 10BaseT Ethernet, Fast Ethernet	Twisted-pair cabling overwhelming favorite for most installations.

While virtually all newly installed networks today with conventional cables use twisted-pair cabling, many networks are mixtures of twisted-pair and older cabling types. Token-Ring Network Interface cards and Ethernet cards with all three of the popular Ethernet connector types are in wide use.

Wire Pairing for Twisted-Pair Cabling

For large multi-office installations, network cables are usually built from bulk cable stock and connectors. Because the twisted-pair cabling has eight wires, many pairings are possible. If you are adding cable to an existing installation, you should match the wire pairings already in use. However, the most popular wiring standard is the Electronic Industry Association/Telecommunications Industry Association's Standard 568B.

Table 10.5 lists the 568B standard wire pairing and placement within the standard RJ-45 connector.

Table 10.5 RJ-45 Connector Wire Pairing and Placement		
Wire Pairing	**Wire Connected to Pin #**	**Pair Used For**
White/blue and blue	White/blue - #5 Blue - #4	Data
White/orange and orange	White/orange - #1 Orange - #2	Data
White/green and green	white/green - #3 Green - #6	Not used
White/brown and brown	White/brown - #7 Brown - #8	Not used

Thus, a completed cable that follows the 568B standard should look like this when viewed from the flat side of the RJ-45 connector (from left to right):

```
orange/white, orange, green/white, blue,
blue/white, green, brown/white, brown
```

Network Cabling Distance Limitations

Network distance limitations must be kept in mind when creating a network. If you find that some users will be "out of bounds" because of these limitations, you can use repeaters, routers, or switches to reach distant users.

Table 10.6 lists the distance limitations of different kinds of LAN cable.

In addition to the limitations shown in the table, keep in mind that you cannot connect more than 30 computers on a single Thinnet Ethernet segment, more than 100 computers on a Thicknet Ethernet segment, more than 72 computers on a UTP Token-Ring cable, or more than 260 computers on an STP Token-Ring cable.

Table 10.6 Network Distance Limitations			
Network Adapter	**Cable Type**	**Maximum**	**Minimum**
Ethernet	Thin*	607 ft.	20 in.
	Thick (drop cable)*	164 ft.	8 ft.
	Thick (backbone)*	1,640 ft.	8 ft.
	UTP	328 ft.	8 ft.
Token Ring	STP	328 ft.	8 ft.
	UTP	148 ft.	8 ft.

Network Adapter	Cable Type	Maximum	Minimum
ARCnet* (passive hub)		393 ft.	Depends on cable
ARCnet* (active hub)		1,988 ft.	Depends on cable

Indicates obsolete for new installations; may be found in existing installations

Cabling Standards for Fast Ethernet

Thanks to low costs for cabling, network interface cards, and now hubs, Fast Ethernet networks can be built today at a cost comparable to conventional Ethernet networks. Note that the distance limitations given for 100BaseTX (the most common type) are the same as for 10BaseT. Consider using 100BaseFX fiber-optic cable with media converters for longer runs.

Table 10.7 lists the cabling standards for Fast Ethernet.

Table 10.7	100BaseT Cabling Standards	
Standard	**Cable Type**	**Segment Length**
100BaseTX	Category 5 (2 pairs)	100 meters
100BaseT4	Category 3, 4, or 5 (4 pairs)	100 meters
100BaseFX	62.5/125* multimode 400 meters (2 strands)	

First figure is core diameter; second figure is cladding diameter; both in micrometers (µm)

Peer-to-Peer Networking Hardware

At a minimum, a two-station peer-to-peer network for printer or drive sharing requires the following hardware:

- *Two NICs (network interface cards);* one per station; use PCI-based 10/100 Ethernet for desktops; 10/100 Ethernet PCMCIA/PC card or CardBus for notebook PCs

- *Sufficient cable to bridge the systems;* use UTP with RJ-45 connectors

- *Connectors and cabling hardware (specific connectors depend upon the cable);* use a stackable hub (one that can be connected to others through an "uplink" port) with at least two unused connectors to allow the network to be expanded with additional users and hubs.

Peer-to-Peer Networking with Windows 9x

For many small businesses, using the built-in peer-to-peer networking features of Windows 9x is a good place to start learning about
and using networks. Table 10.8 shows the basic configuration you'll
need to complete for any workstation (accessing services on
another PC) and server (sharing services with other PCs) using
Windows 9x.

Table 10.8 Minimum Network Software for Peer-to-Peer Networking		
Item	**Workstation**	**Server**
Windows network client	Yes	No
NetBEUI protocol	Yes	Yes
File and print sharing for Microsoft Networks	No	Yes
NIC installed and bound to protocols and services above	Yes	Yes
Workgroup identification (same for all PCs in workgroup)	Yes	Yes
Computer name (each PC needs a unique name)	Yes	Yes

TCP/IP Network Protocol Settings

The Transmission Control Protocol/Internet Protocol (TCP/IP) is
taking over the computing world from the hodge-podge of compet-
ing protocols used earlier in networking (NetBIOS, NetBEUI, and
IPX/SPX). TCP/IP is the protocol of the World Wide Web, as well as
of the latest network operating systems from Novell (NetWare 5)
and Microsoft (Windows 2000). Even though it's used by both dial-
up (modem) users and LAN workstations, the typical configurations
in these situations have virtually nothing in common. Use Table
10.9 as a guide to what must be set, and remember to record the
settings your TCP/IP connections use.

Table 10.9 TCP/IP Properties by Connection Type—Overview			
TCP/IP Property Tab	**Setting**	**Modem Access ("Dial-Up Adapter")**	**LAN Access ("XYZ Network Card")**
IP Address	IP Address	Automatically assigned by ISP	Specified (get value from network administrator)

TCP/IP Property Tab	Setting	Modem Access ("Dial-Up Adapter")	LAN Access ("XYZ Network Card")
WINS[1] Configuration	Enable/ Disable WINS Resolution	Disabled	Indicate server or enable DHCP[2] to allow NetBIOS over TCP/IP
Gateway	Add Gateway/ List of Gateways	None (PPP is used to connect modem to Internet)	IP address of Gateway used to connect LAN to internet
DNS[3] Configuration	Enable/ Disable Host Domain	Usually disabled, unless proxy server used by ISP	Enabled, with host and domain specified (get value from network administrator)

1 WINS = Windows Internet Naming Service; used on NT servers to automatically manage the association of workstation names and locations to IP addresses; used with DHCP (see note 2)

2 DHCP = Domain Host Configuration Protocol; sets up IP addresses for PCs connected to an NT network

3 DNS = Domain Name System; matches IP addresses to Web site names through the use of name servers

TCP/IP Protocol Worksheet

Use the following worksheet shown in Table 10.10 to track TCP/IP settings for either network card or a dial-up connection. The settings are based on the "Networks" icon in Windows 9x. The first worksheet is blank, the second worksheet lists typical (fictitious) settings for a workstation on a LAN.

Table 10.10   TCP/IP Protocol Settings Worksheet

IP Address

Address	Subnet	Automatically assigned			

WINS Configuration

Enable/ Disable	Primary WINS Server	Secondary WINS Server	Scope ID	Use DHCP for WINS Resolution	

Gateway (list in order; top = first)

First	Second	Third	Fourth	Fifth	Sixth

Bindings That Will Use this Protocol (list)

Advanced (list)

Use TCP/IP as Default

(continues)

Table 10.10 TCP/IP Protocol Settings Worksheet Continued					
IP Address					
DNS Configuration					
Disable/ Enable DNS	Host	Domain			
First DNS Server	Second DNS Server	Third DNS Server	Fourth DNS Server	Fifth DNS Server	Sixth DNS Server
First Domain Suffix	Second Domain Suffix	Third Domain Suffix	Fourth Domain Suffix	Fifth Domain Suffix	Sixth Domain Suffix

Table 10.11 shows how TCP/IP protocols could be set up to allow Internet access via a LAN in an office building. If you use TCP/IP for both Internet and LAN access as your only protocol, your settings will vary.

Table 10.11 Completed TCP/IP Protocol Settings Worksheet—LAN Connection					
IP Address					
Address	Subnet	Automatically assigned	Notes		
192.168.0.241	255.255.255.0	No	If automatically assigned = "Yes", no values are used for either address or subnet		

WINS Resolution

Enable/ Disable	Primary WINS Server	Secondary WINS Server	Scope ID	Use DHCP for WINS resolution	Notes
Disable	(blank)	(blank)	(blank)	(blank)	If "disable", no values for other fields

Gateway (list in order; top=1st)

First	Second	Third	Fourth	Fifth	Sixth
192.168.0.1	192.168.0.2	(blank)	(blank)	(blank)	(blank)

Bindings That Will Use this Protocol (list)

Client for Microsoft Networks enabled	File and Print Sharing for Microsoft Networks* disabled	Note *This is a very dangerous setting. While this may be listed as an option, do not enable it if you use another protocol for your LAN. Enabling this setting would allow anybody on the Web access to your system!

Advanced (list)

Use TCP/IP as Default	Other value(s)	Note *This network also uses NetBEUI for internal LAN communications; if TCP/IP were the only protocol, it would be enabled as default.
disabled*	(none)	

DNS Configuration

Disable/ Enable DNS	Host (list)	Domain			
Enabled	smithy	Biz-tech.com			
First DNS Server	Second DNS Server	Third DNS Server	Fourth DNS Server	Fifth DNS Server	Sixth DNS Server
192.168.0.1	(none)	(none)	(none)	(none)	(none)
First Domain Suffix	Second Domain Suffix	Third Domain Suffix	Fourth Domain Suffix	Fifth Domain Suffix	Sixth Domain Suffix
(none)	(none)	(none)	(none)	(none)	(none)

Troubleshooting Networks

Use Tables 10.12 and 10.14 to help find solutions to common networking problems.

Troubleshooting Network Software Setup

Table 10.12   Troubleshooting Network Software Setup

Problem	Symptoms	Solution
Duplicate Computer IDs	You get a "duplicate computer name" message at startup	Make sure that every computer on the network has a unique ID (Use Control Panel, Network – Identification to view this information). Set the ID before connecting to the network.
Workgroup name doesn't match	Don't see other workstations in "Network Neighborhood"	Make sure that every computer that's supposed to be working together has the same workgroup name. Different workgroup names actually create different workgroups, and you'd need to access them by browsing via "Entire Network".
Shared Resources not Available	Can't access drives, printers, or other shared items	Make sure that shared resources have been set for any servers on your network (including "peer servers" on Windows 9x).

(continues)

Table 10.12	**Troubleshooting Network Software Setup Continued**	
Problem	**Symptoms**	**Solution**
		If you can't share a resource through Windows Explorer on the peer server, make sure that File and Printer Sharing has been installed.
Changes to Configuration Don't Show Up	Network doesn't work after making changes	Did you reboot? Any change in the Network icon in Windows 9x Control Panel requires a system reboot!
		Did you logon? Any network resources can't be accessed unless you logon when prompted. You can use the Start, Shutdown, Close all Programs, and log on as a "new" user to recover quickly from a failure to logon.

Troubleshooting Networks in Use

Table 10.13	**Troubleshooting Networks On-the-Fly**	
Problem	**Symptoms**	**Solution**
Connection to network not working for one user	Other users can use shared printers, drives, etc.	First, have user use Start, Close All Programs and logon as "new" user. Pressing Cancel or Esc instead of logging in would keep user off network.
		Next, check cable connections at server and workstation.
Connection to network not working for multiple users	No one can access network	Loose terminators or BNC T-connectors will cause trouble for all workstations on Thinnet cable segment.
		Hub power or equipment failure will cause trouble for all stations using UTP.
Have read-only access instead of full access	Can't save files to shared drive	If you save your passwords in a "password cache,"entering the read-only password instead of the full-access password will limit your access with peer servers.
		Try un-sharing the resource and try to re-share it, or have the user of that peer server set up new full-access and read-only passwords. Or, don't use password caching by unchecking the Save Password box when you log on to a shared resource.

Problem	Symptoms	Solution
		With a client/server network with user lists and rights, check with your network administrator, because he or she will need to change the rights for you.

Troubleshooting TCP/IP

Use Table 10.14, in addition to the TCP/IP information presented earlier, to troubleshoot a TCP/IP connection on either a LAN or Dial-Up connection.

Table 10.14   Troubleshooting TCP/IP Connections

Problem	Symptoms	Solution
Incorrect settings in network properties	Can't connect to any TCP/IP resources	Get correct TCP/IP settings from administrator and enter; restart PC.
Problem with server type or PPP version	Can't keep connection running in Dial-Up Networking	Might have wrong version of PPP running (classic CompuServe uses CISPPP instead of normal PPP); change server type in properties under Dial-Up Networking, not Networks
Duplicate IP addresses	Error message indicates "the (TCP/IP) interface has been disabled" during startup	Duplicate IP addresses will disable both TCP/IP and NetBEUI networking if NetBEUI is being transported over TCP/IP.
One user to an IP address	Can't share the Web	If you're trying to share your Internet connection, use software such as Artisoft's Ishare, or check with your networking hardware vendor for their recommenda-tions. If your LAN uses a proxy server for connection, some sharing products may not work. Windows 98 Second Edition allows Internet sharing under certain conditions.

Direct Cable Connections
Null Modem and Parallel Data-Transfer Cables

A *null modem cable* is a special cable that has its circuits crossed so the transmit data (TD) pin on each serial port connector leads to the receive data (RD) pin on the other. A cable that connects the sys-tems' parallel ports in this way is called a *parallel data-transfer cable*.

Cables like these are usually available at computer stores that sell cables. They are sometimes called *LapLink* cables, after one of the first software products to introduce the concept of the direct cable connection. FastLynx and other parallel-connection cables supplied for MS-DOS and Windows 3.x will also work. A good rule of thumb is this: If the cable works for LapLink or the MS-DOS INTERLNK file transfer utility, you can use it for Direct Cable Connection as well.

You can also build your own null modem or parallel data-transfer cable using the wiring diagrams that follow. Table 10.15 shows the pins that you must connect for a serial cable, using either DB-9 (9-pin) or DB-25 (25-pin) connectors. Table 10.16 shows the connections for a parallel port cable. The parallel cable is slightly harder to build, but is recommended because of its much higher transfer speed and because it will not interfere with existing modems and mouse drivers on the computers.

Table 10.15	3-Wire Serial Null Modem Cable Pinouts				
PC#1	**DB-9**	**DB-25**	**DB-25**	**DB-9**	**PC#2**
TD	3	2 <————>	3	2	RD
RD	2	3 <————>	2	3	TD
SG	5	7 <————>	7	5	SG

Table 10.16	11-Wire Parallel Data-Transfer Cable Pinouts
PC #1	**PC #2**
2 <————>	15
15 <————>	2
3 <————>	13
13 <————>	3
4 <————>	12
12 <————>	4
5 <————>	10
10 <————>	5
6 <————>	11
11 <————>	6
25 <————>	25

Direct Connect Software

After you have the hardware in place, you need the proper software for the two systems to communicate. At one time, you had to purchase a third-party product (such as LapLink) to do this, but the capability is now part of most operating systems, including DOS 6, Windows 9x, and Windows NT.

In DOS, the software consists of two executable files, called INTERSVR.EXE and INTERLNK.EXE. On Windows 9x and Windows NT, the feature is called Direct Cable Connection. The software functions in basically the same way in either case. One computer is designated the host and the other is the guest. The software enables a user, working at the guest machine, to transfer files to and from the host.

In the DOS version, you run the INTERSVR program on the host computer. This system can be running a different version of DOS; you have to copy the INTERSVR.EXE program to it from a DOS 6 machine (using a floppy disk). On Windows 9x, you click the Start menu, and then select Programs, Accessories, Direct Cable Connection (on some systems it might be stored in a Communications folder beneath the Accessories folder). Then choose the Host option button. In both cases, you are prompted to select the COM or LPT port to which you have connected the cable.

On the other computer, you run the INTERLNK.EXE program in DOS or select the same Direct Cable Connection menu item in Windows 9x and choose the Guest option button. Again, you are prompted to choose the correct port, after which the software establishes a connection between the two machines. After this is done, the guest computer mounts the drives from the host in its own file system, assigning them the next available drive letters with Interlink. With the Windows 9x Direct Cable Connection, you can either access the shared drive as a folder or map a drive letter to it with Windows Explorer.

At this point, you can use the drive letters or folders representing the host system just as though they were local resources. You can copy files back and forth using any standard file-management tool, such as the DOS copy command or Windows Explorer. The only difference is that file transfers will, of course, be slower than local hard drive operations.

Troubleshooting Direct Cable Connections

Microsoft's Direct Cable Connection troubleshooter (Windows 95) and DCC Setup Wizard (Windows 95/98) both make a critical mistake in their coverage of setting up DCC: the lack of coverage of networking protocols (protocols aren't required for LapLink or for the MS-DOS Interlink programs). If the same networking protocol isn't set up for both the host and guest PCs, DCC can't work.

To solve problems with DCC, use this checklist:

- Make sure the same networking protocols are installed on both the host and guest machines. The simplest protocol to install is NetBEUI, and that's what Parallel Technologies (creator of DCC) recommends for a basic DCC "mini-network."

- Use the parallel (LPT) ports for DCC; while serial (COM) port transfers will work, they are unbearably slow.

- Make sure that both host and guest LPT ports are working correctly, with no shared IRQ problems. Use the Windows 9x Device Manager to check for IRQ conflicts with the parallel port you're using.

- Make sure the person using the guest computer knows the network "name" of the host computer (set through the Networks icon in Control Panel, Identification tab). With a simple protocol such as NetBEUI, it may be necessary to enter the name to logon to the host machine.

- Install the client for Microsoft Networks on the guest computer.

- Don't print to the printers on the port using DCC; it won't work! Also, allow any print jobs to finish (or delete them) on any port you want to use for DCC before you set up your cables.

- Make sure that the host computer is sharing a drive, so that the guest computer can copy files from it or move files to it. The sharing is done in the same way that peer-to-peer network sharing is done.

Chapter 11

Technician's Survival Kit

General Information

Use this chapter as a guide to help you be well-equipped to solve computer problems. Most of the items in the following lists have been mentioned in other chapters. Here we bring them together to help you "get ready for battle" with computer problems—and win!

Hardware Tools and Their Uses

A well-equipped computer toolbox should contain the items listed in Table 11.1. Compare this list to yours. The list is divided into sections, allowing you to customize the toolkit for the types of servicing you typically perform.

Table 11.1 Basic Hardware Tools Everybody Needs

Item	Purpose	Notes
Phillips-head and flat-blades screwdrivers (#2 size for most jobs)	Opening and removing cases and screws	Magnetic tips are okay if you keep them away from floppies and backup tapes!
		Discard worn screwdrivers
		Use #1 size screwdrivers for attaching and detaching cables
Hex-head drivers (assorted sizes)	Opening and removing cases and screws Tightening cable connectors on cards	Use in place of screwdrivers whenever possible
Needle-nose pliers	Remove and insert jumper blocks; remove cables; cut cable ties; straighten bent pins	Most flexible tool in the basic toolbox; often omitted from low-cost "basic" toolkits; buy assortment of different sizes, offset heads, etc. for flexibility
3-claw parts retrieval tool	Grabs small parts like jumpers and screws from motherboard	It's better than disassembling a PC to find a single screw!
Tweezers	Remove and insert jumper blocks; pick up parts too large for parts retrieval tool; hold small parts for use	Typical set found in low-cost tool set, normally useless; replace with one or both of these: eyebrow tweezers from drugstore, hemostat clamps from medical supply store

(continues)

Table 11.1	Basic Hardware Tools Everybody Needs Continued	
Item	Purpose	Notes
Small flashlight	Illuminate dark places in case	Can be combined with magnifier; for bench use, get arm-mounted magnifier with light
File	Gently trim edges on drive faceplates or case edges	Get file with a very fine "tooth" and use it sparingly
Wire cutter or stripper	Fix damaged power cables or cut away bad connectors	Check gauges to make sure your stripper can handle the small wires inside a PC; never cut a wire unless the power is unplugged (not just turned off—because of power-management features in newer systems)
Canned air	Use to clean out dust from power supplies, keyboards, and cases	Hold can at recommended angle; spread newspapers under and behind what you're cleaning to catch the junk you'll remove
ESD (electrostatic discharge) protection kit	Attach wrist strap to you; cable to ground; unplug system before working inside	Comprises a mat for parts and the wrist strap for you; metal plate on wrist strap must be comfortably tight on your wrist to ground you properly
Soldering iron	Use on conventionally soldered (not surface-mounted!) chips that have bad solder joints	Practice, practice, practice on "dead" boards before you solder a board that's worth fixing
Toothpick or thin wire	Use to probe depth of screw holes	Helps you avoid damaging a drive by using a mounting screw that's too long

Tools of the Trade—Drive Installation

Table 11.2 provides a list of tools and parts you'll need to install disk drives.

Table 11.2	Disk Drive Installation Tools and Parts	
Item	Purpose	Notes
Floppy drive cable	Use as replacement for suspected failures	Some newer Super I/O chips support drive A only
		Use known, working rather than new and unknown
		Use a 5-connector cable if you need support for 5" drives

Item	Purpose	Notes
IDE Hard drive cable (40-pin)	Use as replacement for suspected failures	Should be no more than 18" for use with UDMA drives
		Check spacing between first and second drive connector if you want to use master and slave on drives in non-adjacent bays
		Use known, working rather than new and unknown
IDE hard drive cable with blue end (40-pin, 80-wire)	Use as replacement for suspected failures	Required for UDMA/ATA-66; high-quality for all other drives
		Blue end to motherboard
SCSI ribbon cables	Use as replacement for suspected failures	Use 50-pin or 68-pin depending on device needs
		Use known, working rather than new and unknown
Mounting screws	Attach drives to drive bays	Keep spares from existing or scrapped-out systems
		Use the shortest screws that work, because overly long screws can destroy a drive
Y-cable power splitters	Allows single power connector to run two drives	Examine carefully
		Buy splitters with high-quality construction and wire the same gauge as power supply
Mounting frame	Put 3.5" drives in 5.25" bay	Standard with most 3.5" retail-pack hard drives; save spares
Digital Multimeter I (DMM)	Test power going to drive and cable continuity	Test new and unknown cables before using them
Spare battery for DMM	Keeps tester working	Keep in original blister packaging so it won't short out
Jumper blocks	Adjust IDE drive configuration for master, slave	WD drives use same jumpers as motherboards and add-on cards; some Maxtor and Seagate models use a smaller size
Rails	For mounting 5.25" drives to some cases	Check compatibility since rail types vary—two rails per drive

Tools of the Trade—Motherboard and Expansion Card Installation

Table 11.3 provides a list of helpful tools when installing motherboards and expansion cards.

Table 11.3   Motherboard & Card Installation Parts & Tools

Item	Purpose	Notes
Stand-off connectors	Hold motherboard off bottom or side of case	Use existing stand-offs if in good condition Buy the same size if they must be replaced
Slot covers	Cover rear of case openings for card slots without cards	System cooling is affected if these are missing Keep spares from scrapped systems, or when adding cards
Jumper blocks	Adjust motherboard and add-on card configurations	Buy long-handled jumper blocks for easier configuration changes
Digital Multimeter (DMM)	Test power going to motherboard and expansion slots	Use power supply case as ground
Outlet tester	Quick plug-in tester for bad ground, other wiring faults	Finds real cause of "inexplicable" lockups and system failure—bad power
POST testing card	Use to diagnose bootup problems	Use BIOS tables in Chapter 3 along with board
IRQ/DMA testing card	Use to diagnose IRQ and DMA usage and problems	May be combined with POST on some versions
Spare Pentium, Pentium II, K6, other CPUs	Use to test motherboard when no POST codes appear	Salvage low-speed versions from retired "junk" PCs Be sure to jumper host system appropriately and rejumper after re-inserting original CPU
Spare memory modules	Use to test motherboard that produces memory errors during POST	Salvage compatible small-size types from retired "junk" PCs Two 4MB SIMMs and one 16MB DIMM can test most common PCs

Tools of the Trade—External Device and Networking Installation

Table 11.4 provides a list of tools and parts you'll need to install external devices and network cables.

Table 11.4   External Devices and Networking

Item	Purpose	Notes
Loopback plug for serial port	Use to test serial (COM) ports and cables	Buy or build to match your favorite diagnostic software (see the following) Buy or build 25-pin version as well as 9-pin if you want to test modem cables or if your systems have 25-pin serial ports

Item	Purpose	Notes
Loopback plug for parallel port	Use to test parallel (LPT) ports and cables	Buy or build to match your favorite diagnostic software (see the following) May aid in detection of IRQ usage
IEEE-1284 parallel cable	Known, working spare for all types of parallel printers	Buy 10' cable to have extra distance in tricky cabling situations
"Silver satin"phone cable	Known, working spare for modems and all-in-one units	Carry 10'–15' at least (it's small!)
RJ-45 network cable	Known, working spare for Ethernet, Fast Ethernet and Token-Ring networks	Use along with hub to test card and port Two pieces at 15'–25' to make an impromptu network
5-Port Ethernet hub	Known-working connection for RJ-45 cable	Attach spare cable to hub, check connection with lights
USB cables and hub	Known, working spares for USB devices	Use powered hub Have at least one "A" to "A" extension cable and at least one "A" to "B" device cable
RS-232 breakout box	Analyzes serial signals for use in cable-building, troubleshooting	Allows prototyping of a serial cable

Tools of the Trade—Data Transfer

Use Table 11.5 to "be prepared" to pull vital data from systems.

Table 11.5 Data-Transfer Tools, Parts, and Supplies		
Item	**Purpose**	**Notes**
Parallel data-transfer cable (LapLink or Interlink type)	Use with Interlink, Direct Cable Connection, or LapLink to move files without a network	Preferred version because of speed advantage over serial
Null-modem serial cable (LapLink or Interlink type)	Use with Interlink, Direct Cable Connection, or LapLink to move files without a network	Parallel version above preferred Carry this one as a fallback Select from the following, depending on the drive tech-nologies you support
3.5" floppy diskettes	3.5" SuperDisk LS-120	Zip 100
CD-R	CD-RW	SyQuest SparQ

(continues)

Table 11.5 Data-Transfer Tools, Parts, and Supplies Continued		
Item	Purpose	Notes
Tape backup cartridges	You should carry two of each magnetic device, and one of each optical device you support for use as a backup for vital data	

Tools of the Trade—Cleaning and Maintenance

Table 11.6 provides a list of supplies you should keep on hand for cleaning and maintaining PC hardware.

Table 11.6 Cleaning and Maintenance Supplies		
Item	Purpose	Notes
Floppy drive cleaning kit	Removes gunk from read/write heads	Use wet-type cleaner Not for use on SuperDisk drives! Works best when software-driven with a program such as TestDrive
SuperDisk LS-120 Cleaning kit	Removes gunk from read/write heads of SuperDisk/LS-120 drives only	Use Imation-brand or Imation-approved kits
Tape drive cleaning kit	Removes gunk from read/write heads	QIC models may also be used with QIC-wide and Travan Consult drive manufacturer for service interval
Endust for Electronics	Effective surface cleaner for monitor cases, monitor glass, keyboards, other PC parts	Blue and silver can Never spray directly on object to be cleaned! Spray on lint-free cloth till damp; then wipe
Electronic contact cleaner	"Tweek" or other dilute forms of Stabilant 22	Great for lubricating and protecting contacts on card slots, disk drive connectors, etc.
ESD-safe vacuum cleaner	Eliminates dust and gunk instead of blowing it around	Make sure unit is designed for computer use
Foam or chamois cleaning swabs	Useful for drive-head and contact cleaning	Use in place of cotton swabs, which shed
Silicone sprays	Lubricates moving parts	Check label Spray onto swab and apply sparingly to item Don't spray item directly

Software Toolkit

Tables 11.7 through 11.9 list the software tools you should have to perform important tests.

> **Tip**
>
> If you have a CD-R or CD-RW drive and licenses permit, create a CD-R with an entire collection of tools you can take with you.

Table 11.7   Operating System Software and Drivers

Item	Purpose	Notes
Your operating system files on CD	Fast reloading to fix numerous problems	Verify exact operating system on computer before reloading
Bootable diskette with CD-ROM driver(s) for each operating system supported	Allows operating system reload when Windows isn't working	Verify exact operating system on computer before reloading
Standard system image on bootable CD-R	Can be restored in minutes to a system with a standard hardware configuration	Create with Drive Image, Norton Ghost, PowerQuest EasyRestore, or ImageCast plus bootable option in CD-R creation software Bootable CD-ROM requires boot files onboard, boot CD-ROM first setting in BIOS, and boot-compatible drive
Windows 98 Emergency diskette	Has drivers for most CD-ROM drives	Can be used to "cheat" by making a CD-ROM drive available for a Windows 95 installation
Network card software	Including drivers, test, diagnostic software	Use to verify proper operation and test network communication

Table 11.8 includes the most popular testing, maintenance, and reference programs and files found in Microsoft Windows and MS-DOS.

Table 11.8   Testing, Maintenance, and Reference Software included in Major Operating Systems

Item	Name	Notes
MSD.EXE	Microsoft Diagnostics	Found in MS-3Offers printer testing that works for laser, inkjet, and even PostScript printers. Inaccurate IRQ listings are a major limitation.
WINMSD.EXE	Microsoft Diagnostics	Standard Windows NT system reporting tool.

(continues)

Table 11.8   Testing, Maintenance, and Reference Software included in Major Operating Systems Continued

Item	Name	Notes
HWDIAG.EXE	Hardware Diagnostics	Found on OEM CD-ROM versions of Windows 95 OSR 2.x.
		Can be downloaded from
		User.aol.com/AXCEL216/osr2.htm
		(the ©Tricks + Secrets Files database) for Win95 users who don't have it on their CD-ROMs.
		More thorough and accurate than the Windows 95 Device Manager information about hardware drivers and resources. Also lists INF files and Registry keys. Works with all releases of Windows 95.
HWINFO.EXE	System Diagnostics	Similar to HWDIAG.EXE, but for Windows 98.
MSIE32.EXE	System Information	Standard part of Windows 98 and Office 97. Provides information superior to Device Manager reports in Windows 95. Office 97 and newer versions can be used with Windows 95/98/NT4.
		Maintains history of device drivers and links to other repair tools.
Win95rk.hlp	Windows 95 Resource Kit	The entire 1,200-plus page text of Windows 95 Resource Kit book is stored on the Windows 95 CD-ROM as a help file in \Admin\Reskit\Helpfile.
		Windows 98 Resource Kit Online is similar product stored in Tools\Reskit\Help on Windows 98 CD.
		Both provide large amounts of technical references and troubleshooters not found in standard help system.
Help.exe	MS-DOS 6.x Help file	Standard part of the MS-DOS 6.x installation.
		Contained on some CD-ROM versions of Windows 95.
		Lists all internal and external MS-DOS 6.x commands along with syntax and usage notes. Most command-line utilities in Windows 9x are similar, so it's still useful to refer to.
		Limited help is available with most DOS or Windows command-line utilities by typing /? after the command.
Scandisk.exe	Scandisk	Standard utility in MS-DOS 6.x, Windows 9x, and Windows NT/2000.
		Performs check of disk structures and (optional) surface testing.

Item	Name	Notes
		Runs automatically in Windows 95 OSR2.x and Windows 98 if Windows isn't shut down properly. Best used from drive properties sheet in Windows 9x/NT/2000 as it tracks last use. Run before defrag or backup.
Defrag.exe	Defrag	Standard utility in MS-DOS 6.x, Windows 9x. Realigns all files into contiguous clusters in full defrag mode. Windows 98 offers enhanced options for faster program loading. Windows NT 4.0 and earlier must use a third-party defragmenter such as Diskeeper.

Table 11.9 lists third-party diagnostic and testing utilities, most of which go beyond what can be done with built-in operating system utilities. Web sites are listed for products that aren't widely found at retail locations.

Table 11.9   Third-Party Test and Diagnostic Utilities

Program	Uses	Notes
Norton Utilities	Hardware testing, data protection, data recovery, system information, system speedups, antivirus; defragment and disk testing routines significantly better than standard Microsoft utilities	Best buy when purchased as part of System Works Professional, which includes many other programs; loopback plugs are available for serial and parallel port testing
AMIDiag (www.ami.com)	Hardware testing, system information; burn-in test routines included for stress testing of new equipment	From the makers of the AMI BIOS; loopback plugs are available for serial and parallel port testing
CheckIt 98, CheckIt Diagnostic Suite (www.checkit.com)	Hardware testing, system information; burn-in test routines included for stress test of new equipment	Can be used to gather information from multiple PCs and analyze reports at a single PC; loopback plugs are available for serial and parallel port testing; included in Diagnostic Suite
TestDrive (www.msd.com)	Floppy drive testing and diagnostic utility	Provides thorough information, especially when used with the appropriate Accuride Digital Diagnostic Diskette
SpinRite (www.grc.com)	Hard disk testing and data recovery	Dynastat Data Recovery extremely accurate at recovering data from damaged drives; same vendor offers Trouble in Paradise tester for Zip drive media

(continues)

Table 11.9 Third-Party Test and Diagnostic Utilities Continued		
Program	**Uses**	**Notes**
AntiVirus Available from Trend Micro, Norton, DrSolomon, McAfee, and others	Detect, clean, and prevent viruses and attacks	Use against program, macro, data, and Web-based viruses; use more than one for maximum protection

Chapter 12

Vendor Listing and Useful Web Sites

Using this Listing

This vendor listing includes the "top 100" of the over 400 vendors found in *Upgrading and Repairing PCs, Eleventh Edition*, from Que. These vendors have been specially selected for this volume, and all references have been updated with the latest contact information.

Whenever possible, FAXback and BBS numbers are listed for situations in which an Internet connection is not available.

Other useful Web sites can be found after the vendor listing.

3Com Corp.

Network adapters, modems, and other networking equipment

Phone	(408) 326-5000
Sales	(800) 326-5001
Fax	(408) 764-5001
3ComFacts FAXback	(408) 727-7021
BBS	(847) 262-6000
Web	www.3com.com

3Dfx Interactive, Inc.

3D graphics accelerators including Voodoo series. Now owns STB

Phone	(888-FOR-3Dfx
Fax	(408) 262-8874
Web	www.3dfx.com
Email	info@3dfx.com

ABIT Computer (USA) Corporation

AT/ATX motherboards with jumperless configuration

Phone	(510) 623-0500
Fax	(510) 623-1092
Web	www.abit-usa.com
Email	sales@abit-usa.com or technical@abit-usa.com

Accurite Technologies, Inc.

Floppy diagnostic hardware and software, plus PC card/PCMCIA devices

Phone	(510) 668-4900
Fax	(510) 668-4905
Web	www.accurite.com
Email	sales@accurite.com or tech@accurite.com

Acer America Corp.

U.S. division of Acer Group, makers of PCs, notebook computers, displays, and peripherals

Phone	(408) 432-6200
Toll-free	(800) SEE-ACER
FAXback	(800) 554-2494
Tech Support	(800) 873-7255
Fax	(408) 922-2933
Web	www.acer.com/aac/ or www.acersupport.com

Acer Laboratories, Inc. (Ali) Pacific Technology Group

Makes chipsets, including Aladdin series for Pentiums

Phone	(408) 764-0644
Fax	(408) 496-6142
Web	www.ali.com.tw

Adaptec

Leading producer of SCSI host adapters, Easy CD-Creator, and owners of Trantor and Future Domain

Phone	(408) 945-8600
FAXback	(303) 684-3400
Fax	(408) 262-2533
Web	www.adaptec.com

Advanced Integration Research (AIR)

Pentium-class motherboards

Phone	(408) 428-0800
Fax	(408) 428-0950 or (408) 428-1736
Web	www.airwebs.com
Email	sales@airwebs.com or support@airwebs.com

Advanced Micro Devices (AMD)

K5/K6/Athlon CPU's and chipsets; owns NexGen

Phone	(408) 732-2400
Toll-free	(800) 538-8450
Tech Support	(408) 749-3060
Fax	(408) 749-4753
Web	www.amd.com
Email	hw.support@amd.com

America Online

Provides a popular online service that allows access to their own network and the Internet

Phone	(703) 448-8700
Headquarters	(703) 265-2120
Web	www.aol.com/corp

American Megatrends, Inc. (AMI)

Maker of AMIBIOS and chipsets, motherboards, and RAID host adapters

Phone	(770) 246-8600
Fax	(770) 246-8791
Sales	(800) 828-9264
Tech Support	(770) 246-8645
BBS	(770) 246-8780
Web	www.ami.com
Email	support@ami.com

American Power Conversion (APC)

Manufactures a line of power protection equipment.

132 Fairgrounds Rd.
West Kingston, RI 02892

Phone	(401) 789-5735
Tech Support	(800) 800-4272
Fax	(401) 789-3710
Web	www.apcc.com

AMP, Inc.

Manufactures a variety of computer connectors, sockets, voltage adapters, and cables used by many OEMs.

AMP Building
P.O. Box 3608
Harrisburg, PA 17105

Phone	(717) 564-0100
Sales & Technical Support	(800) 522-6752
Fax	(717) 986-7575
Web	www.amp.com
Email	product.info@amp.com

AOpen USA

The components division of Acer, makers of many popular motherboard, case, optical drive, video, and other PC components used in "generic" PCs

1911 Lundy Ave.
San Jose, CA 95131

Phone	(650)827-9688
Fax	(408)922-2935
Web	www.aopenusa.com

Apple Computer, Inc.

Manufactures a line of personal computers under the Macintosh (Mac) brand name, peripherals, and software

> 1 Infinite Loop
> Cupertino, CA 95014

Phone	(408) 996-1010
Sales	(800) 538-9696
Fax	(408) 974-2113
Web	www.apple.com

Asus Computer International (ASUStek)

Manufactures a line of PC-compatible motherboards, including Pentium- and Pentium II-class motherboards

> 6737 Mowry Ave.
> Mowry Business Center, Bldg 2.
> Newark, CA 94560

Phone	(510) 739-3777
Fax	(510) 608-4555
BBS	(510) 739-3774
Web	www.asus.com
Email	tsd@asus.com.tw

ATI Technologies, Inc.

High-performance PC video adapters and chipsets including RAGE series

Phone	(905) 882-2600
Tech Support	(905) 882-2626
Fax	(905) 882-2620
BBS	(905) 764-9404
Web	www.atitech.com or support.atitech.ca
Email	support@atitech.ca

Award Software International, Inc. (see Phoenix Technologies—Award BIOS)

Best Power (a unit of General Signal Power)

Makers of backup power systems and line conditioners

Phone	(608) 565-7200
Sales	(800) 356-5794
Fax	(608) 565-2221
Web	www.bestpower.com
Email	info@bestpower.gensig.com

Black Box Corporation

Network equipment, power protection, cables, and connectors

Phone & FAXback	(724) 746-5500
Fax	(724) 746-0746
Web	www.blackbox.com
Email	info@blackbox.com

Boca Research, Inc.

Makers of Boca Research and Global Village modem, I/O, and network products

Phone	(561) 997-6227
Tech Support Boca	(561) 241-8088
Tech Support Global Village	(408) 523-1050
Fax	(561) 997-9657
FAXback	(561) 995-9456
BBS	(561) 241-1601
Web	www.bocaresearch.com

Byte Runner Technologies

High-performance I/O cards with FIFO serial, EPP/ECP parallel ports, hi-IRQs, and more

Phone	(423) 470-4938
Sales	(800) 274-7897
Tech Support	(423) 693-5560
Fax	(423) 693-6785
Web	www.byterunner.com
Email	sdudley@byterunner.com

Centon Electronics, Inc.

Memory, Flash, and PC card upgrades

Phone	(949) 855-9111
Toll-free	(800) 234-9292
Tech Support	(800) 9-Centon
Fax	(949) 855-6035
Web	www.centon.com
Email	techsupport@centon.com

Chips and Technologies, Inc. (Intel)

Now Intel's Graphic Components Division, makers of HiQVideo product line

Phone	(408) 765-8080
Web	www.chips.com or developer.intel.com/design/ graphics/mobilegraphics/

Cirrus Logic, Inc.

Maker of chipsets for disk controller, video, and communications circuits. Cirrus graphics accelerator chipsets now supported by Integrated Software and Devices Corporation at www.isdcorp.com/ downloads/cirruslogic/graphics/.

Phone	(510) 623-8300
Fax	(510) 252-6020
FAXback	(800) 359-6414
BBS	(510) 440-9080
Web	www.cirrus.com

Colorado Memory Systems, Inc. (see Hewlett-Packard Storage Division)

Compaq Computer Corporation

Leading maker of desktop, server, and notebook PCs, owner of Digital Equipment Corporation products

Phone	(281) 370-0670
Sales	(800) 231-0900
Tech Support	(800) 652-6672
Product Info	(800) 345-1518
Fax	(281) 514-1740
BBS	(281) 378-1418
Web	www.compaq.com
Email	support@compaq.com

CompTIA (Computing Technology Industry Association)

Sponsors A+ Certification programs

Phone	(630) 268-1818
Fax	(630) 268-1384
Web	www.comptia.org
Email	info@comptia.org

Conner Peripherals, Inc. (see Seagate Technology)

Creative Labs, Inc.

SoundBlaster, Live!, and Blaster-series video cards; owns former Opti audio chipset business; see www.ectiva.com

Phone	(408) 428-6600
Sales	(800) 544-6146
Customer Service	(800) 998-1000
Tech Support	(405) 742-6622
Fax	(405) 428-6633
FAXback	(405) 372-5227
BBS	(405) 742-6660
Web	www.creaf.com

CST
Memory/SIMM/DIMM testers

Phone	(972) 241-2662
Fax	(972) 241-2661
BBS	(972) 241-3782
Web	www.simmtester.com
Email	cst@simmtester.com

Cyrix Corporation
6x86 and MII CPUs

Phone	(972) 968-8388
Sales	(800) 462-9749
Fax	(972) 699-9857
FAXback	(800) GO-CYRIX (462-9749)
BBS	(972) 968-8610
Web	www.cyrix.com
Email	tech_support@cyrix.com

Diamond Flower, Inc. (DFI)
Motherboards, adapter cards, and PCs

Phone	(916) 568-1234
Toll-free	(800) 909-4334
Fax	(916) 568-1233
Web	www.dfiusa.com
Email	support@dfiusa.com

Diamond Multimedia Systems, Inc.
Diamond and Orchid video, Micronics motherboards, RIO MP3 players, Supra modems (Now owned by S3)

Sales	(800) 468-5846
Fax	(408) 325-7070
FAXback	(800) 380-0030 or (541) 967-2424
Support Phone	(541) 967-2450
Web	www.diamondmm.com
Email	techsupt@diamondmm.com

Electrocution

Publishers of *The BIOS Companion*, an outstanding reference for BIOS configuration and troubleshooting

Phone	(204) 582-1943
Web	www.electrocution.com
Email	paco@electrocution.com

First International Computer, Inc. (FIC)

Largest Taiwan-based motherboard builder

Phone	(510) 252-7777
Sales	(800) FICA-OEM (342-2636)
Fax	(510) 252-8895
Web	www.fica.com
Email	support@fica.com

Fujitsu Computer Products of America, Inc.

High-capacity hard drives, printers, scanners, optical, and tape drives

Phone	(800) 591-5924
Fax	(408) 432-6333
Web	www.fcpa.com

Future Domain Corporation (see Adaptec)

Giga-Byte Technology Co., Ltd.

One of the top-10 Taiwan motherboard manufacturers

Phone	(626) 854-9338
Fax	(626) 854-9339
Web	www.giga-byte.com
Email	tech-gbt@giga-byte.com

IBM National Publications

Current reference materials, software, docs for IBM systems. For discontinued publications, contact Fantasy Productions or Annabooks

Phone	(800) 879-2755
Fax	(800) 445-9269
Web	elink.ibmlink.ibm.com/pbl/pbl

IBM OEM Division

Manufacturer and distributor of IBM hard drives, network, and chipset products

Phone	(914) 288-3000
Web	www.ibm.com

IBM Parts Order Center

Nationwide service parts

Phone	(800) 338-7080 (option 2)

IBM PC Direct

Direct-mail catalog sales

Sales	(800) 772-2227
Canada Sales	(800) 465-7999
Fax	(800) 426-4182
General Information	(800) 426-3332
Tech Support	(800) 772-2227
Orders	(800) 426-2968
Web	www.pc.ibm.com

Intel Corporation

Pentium family of CPUs, motherboards, chipsets, and networking products

Phone	(408) 765-8080
Customer Service	(800) 628-8686
Tech Support	(800) 321-4044
Fax	(408) 765-9904
Web	www.intel.com

Iomega Corporation

Bernoulli, Jaz, ZipCD, Clik and Zip drives; Buz multimedia; Ditto
drive products now sold by Tecmar

Phone	(801) 778-1000
Sales	(800) 777-6654
Tech Support	(888) 4-IOMEGA
Fax	(801) 778-3461
BBS	(801) 778-5888
Web	www.iomega.com

JVC Information Products

Optical and recordable-optical drives

Phone	(714) 816-6500
Sales Fax	(714) 816-6519
Web	www.jvc.net

Kensington Technology Group

Computer accessories

Phone	(650) 572-2700
Tech Support	(800) 535-4242
Reseller Support	(800) 280-8318
Fax	(650) 572-9675
Tech Support Fax	(610) 231-1022
Web	www.kensington.com

Kingston Technology Corporation

Leading memory module and CPU upgrade vendor

Phone	(714) 435-2600
Tech Support	(800) 435-0640 or (714) 435-2639
Sales	(800) 337-8410
Fax	(714) 435-2699
Technical Fax	(714) 424-3939
Web	www.kingston.com
Email	tech_support@kingston.com

LSI Logic, Inc.

Motherboard logic, chipsets, Symbios SCSI host adapters, NCR Microelectronics

Phone	(408) 433-8000
Tech Support (Symbios)	(719) 533-7230
Sales	(800) 433-8778
Fax	(408) 433-2882
Tech Support Fax (Symbios)	(719) 533-7271
Web	www.lsilogic.com
Email	support@lsil.com

MAG InnoVision

Flat Square Technology monitors

20 Goodyear
Irvine, CA 92678-1813

Phone	(949) 855-4930
Sales	(800) 827-3998
Fax	(949) 855-4535
Tech Support Fax	(949) 598-4920
Web	www.maginnovision.com
Email	tech@maginnovision.com

Matrox Graphics, Inc.

Major graphics chipset and adapter maker, featuring the Millennium series

Phone	(514) 685-7230
Fax	(514) 685-2853
FAXback	(514) 685-0174
Sales	(800) 361-1408
BBS	(514) 685-6008
Web	www.matrox.com/mga

Maxell Corporation of America

Magnetic and optical media

Phone	(201) 794-5900
Toll-free	(800) 533-2836
Tech Support	(800) 377-5887
Fax	(201) 796-8790
FAXback	(888) MAXLFAX (629-5329)
Web	www.maxell.com
Email	techsupp@maxell.com

Maxtor Corporation

High-performance IDE drives

Phone	(408) 432-1700
Customer Service/FAXback	(800) 262-9867
Fax	(408) 922-2085
BBS	(303) 678-2222
Web	www.maxtor.com

Micro House International (an Earthweb Company), now SupportSource

MicroHouse Technical Library, Support on Site, SupportSource online hardware references

Phone	(303) 443-3388
Tech Support	(303) 443-3389
Sales	(800) 926-8299
Fax	(303) 443-3323
BBS	(303) 443-9957
Web	www.supportsource.com
Email	support@microhouse.com

Contact StorageSoft (www.storagesoft.com) for former MicroHouse DrivePro, EZ Drive, EZ Copy, and many other hard-drive formatting and protection products.

Contact ImageCast Corporation (www.imagecast.com) for former MicroHouse ImageCast software.

Micron Technologies (parent company of Micron Electronics and Micron Custom Manufacturing)

PC systems, RAM, and owner of Rendition graphics accelerators

8000 S. Federal Way
Boise, ID 83707-0006

Phone	(208) 368-4000
Sales	(800) 209-9686
Fax	(208) 368-2536
BBS	(208) 368-4530
Web	www.micron.com

Micronics Computers, Inc. (see Diamond Multimedia Systems)

Microsoft Corporation

Phone	(425) 882-8080
Sales	(800) 426-9400
Fax	(425) 936-7329
BBS	(425) 936-6735
Web	www.microsoft.com

Micro-Star International

One of the top-10 Taiwan motherboard manufacturers

Phone	(510) 623-8818
Fax	(510) 623-8585
BBS	(510) 623-7398
Web	www.msicomputer.com

MicroSystems Development, Inc.

Hardware diagnostics products: Post Code Master, Port Test, and Test Drive

Phone	(408) 296-4000
Fax	(408) 296-5877
BBS	(408) 296-4200
Web	www.msd.com/diags

Mitsumi Electronics Corporation

Optical and floppy drives; keyboards and mice

Phone	(972) 550-7300
Tech Support	(800) 801-7927
Fax	(972) 550-7424
Web	www.mitsumi.com

Mylex Corporation

SCSI, SCSI RAID host adapters, formerly made video cards and motherboards

Phone	(510) 796-6100
Sales	(800) 776-9539
Fax	(510) 745-8016
Tech Support Fax	(510) 745-7715
BBS	(510) 793-3491
Web	www.mylex.com
Email	support@mylex.com

National Semiconductor Corporation

UART and super I/O chips

Phone	(408) 721-5000
BBS	(408) 245-0671
Web	www.nsc.com

NEC Computer Systems Division

Desktop, server, handheld, and notebook PCs

Phone	(800) 524-0819
Tech Support (Ready & Z1)	(801) 578-5104
Tech Support for Versa, PowerMate, Express5800, MobilePro	(800) 457-7777
Tech Support (Direction)	(888) 632-2678
FAXback	(888) 329-0088
BBS	(916) 379-4499
Web	www.nec-computers.com/
Email	tech-support@neccsd.com

NEC Technologies, Inc.

Monitors and peripherals

Phone	(800) 632-4636
Tech Support numbers:	
Monitors	(800) 632-4662
Printers	(800) 632-4650
CD-ROMs and SCSI interfaces	(800) 632-4667
CRT projectors, portable projection systems:	
Direct View Display (Technical support only)	(800) 366-5213
Fastfax	(800) 366-0476
BBS	(978) 742-8706
Web	www.nectech.com

NexGen, Inc. (see AMD)

Number Nine Visual Technology Corporation

High-end PC graphics accelerator cards

Phone	(781) 674-0009
Toll-free/FAXback	(800) GET-NINE (438-6463)
Fax	(781) 869-7190
BBS	(781) 862-7502
Web	www.nine.com

Oak Technology, Inc.

Now manufactures semiconductors, formerly produced video and audio chipsets

Phone	(408) 737-0888
Fax	(408) 737-3838
BBS	(408) 774-5308
Web	www.oaktech.com

Ontrack Data International, Inc.

Remote and standard Data Recovery, drive repair, Disk Manager, DiscWizard, and DiskGo

Sales & Technical	(800) 872-2599 or (612) 937-5161
Fax	(612) 937-5815
BBS	(612) 937-0860
Web	www.ontrack.com

Opti, Inc.

Viper chipset for Pentiums, audio chipsets, PC video, USB, embedded, and mobile chipsets

Phone	(408) 486-8000
Sales	(408) 486-8686
Fax	(408) 486-8001
BBS	(408) 486-8051
Web	www.opti.com

Orchid Technology (see Diamond Multimedia Systems)

Packard Bell

Popular low-cost computer systems

Phone	(818) 673-4800
Tech Support	(801) 578-5108
Sales Fax	(818) 673-4883
Tech Support Fax	(801) 579-0092
Customer Service	(800) 244-0049
Web	www.packardbell.com

PC Power and Cooling, Inc.

Leader in power supplies, cases, and cooling fans

Phone	(760) 931-5700
Sales	(800) 722-6555
Fax	(760) 931-6988
Web	www.pcpowercooling.com
Email	PCPower@ix.netcom.com

PCMCIA-Personal Computer Memory Card International Association

PC card and CardBus standards organization

Phone	(408) 433-2273
Fax	(408) 433-9558
BBS	(408) 433-2270
Web	www.pc-card.com

Philips Consumer Electronics North America

Magnavox/Philips monitors and optical/recordable drives

Phone	(770) 821-2400
Toll-free	(800) 531-0039
Web	www.magnavox.com

Phoenix Technologies, Ltd.

Phoenix and Award BIOS

Phone	(408) 570-1000
Fax	(408) 570-1001
BBS	(714) 440-8026
Web	www.phoenix.com

Plextor

High-performance optical drives

Phone	(408) 980-1838
Sales	(800) 886-3935
Fax	(408) 986-1010
BBS	(408) 986-1569
Web	www.plextor.com
Email	support@plextor.com

PowerQuest Corporation

Partition Magic, DriveCopy, Drive Image, EasyRestore, Lost and Found, ServerMagic

Phone	(801) 437-8900
Sales	(800) 379-2566
Fax	(801) 226-8941
Tech Support Fax	(801) 437-4218
FAXback	(800) 720-0391 or (801) 437-7921
Web	www.powerquest.com
Email	support@powerquest.com

Quantum Corporation

IDE and SCSI hard drives, also DLT and SSD drives; major supplier to Compaq, IBM, Dell, and HP

Phone	(408) 894-4000
Sales	(800) 624-5545
Tech Support	(800) 826-8022
Fax	(408) 894-3218
FAXback	(800) 434-7532
Automated Phone Support	(800) 826-8022
Web	www.quantum.com

S3, Inc.

Savage, Virge, and Trio video chipsets; now owns Diamond Multimedia

Phone	(408) 588-8000
Fax	(408) 980-5444
Web	www.s3.com
Email	support@s3.com

Seagate Technology

IDE and SCSI hard drives, Backup Exec software; owns and supports
Conner Peripherals product lines

Phone	(408) 438-6550
Fax	(408) 438-7612
Customer Service	(800) 468-3472
Automated Support/FAXback	(800) SEAGATE (732-4283)
Tech Support Disc	(405) 936-1200
Tech Support Tape	(405) 936-1400
Tech Support Fax Disc	(405) 936-1685
Tech Support Fax Tape	(405) 936-1683
FAXback	(405) 936-1220
BBS Disc	(405) 936-1600
BBS Tape	(405) 936-1630
Web	www.seagate.com

Silicon Integrated Systems Corp. (SiS)

PC motherboard and video chipsets featuring integrated AGP

Phone	(408) 730-5600
Fax	(408) 730-5639
Web	www.sis.com.tw

Sony Electronics

VAIO desktop and notebook computers, optical and magnetic storage, displays

Phone	(800) 326-9551
Tech Support Computers	(888) 476-6972
Tech Support Peripherals	(800) 326-9551
Fax	(408) 955-5171
FAXback	(888) 476-6972
BBS	(408) 955-5107
Web	www.sel.sony.com

SOYO Tek, Inc.

One of the top-10 Taiwan motherboard makers

Phone	(510) 226-7696
Fax	(510) 226-9218
Web	www.soyo.com
Email	support@soyousa.com

STB Systems, Inc.

Now owned by 3dfx (makes video boards)

Phone	(972) 234-8750
Fax	(972) 234-1306
BBS	(972) 437-9615
Web	www.3dfx.com

Supermicro Computer, Inc.

Major maker of Pentium-class motherboards, chassis, and server/workstation components

Phone	(408) 895-2000
Fax	(408) 895-2008
Tech Support Fax	(408) 895-2012
BBS	(408) 895-2022
Web	www.supermicro.com
Email	support@supermicro.com

SYQT, Inc. (formerly SyQuest Technologies)

Sales and support of SyQuest drives and media

Fax (Sales)	(510) 770-9543
Web	www.syqt.com

Teac America, Inc.

Floppy, tape, and optical drives

Phone	(323) 726-0303
Tech Support	(323) 727-4860
Fax	(323) 727-7656
Tech Support Fax	(323) 869-8751
BBS	(323) 727-7660
FAXback	(323) 727-7629
Web	www.teac.com
Email	dspdtsg@teac.com

Tekram Technologies

Motherboards, SCSI host adapters, and infrared devices

Phone	(512) 833-6550
Tech Support	(512) 833-8158
Fax	(512) 833-7276
Web	www.tekram.com
Email	support@tekram.com

Toshiba America Information Systems, Inc.

Printers, computers, drives, and copiers

Phone	(949) 583-3000
Sales	(800) TOSHIBA
Customer Service	(800) 457-7777
FAXback	(888) 598-7802
BBS	(949) 837-4408
Web	www.csd.toshiba.com (computers)
	www.toshiba.com/taiseid (printers)

Trident Microsystems

Video chipsets and multimedia video adapters

Phone	(408) 496-1085
Fax	(408) 496-6461
Web	www.tridentmicro.com
Email	techsupport@tridentmicro.com

TriniTech, Inc.

PC diagnostic products and training courses

Phone	(727) 532-4151
Sales	(800) 909-3424
Fax	(727) 532-0457
Web	www.pcanalyzer.com

Tripp Lite Manufacturing

Power-protection devices including Isobar, Isotel, and UPS

Phone	(773) 869-1111
Tech Support	(773) 869-1234
Fax	(773) 869-1329
FAXback	(773) 869-1877
Web	www.tripplite.com
Email	techsupport@tripplite.com

Tyan Computer Corporation

ATX/Baby-AT motherboards

Phone	(510) 651-8868
Fax	(510) 651-7688
Tech Support	(510) 440-8808
Tech Support Fax	(510) 659-8288
Web	www.tyan.com
Email	techsupport@tyan.com

U.S. Robotics, Inc. (see 3Com)

VIA Technologies, Inc.

Motherboard chipsets, used by FIC and others

Phone	(510) 683-3300
Fax	(510) 683-3301
Web	www.viatech.com
Email	support@via.com.tw

Western Digital Corporation

Major maker of IDE and SCSI hard drives

Phone	(949) 932-5000
Fax	(949) 932-6294
Tech Support	(949) 932-4900
Sales	(800) 832-4778
FAXback	(949) 932-4300
BBS	(949) 753-1234
Web	www.westerndigital.com

Xircom

PC card/PCMCIA modem/LAN and combo cards

Phone	(805) 376-9300
Sales	(800) 438-4562
Tech Support	(805) 376-9200
Tech Support Fax	(805) 376-9100
BBS	(805) 376-9130
Web	www.xircom.com

Web Site List

There are many Web sites not affiliated with any specific product. These range from professional standards organizations that publish documents about the hardware they write specifications for, to individuals who collect and disseminate useful hardware informa-tion as a hobby, to vendors who distribute general information that doesn't support a specific product. Several of these are *meta-sites* that collect and index information from other sites. This chapter lists the sites in those areas that I have found most useful.

Site URL	Description	Drivers	Reviews	Links	Troubleshooting
elaine.teleport.com/%7Ecurt/modems.html	High speed modem FAQ			X	X
hardware.pairnet.com	Links to hardware news and reviews		X	X	
infopad.eecs.berkeley.edu/CIC	CPU information			X	
pan.mdronline.com/	Microprocessor design resources		X		
pclt.cis.yale.edu/pclt/PCHW/PLATYPUS.HTM	General overview of PC hardware technologies			X	X
selectsystems.com	Co-author Mark Soper's company Web site, featuring subject list of articles and tech writing projects		X	X	X
www.56k.com	News and information on KFlex, X2, and v.90 standard modems	X	X	X	X
www.anandtech.com	Reviews of motherboards, processors, and more		X		
www.atipa.com/InfoSheets/irqs.shtml	Troubleshooting COM and IRQ conflicts				X
www.cd-info.com	Compact disc development and production technology		X	X	
http://www.cis.ohio-state.edu/hypertext/faq/usenet/scsi-faq/top.html	SCSI FAQs from USENET/scsi-faq/top.html			X	X
www.cis.ohio-state.edu/hypertext/faq/usenet-faqs/bygroup/comp/sys/ibm/pc/hardware/top.html	Links to several hardware-related Usenet group FAQs			X	X

Site URL	Description	Drivers	Reviews	Links	Troubleshooting
www.cpu-central.com	CPU specifications, information, and reviews		X	X	X
www.drivershq.com	Links to hardware drivers	X		X	X
www.driverupdate.com	Hardware drivers for Windows, UNIX, NetWare, Linux, and other operating systems	X			X
www.erols.com/chare/main.htm	Links to processors specifications and FAQs	X		X	X
www.hardwarecentral.com	Reviews, FAQs, and more about most PC hardware components	X	X	X	X
www.irda.org	Infrared technology standards				X
www.itu.int	International Telecommunication Union (standards body for modems and other telecommunications)				X
www.lexology.com/bios/bios_sg.htm	The BIOS survival guide			X	X
www.motherboards.org	Motherboard reviews, tips, and performance comparisons		X	X	X
www.mrdriver.com	Links to hardware drivers for many operating systems; offers FCC-ID lookup	X		X	
www.pc-card.com	PC card and PCMCIA standards			X	

(continues)

(continued)

Site URL	Description	Drivers	Reviews	Links	Troubleshooting
www.pcengines.com/simm.htm	Memory buyer's guide		X	X	X
www.pcguide.com	General PC hardware information		X	X	X
www.pcisig.com	PCI specifications and developments			X	
www.pcWebopedia.com	PC technology encyclopedia and search engine			X	
www.ping.be/bios/	Wim's BIOS page; BIOS updates, identifies BIOS by ID numbers	X		X	X
www.scsita.org	SCSI Trade Association's SCSI information			X	X
www.sig.net/~slogan/hardware.htm	Hardware advice, reviews, and links		X	X	X
www.sldram.com	Information on new SLDRAM memory technology			X	
www.storagereview.com	Reviews and benchmarks of SCSI and ATA IDE hard drives			X	
www.sysopt.com	System optimization and performance with special emphasis on motherboards		X	X	X
www.t10.org/	ANSI Web site with I/O information, mainly about SCSI			X	
www.teleport.com/~atx/	ATX motherboard specifications			X	X
www.teleport.com/~nlx/	NLX motherboard specifications			X	X

Site URL	Description	Drivers	Reviews	Links	Troubleshooting
www.the-view.com	Hardware reviews and news		X	X	
www.tomshardware.com	Reviews and analysis of motherboards, processors, video cards, and more		X	X	X
www.twinight.org/chipdir/	Directory of chips, manufacturers, pinouts, and so on			X	X
www.usb.org	USB specifications and information		X	X	
www.vesa.org	VESA standards			X	
www.west.net/~jay/modem	Modem initialization strings	X			X
www.whatis.com	Online dictionary of computer terms with many useful technical references			X	X
www.windrivers.com	Hardware drivers for all Windows versions	X	X	X	X
www.winfiles.com	Windows 9x hardware drivers, bug reports, and fixes	X	X	X	X
www.x86.org	"Secrets" about Intel and compatible processors and technologies from Dr Dobbs' Journal			X	X
wwwcsif.cs.ucdavis.edu/ ~wen/intel.html	Guide to Intel chipsets			X	

Symbols

0 bit, 135
101-key Enhanced keyboards, 169, 176-179
102-key Enhanced keyboards, 169, 176-179
104-key Enhanced keyboards, 179
104-key Windows keyboards, 169-170
16-bit ISA interrupts, 38-39
16-bit serial driver (COMM.DRV), 142
16.8 million color (memory requirements), 195
168-pin DIMMs, 33
25-pin SCSI cables, 94
25-pin SCSI connectors, 94
25-pin serial-port, 137-138
3-claw parts retrieval tool, 229
3D chipsets, 201
30-pin SIMMs, 29, 32
32-bit serial driver (SERIAL.VXD), 142
32-bit VL-Bus/PCI interrupts, 38-39
40-pin IDE hard drive cable, 231
40-pin, 80-wire IDE hard drive cable, 231
5-pin DIN keyboard connectors, 180
5-port Ethernet hub, 233
56Kbps modems, 146

6-pin mini-DIN keyboard connectors, 180
72-pin SIMMs, 29, 32
8-bit SCSI Centronics 50-pin connector, 93
80-pin SCSI connector, 94
9-pin serial port, 136
9-pin-to-25-pin serial-port, 138

A

A cables, 91
AC (alternating current), 24
Accelerated Graphics Port (AGP), 53
access control (networking), 213
accessing
    BIOS Setup program, 68-69
    Iomega Zip drives, 123
Accessories command (Programs menu), 227
Accessories menu commands (Direct Cable Connection), 227
Accupoint, 185
ACPI (Advanced Configuration and Power Interface), 190
adapter cards, 36
adapters
    SCSI, 92
    video
        memory, 193-194
        RAMDACs (RAM Digital-to-Analog Converter), 197
    video display, 194-195

add-on cards, 37-38
Add/Remove Programs
    icon, 124
adding cards, 37-38
addresses
    I/O, 142, 159
    I/O ports, 41
        bus-based devices,
            42-44
        chipset devices, 41
        determining ranges,
            44
        motherboards, 41
adjusting
    parameters, 175
    refresh rates (video
        cards), 198-199
    typematic repeat
        rate, 175
Advanced Configuration
    and Power Interface
    (ACPI), 190
Advanced Graphics Port
    (AGP), 196
Advanced Power
    Management
    (APM), 190
AGC (Automatic Gain
    Control), 206
AGP (Accelerated
    Graphics Port), 53
AGP (Advanced
    Graphics Port), 196
AGP expansion slots, 53
alphanumeric codes
    (BIOS), 71-72
Alps keyswitches, 174
alternating current
    (AC), 24
Alternative Single Drive
    configuration, 87

alternative to BIOS
    upgrades, 58
AMI BIOS
    ID strings, 66-67
    identifying
        motherboards, 66
    reporting errors, 70
AMI Web site, 67, 237
AMIDiag, 237
APM (Advanced Power
    Management), 190
applications (printers),
    troubleshooting,
    165-166
ARCnet (network
    protocols), 216
arrays (RAID), 94
ASCII
    hexadecimal/ASCII
        conversions, 2-9
    line-drawing
        characters, 2
ASCII control code, 1
assigning drive
    letters, 104-106
assignments (DMA
    channels), 39
asynchronous serial
    interface, 135
AT systems, 12
ATA (AT Attachment)
    drives, 76. *See also*
    IDE drives
ATA-2 translation
    methods, 80
ATAPI driver,
    downloading, 125
ATI video card
    chipsets, 200
ATX cases, 23
ATX motherboard, 23

ATX power supplies,
comparing to
LPX, 25-26
audio, 207
    quality standards, 207
    troubleshooting, 207
audio in connectors, 205
audio out connectors,
205
automatic drive
detection, 89
Automatic Gain Control
(AGC), 206
automatic settings (SCSI
IDs), 96
Award BIOS
    identifying
        motherboards, 67-68
    reporting errors, 71
Award Software
manufacturer codes
Web site, 68

B

Baby-AT motherboard,
21
backing up
data, 129-132
backups, networking,
214
banks (memory), 33
basic input/output
system. *See* BIOS
batteries, 231
beep codes (BIOS), 69-70
    AMI, 70
    Award, 71
    IBM, 71-72
    MR, 72-73
    Phoenix, 71

binary values, 10
BIOS (basic input/output
system), 55
    alternative to
        upgrades, 58
    AMI
        ID strings, 66-67
        reporting errors, 70
    Award, reporting
        errors, 71
    determining
        compatibility with
            hard drive, 83-84
        version/brand,
            65-66
    enhanced, 79
    error/status codes, 74
    errors, reading, 74
    flash update failure,
        recovery, 61
    flash-upgradable, 59
    IBM, reporting
        errors, 71
    modes
        Extended CHS, 80
        Large, 80
        LBA (Logical Block
            Addressing), 80-82
        Normal, 80
    MR, reporting
        errors, 72
    Phoenix, reporting
        errors, 71
    PnP, 62-64
    reporting errors, 69-70
    troubleshooting, 65
    updating, 55-56
        motherboard, 59
        precautions, 60
        sources for, 59
    upgrading, 86-87

USB Legacy support, 181
Y2K testing, 56
  power-off BIOS date rollover test, 57
  power-off DOS date rollover test, 57-58
  power-on BIOS date rollover test, 57
  power-on DOS date rollover test, 57
BIOS chip, 55
BIOS Setup program, accessing, 68-69
BIOS upgrades, 59
bits, 10, 135
bootable CDs, troubleshooting, 128-129
bootable diskettes, creating, 124
brand (BIOS), determining, 65-66
building cables, 226
built-in testing/ diagnostic utilities, 235-237
bus mouse, 184
bus-based devices, 42-44
bus-card interface, 184
bus-mastering
  chipsets, 126
  drivers, 125
buses (SCSI terminators), 97
buttons, Change Setting, 143
bytes, 9-10

C

/C switch, 109
cables
  external modem pinouts, 151-152
  floppy drive, 230
  IDE drive
    40-pin, 231
    40-pin, 80-wire, 231
  LapLink, 226
  network
    RJ-45, 233
    tools for installing, 232-233
  null modem, 225-226
  parallel, IEEE-1284, 233
  parallel data-transfer, 226
  phone (silver satin), 233
  ribbon, 231
  SCSI
    A, 91
    identifying, 93
    P, 91
  SCSI 25-pin, 94
  SCSI-3 68-pin P, 94
  serial (Null-modem), 233
  STP Token-Ring, 218
  USB, 233
  UTP Token-Ring, 218
cabling loopback tests, 144-145
cabling standards (Fast Ethernet network), 219
canned air, 230

capacities
168-pin DIMMs, 33
30-pin SIMMs, 32
72-pin SIMMs, 32
cards, adding, 37-38
cases (ATX), 23
CD-R disks,
troubleshooting,
127-128
CD-ROM drives
reloading Windows,
124-125
troubleshooting,
127-128
CD-Rs, 233
CD-RWs, 127-128, 233
CDs (bootable),
troubleshooting,
128-129
Centronics 36 connector,
157
chamois cleaning
swabs, 234
Change Setting
button, 143
character sets
PC-50, 2
PC-8, 2
Roman-8, 2
characters, 9
CheckIt 98, 237
CheckIt Diagnostic
Suite, 237
CheckIt Web site, 237
chip swaps, 59
Chips and Technologies
65554 Graphics
Accelerator Chipset
video modes, 192-193

chipset devices, 41
chipsets
3D, 201
bus-mastering, 126
Permedia, 200
RAMDAC speed, 197
Cirrus video card
chipsets, 201
cleaning
floppy drives, 115
keyswitches, 174-175
PCs, 234
cleaning kits, 234
cleaning swabs, 234
client/server
networking, 213-214
cluster sizes
comparing FAT-16 to
FAT-32, 103
FAT-16, 103
color depth, 194-195
COM ports, 135. *See also*
serial ports
combo expansion
slots, 54
COMM.DRV (16-bit
serial driver), 142
commands
Accessories menu
(Direct Cable
Connection), 227
keyboards, 171-172
Programs menu
(Accessories), 227
XCOPY, 108
XCOPY32, 109-110
comparing
cluster sizes (FAT-16 to
FAT-32), 103
keyboards (standard to
portable), 173
multimedia devices,
202

networking
(client/server to peer-
to-peer), 213-214
power management
standards, 190-191
power supplies (ATX to
LPX), 25-26
printers (host-based to
PDL-based), 162
refresh rates, 198
ribbon cables, 117
sound cards (PCI to
ISA), 208
USB and IEEE-1394,
154
video cards, 199
**compatibility (BIOS and
hard drive),
determining, 83-84**
**CONFIG.SYS files,
creating, 125**
configuration options
PCI bus, 63-64
PnP BIOS, 62-64
configuring
drives
IDE, 78
SCSI, 95
parllel ports, 159
SCSI, troubleshooting,
97-98
serial ports, 141
sound cards, 207
**Conflicting Devices
List, 143**
conflicts
hardware, 210
resource
detecting, 209
sound cards,
208-210
serial ports, 142

connections
direct cable
null modem
cables, 225
software, 226-227
troubleshooting,
227
printers,
troubleshooting,
164-165
connector shells, 145
**connector specifications
(keyboards), 182-183**
connectors
8-bit SCSI Centronics
50-pin, 93
Centronics 36, 157
IDE drives, 77
keyboard, 180
5-pin DIN, 180
6-pin mini-DIN,
180
signals, 180-181
loopback, 145
mouse, 184
network cable, 217
parallel ports, 157
SCSI
25-pin, 94
80-pin, 94
SCSI-2 high-density, 93
sound card
audio in, 205
audio out, 205
internal pin-type,
206
joystick, 206
line in, 205
line out, 205
microphone, 206
MIDI, 206

mono in, 206
speaker/headphone, 205
sound cards, 205
stand-off, 232
Type B, 157
Type C, 157
USB, 153
video, 191
VL-Bus, 52
constructing loopback plugs, 144-145, 159-160
control codes (ASCII), 1
conventional memory barrier, 34
conversions, hexadecimal/ASCII, 2-9
converting FAT-16 to FAT-32, 103
CPUs, 232
creating
bootable diskettes, 124
CONFIG.SYS files, 125
Windows 95 Emergency Diskette, 124
CRT monitors, 187-189
cylinders (hard drives), 76

D

/d: switch, 125
data
backing up, 129-132
restoring, 132
data bus width, 11, 33
data connectors (floppy drives), 116

data transfer, 39
tools, 233-234
Windows 9x (XCOPY32 command), 109-110
DC (direct current), 24
decimal values, 10
dedicated motherboard mouse port (PS/2 port), 184
Defrag, 237
Defrag.exe, 237
delay parameters, adjusting, 175
detecting
full capacity (hard drives), 84-86
resource conflicts, 209
support (LBA mode), 82-83
determining
compatibility (BIOS and hard drive), 83-84
LBA mode, need for, 81
ranges
I/O port addresses, 44
memory addresses, 37
type of motherboard, 24
version/brand
BIOS, 65-66
UART chips, 140
Device Manager, 40, 45
Device Manager tab, 143
Device Manager's System Properties sheet, 37

devices, external
setting SCSI ID for, 97
tools for installing,
232-233
diagrams, drawing, 2
dialog boxes (Windows),
171
differential SCSI, 92
Digital Multimeter
(DMM), 231
DIMMs, 30, 33
DIP switches, 68
Direct Cable Connection
command (Accessories
menu), 227
direct cable connections
null modem
cables, 225
software, 226-227
troubleshooting, 227
direct current (DC), 24
Direct Memory Access
(DMA), 37
disabling LBA mode,
81-82
disk space, 10
disks. *See also* drives
CD-R, 127-128
CD-RW, 127-128
hard, 75. *See also* hard
drives
Display Power-
Management Signaling
(DPMS), 190
divide by 3 rule, 32
divide by 9 rule, 32
DMA (Direct Memory
Access), 37
data transfer, 39
settings, 40-41
DMA channels, 39
DMM (Digital
Multimeter), 231-232

DMPS modes, 190
DOS direct cable
connection
software, 227
downloading
drivers, 125
DPMS (Display Power-
Management
Signaling), 190
DRAM, 30
drawing diagrams, 2
drive cover (floppy
drives), 114
drive letters
assigning, 104-106
extended
partitions, 106
primary partitions, 106
drive migration
MS-DOS, 108
Windows 9x, 109
drive typing, 89-90
drive-letter size
limits, 101
drivers
ATAPI, 125
bus-mastering, 125
mouse, 184
printers, 165-166
drives
ATA (AT
Attachment), 76
CD-ROM
reloading windows,
124-125
troubleshooting,
127-128
DVD, 127-128
floppy, 113
cable, 230
cleaning kits, 234
data connectors,
116

drive cover, 114
error messages,
    120-121
hardware conflicts,
    116
hardware resources,
    115
interface circuit
    boards, 115
parameters,
    117-118
power connectors,
    116
read/write heads,
    115
stepper motor,
    114-115
troubleshooting,
    119
formatting (FDISK),
    101
hard
    cylinders, 76
    detecting full
        capacity, 84-86
    determining
        compatibility
        with BIOS, 83-84
    formatting, 100
    drive heads, 75
    high-level format,
        106-108
    improving
        speed, 88
    partitioning, 102
    repairing, 110-111
    replacing, 108
    sectors per track, 75
    setting parameters,
        75
    troubleshooting,
        110-111

IDE (Integrated Drive
    Electronics), 76
    40-pin cable, 231
    40-pin, 80-wire
        cable, 231
    configuring, 78
    connectors, 77
    jumper settings, 78
IDE/ATAPI CD-ROM,
    127-128
installing, 230-231
logical DOS, 104
master, 77
media, removable,
    123-124
MS-DOS,
    downloading, 125
power connectors,
    26-27
SCSI, 76, 95
slave, 77
storage, 121-122
tape, 129
    cleaning kit, 234
    media
        compatibility, 129
    Travan, 130
Zip (Iomega), 123
**Dual Inline Memory
Modules (DIMMs), 30
DVD drives, 127-128**

E

/E switch, 109
**ECC (Error Correction
Code), 31
ECP ports, 158
EISA (Enhanced ISA), 50
EISA expansion
slots, 50-52**

electronic contact
cleaner, 234
electrostatic discharge
protection kit
(ESD), 230
enabling
DPMS, 190
LBA mode, 80
Endust for Electronics,
234
enhanced BIOS, 79
enhanced IDE, 79
Enhanced Int13h, 86
Enhanced ISA (EISA), 50
Enhanced
keyboards, 169
Enhanced Serial Ports
(ESP), 141
EPP ports, 158
error codes
(keyboards), 183
Error Correction Code
(ECC), 31
error messages
floppy drives, 120-121
onscreen, 69, 74
error/status codes, 69, 74
errors
AMI BIOS, 70
Award BIOS, 71
BIOS
reading, 74
reporting, 69-70
fatal, 69
IBM BIOS, 71-72
MR BIOS, 72-73
non-fatal, 69
Phoenix BIOS, 71
Escape code (decimal
27), 1
ESD (electrostatic dis-
charge protection
kit), 230

ESP (Enhanced Serial
Ports), 141
Ethernet network
protocols, 216
Ethernet hub, 233
ex-K56flex modems,
upgrading to
V.90, 147-148
expanding memory, 33
expansion cards,
installing, 231-232
expansion slots, 48, 54
AGP (Accelerated
Graphics Port), 53
combo, 54
EISA, 50-52
ISA (Industry Standard
Architecture), 49-50
PCI (Peripheral
Component
Interconnect), 53
shared, 54
Extended CHS mode, 80
eXtended Graphic Array
(XGA), 188
extended partitions,
104-106
external
devices, 97, 232-233
loopback tests, 144
modems, 145, 149-152

F

Fast Ethernet networks
cabling standards, 219
protocols, 216
FAT high-level format
program, 107
FAT-16, 102-103
FAT-32, 102-103

fatal errors, 69
FDISK, 101
  assigning drive
    letters, 104-106
  determining BIOS/hard
    drive compatibility,
    83-84
  formatting drives, 101
  large hard disk
    support, 102
  partitions, 104
files (CONFIG.SYS),
  creating, 125
files (tool), 230
FireWire, 154
firmware, 35-36
fixed-pitch fonts, 2
Flash BIOS, 55, 61
flash upgrades, 147-148
flash-upgradable
  BIOS, 59
flashlights, 230
flat-blade
  screwdrivers, 229
flex-ATX
  motherboard, 23
flicker-free refresh
  rate, 198
floppy diskettes, 233
floppy drive cleaning
  kit, 234
floppy drives, 113
  cable, 230
  data connectors, 116
  drive cover, 114
  error messages,
    120-121
  hardware
    conflicts, 116

hardware
  resources, 115
  interface circuit
    boards, 115
  parameters, 117-118
  power connectors, 116
  read/write heads, 115
  stepper motor, 114-115
  troubleshooting, 119
foam cleaning
  swabs, 234
foam element
  keyswitches, 173-175
folder/shortcut controls
  (keyboard
  commands), 172
fonts, fixed-pitch, 2
form factors, 21, 24
FORMAT.COM, 106
formats, high-level,
  106-108
formatting
  drives (FDISK), 101
  hard drives, 100-102
freeing IRQ 5, 210
full capacity (hard
  drives), detecting,
  84-86

G-H

geometries, 75-76
gigabytes, 10
glass-tube monitors,
  187-189
Guest option
  button, 227

/H switch, 109
hard disks. *See* hard
  drives
hard drive heads, 75

hard drives
cylinders, 76
detecting full
capacity, 84-86
determining
compatibiilty with
BIOS, 83-84
formatting, 100
geometries, 76
high-level
format, 106-108
large (support), 102
parameters, setting, 75
partitioning, 102
repairing, 110-111
replacing, 108
sectors per track, 75
speed, improving, 88
troubleshooting,
110-111
"hard" problems (hard
drive), 110
hardware
memory addresses,
35-36
peer-to-peer
networking, 219
printers,
troubleshooting,
162-164
hardware conflicts, 116,
210
hardware cost
(networking), 214
Hardware Diagnostics
(HWDIAG.EXE), 236
hardware interrupts, 38.
See also IRQs
hardware resources
(floppy drives), 115
hardware tools, 229-230
Help files (MS-DOS 6.x),
236

Help.exe (MS-DOS 6.x
Help file), 236
Hewlett-Packard Printer
Control Language (HP
PLC), 161
Hex-head screwdrivers,
229
hexadecimal/ASCII
conversions, 2-9
HI-Flex AMI BIOS ID
strings, 66-67
High-Flex BIOS, 66
high-level format,
106-108
Host option button, 227
host-based printers,
161-162
hot swappable, 94
HP PLC (Hewlett-
Packard Printer
Control Language), 161
hubs, 233
HWDIAG.EXE
(Hardware
Diagnostics), 236
HWINFO.EXE (System
Diagnostics), 236

I

I/O addresses, 142, 159
I/O ports, 41. *See also*
radio channels
addresses, 41
bus-based
devices, 42-44
chipset devices, 41
determining
ranges, 44
motherboards, 41
troubleshooting,
142-143

IBM 25-pin parallel (male DB25P) loopback connector (wrap plug), 159

IBM BIOS, reporting errors, 71-72

IBM type 25-pin serial (Female DB25S) loopback connector (wrap plug), 144

IBM type 9-pin serial (Female DB9S) loop-back connector (wrap plug), 144

icons
  Add/Remove Programs, 124
  My Computer, 143
  Networks, 221
  System, 143

ID strings (BIOS), 66-67

IDE (Integrated Drive Electronics)
  enhanced, 79
  installation, 90-91

IDE drives (Integrated Drive Electronics), 76
  cables, 231
  configuring, 78
  connectors, 77
  jumper settings, 78
  support, 86-87

IDE/ATAPI CD-ROM drives, 127-128

identifying
  modems, 145-146
  motherboards, 66
    AMI BIOS, 66
    Award BIOS, 67-68
    MR (Microid Research) BIOS, 68
    non-AMI BIOS, 67
    Phoenix BIOS, 68
    SCSI cables, 93
    SCSI connectors, 93
    USB ports, 152-153

IDs (SCSI), 95
  jumper settings, 96
  setting, 96-97

IEEE-1284 parallel cables, 233

IEEE-1284 printer cable, 158

IEEE-1394, 154-155

iLINK, 154

improving hard drive speed, 88

Industry Standard Architecture (ISA) expansion slots, 49-50

Inport mouse, 184

installation (IDE), troubleshooting, 90-91

installing
  drives, 230-231
  expansion cards, 231-232
  external devices, 232-233
  motherboards, 231-232
  network cables, 232-233

Integrated Drive Electronics drives. *See* IDE drives

Intel processor socket types and specifications, 18

Intel processor specifications, 13-14

Intel-compatible Pentium-class processor specifications, 13, 16

Intel-compatible
  processor socket types
  and specifications, 18
interface circuit
  boards, 115
interfaces
    bus-card, 184
    mouse, 184
    serial, 184
    serial ports
      (asynchronous), 135
    USB, 184
INTERLNK.EXE (DOS
  direct cable
  connections), 227
internal loopback
  tests, 143
internal modems, 145,
  149
internal pin-type
  connectors, 206
Internet service provider
  (ISP), 146
interrupt request line.
  See IRQ
interrupts, 142
    16-bit ISA, 38-39
    32-bit VL/PCI, 38-39
    parallel ports, 159
INTERSVR.EXE (DOS
  direct cable
  connections), 227
Iomega Web site, 123
Iomega Zip drives, 123
IRQ 5, freeing, 210
IRQ/DMA testing
  cards, 232
IRQs (interrupt request
  lines), 37-38, 141
    settings, 40-41
    sharing, 37

ISA (Industry Standard
  Architecture)
    devices, 63
    expansion slots, 49-50
    sound cards, 208
    (Internet service
      provider), 146

J-K

joystick connectors, 206
jumper blocks, 231-232
jumper settings, 87
    Alternative Single
      Drive configuration,
      87
    IDE drives, 78
    Normal Single Drive
      configuration, 87
    SCSI IDs, 96

/K switch, 109
key combinations
  (104-key Windows
  keyboards), 170
keyboard commands
    selected objects, 172
    Windows, 171
    Windows dialog
      box, 171
    Windows Explorer, 172
    Windows
      folders/shortcut
      controls, 172
keyboard connectors,
  180-181
Keyboard Control Panel
  (Windows), adjusting
  parameters, 175

keyboards
101-key Enhanced, 169
102-key Enhanced, 169
104-key Windows,
169-170
connectors
5-pin DIN, 180
6-pin mini-DIN,
180
specifications, 182
error codes, 183
layouts, 175-176
parameters,
adjusting, 175
portable, 173
POST codes, 183
scan codes, 175
101-/102-key
Enhanced,
176-179
104-key
Enhanced, 179
standard, 173
troubleshooting,
181-183
USB (requirements),
181
keyswitches, 173-174
Alps, 174
cleaning, 174-175
stuck, 175

L

LAN (TCP/IP protocol
settings), 222-223
LapLink cables, 226
large hard disk
support, 102
Large mode, 80

layouts (keyboards),
175-176
LBA (Logical Block
Addressing) mode, 80
determining need, 81
disabling, 81-82
enabling, 80
problems with support
in BIOS, 81
support, detecting,
82-83
LCD panels, 188-189
legacy ISA devices,
reserving resources, 63
levels (RAID), 215
line in connectors, 205
line out connectors, 205
lists, Conflicting
Devices, 143
local-bus
specifications, 196
logic boards, 115
Logical Block Addressing
mode. *See* LBA mode
logical DOS drives, 104
loopback plugs, 144-145,
159-160, 232
loopback tests (serial
ports), 143
Low-Voltage Differential
devices (LVD
devices), 92
LPX motherboard, 21
LPX power supplies,
25-26
LVD (Low-Voltage
Differential)
devices, 92

M

Macintosh serial
    interface, 138
maintaining PCs, 234
maintenance programs,
    235-237
manual drive
    typing, 89-90
master drives, 77
MDRAM (Multibank
    DRAM), 194
measuring memory, 9-10
media compatibility
    (tape drives), 129
media drives
    (removable),
    troubleshooting,
    123-124
megabytes, 10
membrane keyswitches,
    173-174
memory, 10, 34-35,
    194-195
    banks, 33
    conventional memory
        barrier, 34
    expanding, 33
    measuring, 9-10
    non-parity, 31-32
    parity, 31-32
    RAM (random access
        memory), 28
    RDRAM (Rambus
        DRAM), 30
    troubleshooting, 34
    video, 195
    video adapters,
        193-194
    video card, 195-196
memory addresses, 35
    adapter cards, 36
    firmware, 36
    hardware, 36
    network cards, 36
    ranges, determining,
        37
memory aperture, 37
memory modules, 37,
    232
    DIMMs, 30, 33
    RIMMs, 31
    SIMMS, 32
memory requirements
    (video display
    adapters), 194-195
menus, Resource
    Configuration, 62-63
Micro Firmware
    Web site, 59
micro-ATX
    motherboard, 23
MicroChannel
    architecture, 52
Microid Research BIOS
    (MR BIOS), 68, 72-73
microphone
    connectors, 206
Microsoft Diagnostics
    (MSD.EXE), 235
Microsoft Diagnostics
    (WINMSD.EXE), 235
Microsoft IntelliType
    Software, 170
MIDI connectors, 206
migrations (drives)
    MS-DOS, 108
    Windows 9x, 109
mini-ATX
    motherboard, 23
minidrivers, 200
modems, 145
    56Kbps, 146
    external, 145, 149-152
    identifying, 145-146

internal, 145, 149
protocols, 145-146
speed, 10
standards, 146
troubleshooting,
149-151
upgrading to V.90,
146-148
modes
Extended CHS, 80
Large, 80
LBA (Logical Block
Addressing), 80
detecting
support, 82-83
determining
need, 81
disabling, problems
as result of, 81-82
enabling, 80
problems with
support in
BIOS, 81
Normal, 80
PIO, 88
scanning, 167-168
UDMA, 88-89
**Molex power
connector, 116**
monitors
CRT, 187
glass-tube, 187
multiple, 200-201
power management
standards, 190
purchasing, 198,
203-204
resolution, 188
pixels, 188
screen size
recommendation,
189

size recommenda-
tion, 189
SVGA (Super
VGA), 188
UVGA (Ultra
VGA), 188
VGA (Video
Graphics
Array), 188
XGA (eXtended
Graphics
Array), 188
testing, 203-204
troubleshooting,
204-205
viewing areas, 187
mono in connectors, 206
**motherboard BIOS,
updating, 59**
**motherboard form
factors, 24**
motherboards
ATX, 23
Baby-AT, 21
determining type, 24
form factors, 21
I/O port addresses, 41
identifying, 66
AMI BIOS, 66
Award BIOS, 67-68
MR (Microid
Research)
BIOS, 68
non-AMI BIOS, 67
Phoenix BIOS, 68
installing, 231-232
LPX, 21
NLX, 23
power supplies, 25
mounting frames, 231
mounting screws, 231

mouse
  bus, 184
  connectors, 184
  drivers, 184
  Inport, 184
  interfaces, 184
  opto-mechanical, 183
  troubleshooting,
    183-186
MR (Microid Research)
  BIOS, 68, 72-73
MS-DOS
  drive migration, 108
  UART chip, 140
MS-DOS 6.x Help
  file, 236
MS-DOS driver,
  downloading, 125
MSD Web site, 237
MSD.EXE (Microsoft
  Diagnostics), 235
MSIE32.EXE (System
  Information), 236
Multibank DRAM
  (MDRAM), 194
multimedia devices,
  201-202
multiple monitors,
  200-201
My Computer icon, 143

N

needle-nose pliers, 229
network cable
  connectors, 217
network cables
  installing, 232-233
  RJ-45, 233
Network card
  software, 235
network cards, 36

network distance
  limitations, 218-219
network interface cards
  (NICs), 219
network protocols, 216
networking, 213
  access control, 213
  backups, 214
  client/server, 213-214
  direct cable
    connections
      null modem
        cables, 225
      software, 226-227
      troubleshooting,
        227
  hardware cost, 214
  peer-to-peer, 213-214
    hardware, 219
    Windows 9x, 220
  performance, 213
  redundancy, 214
  security, 213
  software cost, 214
networks
  Fast Ethernet cabling
    standards, 219
  troubleshooting, 223
    software setup,
      223-224
    while in use,
      224-225
Networks icon, 221
nibbles, 10
NICs (network interface
  cards), 219
NLX motherboard, 23
non-AMI BIOS,
  identifying
  motherboards, 67
non-fatal errors, 69

non-parity memory,
31-32
Normal mode, 80
Normal Single Drive
configuration, 87
Norton Utilities
(Symantec) 25-pin
serial (Female DB25S)
loopback connector
(wrap plug), 144
Norton Utilities
(Symantec) 9-pin serial
(Female DB9S) loop-
back connector (wrap
plug), 144
Norton Utilities 25-pin
parallel (male DB25P)
loopback connector
(wrap plug), 160
notebook computers,
185
null modem cables,
225-226
null modem serial
cable, 233

O-P

onscreen error
messages, 69, 74
operating system
files, 235
option buttons
Guest, 227
Host, 227
opto-mechanical
mouse, 183
OS/2 UART chip,
determining
version, 140
outlet tester, 232

P cables, 91
Page Description
Language (PDL), 161
parallel cables (IEEE-
1284), 233
parallel data-transfer
cables, 226
parallel port Iomega Zip
drives, 123
parallel ports, 158
configuring, 159
connectors, 157
ECP, 158
EPP, 158
I/O addresses, 159
interrupts, 159
loopback plugs,
159-160
performance, 157
testing, 159
troubleshooting, 160
types of, 158
parameters
/S, 107
/V, 107
delay, 175
floppy drives, 117-118
hard drives, 75
keyboards, 175
parity memory, 31-32
partitioning hard
drives, 100-102
partitions, 104-106
PC-50 character set, 2
PC-8 character set, 2
PC/XT systems, 12
PCI (Peripheral
Component
Interconnect), 53, 196
PCI bus, 63-64
PCI expansion slots, 53
PCI sound cards, 208

PCL (Printer Control
Language), 161
PCs
    cleaning supplies, 234
    maintaining, 234
PDL (Page Description
Language), 161
PDL-based printers,
161-162
peer-to-peer networking,
213-214
    hardware, 219
    Windows 9x, 220
pels (picture
elements), 188
performance
    networking, 213
    parallel ports, 157
Peripheral Component
Interconnect
(PCI), 53, 196
peripherals, 153
Permedia chipset, 200
Phillips-head
screwdrivers, 229
Phoenix BIOS
    identifying
        motherboards, 68
    reporting errors, 71
phone cables (silver
satin), 233
picture elements
(pels), 188
pinouts
    external modem
        cables, 151-152
    null modem
        cables, 226
    parallel data-transfer
        cables, 226

serial ports, 136
    25-pin, 137-138
    9-pin, 136
    9-pin-to-25-pin,
        138
USB connectors, 153
VGA video
    connectors, 191
pins
    RD, 226
    TD, 226
PIO modes, 88
pixels, 188
PLC HP, 161
pliers, needle-nose, 229
Plug-and-Play (PnP), 38,
62-64
plugs
    loopback, 144, 232
        constructing,
            144-145
        parallel ports, 159.
        See also loopback
            plugs, parallel
            ports
    VGA, 188
    wrap, 144
PnP (Plug-and-Play), 38,
62-64
pointing devices, 185.
See also mouse
portable keyboards, 173
ports
    COM, 135
    dedicated motherboard
        mouse (PS/2), 184
    I/O
        addresses, 41-44
        bus-based
            devices, 42-44

chipset devices, 41
motherboards, 41
troubleshooting in
Windows 95/98,
142-143
parallel
configuring, 159
connectors, 157
constructing
loopback plugs,
159-160
ECP, 158
EPP, 158
I/O addresses, 159
interrupts, 159
performance, 157
testing, 159
troubleshooting,
160
types of, 158
serial, 135
25-pin, 137-138
9-pin, 136
9-pin-to-25-pin,
138
configuring, 141
conflicts, 142
pinouts, 136
troubleshooting,
143
UART chips, 139
USB
identifying,
152-153
requirements, 153
**POST (power-on self
test), 71**
**POST codes
(keyboards), 183**
POST testing card, 232

power connectors
drives, 26-27
floppy drives, 116
Molex, 116
**power management
standards, 190-191**
power supplies, 24
ATX, 25-26
LPX, 25-26
motherboards, 25
troubleshooting, 28
**power-off BIOS date
rollover test, 57**
**power-off DOS date
rollover test, 57-58**
**power-on BIOS date
rollover test, 57**
**power-on DOS date
rollover test, 57**
**power-on self test
(POST), 71**
**precautions when
updating BIOS, 60**
**primary partitions,
104-106**
**primary video adapter,
setting, 201**
**printer cables (IEEE-
1284), 158**
printers, 160
applications, 165-166
connections, 164-165
drivers, 165-166
hardware, 162-164
host-based, 161-162
PDL-based, 161-162
testing, 162
**processor speeds (socket
type), 19**

processors
  data bus widths, 11
  Intel
    socket types and
      specifications, 18
    specifications,
      13-14
  Intel-compatible
    Pentium-class
    specifications, 13, 16
  Intel-compatibles,
    socket types and
    specifications, 18
  trouble-shooting
    problems, 19-20
Programs menu
  commands
  (Accessories), 227
properties (TCP/IP),
  220-221
protocol
  identifying modems,
    145-146
  TCP/IP, settings,
    221-223
purchasing monitors,
  198, 203-204
pure mechanical
  keyswitches, 173-174

Q-R

QIC (Quarter Inch
  Committee), 129
QIC compatibility
  (Travan tape
  drives), 130
QIC-EX tape
  cartridges, 132-133
QIC-Wide tape
  format, 129-130

QRC Web sites, 237
quality standards
  (audio), 207
Quarter Inch Committee
  (QIC), 129

/R switch, 109
radio channels, 41. *See
  also* I/O ports
RAID (Redundant Array
  of Inexpensive
  Drives), 214
RAID arrays, 94
RAID levels, 215
rails, 231
RAM (random access
  memory), 10, 28-30
Rambus DRAM
  (RDRAM), 30
Rambus Inline Memory
  Modules (RIMMs), 31
RAMDAC (Digital-to-
  Analog Converter), 197
random access
  memory, 10, 28-30
ranges, determining
  I/O port addresses, 44
  memory addresses, 37
RD (receive data)
  pin, 226
RDRAM (Rambus
  DRAM), 30
read/write heads (floppy
  drives), cleaning, 115
reading erros (BIOS), 74
receive data pin (RD
  pin), 226
recording system
  settings, 45
recovery (BIOS flash
  update failure), 61

redundancy (networking), 214
Redundant Array of Inexpensive Drives (RAID), 214
reference programs, 235-237
refresh rates, 198
    comparing, 198
    flicker-free, 198
    RAMDAC, 197
    video cards, 198-199
reloading Windows (CD-ROM drives), 124-125
removable media drives, troubleshooting, 123-124
removable storage drives, 121-122
repairing
    floppy drives
        drive cover, 114
        interface circuit board, 115
        stepper motor, 114-115
    hard drives, 110-111
Repeat Delay slider, 175
Repeat Rate slider, 175
replacing hard drives, 108
reporting errors
    AMI BIOS, 70
    Award BIOS, 71
    BIOS, 69-70
    IBM BIOS
        alphanumeric codes, 71-72
        beep codes, 71-72
    MR BIOS, 72-73
    Phoenix BIOS, 71

requirements
    peripherals, 153
    UDMA/66, 89
    USB keyboards, 181
    USB ports, 153
reserving resources (legacy ISA devices), 63
resolution (monitors), 188, 194-195
    pixels, 188
    screen size recommendation, 189
    size recommendation, 189
    SVGA (Super VGA), 188
    UVGA (Ultra VGA), 188
    VGA (Video Graphics Array), 188
    XGA (eXtended Graphics Array), 188
resolving resource conflicts, 48
Resource Configuration menu, 62-63
resource conflicts, 210
    detecting, 209
    resolving, 48
    sound cards, 208, 210
    troubleshooting, 44-45
resources, reserving (legacy ISA devices), 63
Resources tab, 143
restoring data, 132
ribbon cables
    comparing, 117
    SCSI, 231
RIMMs (Rambus Inline Memory Modules), 31

RJ-45 connector wire
  pairing, 218
RJ-45 network cable, 233
ROM BIOS, 55
Roman-8 character set, 2
RS-232, 138
RS-232 breakout
  box, 233
RS-422, 138
rubber dome
  keyswitches, 173-174

S

/S parameter, 107
/S switch, 109
S3 video card
  chipsets, 200
SCAM (SCSI Configure
  AutoMagically), 96
scan codes
  (keyboards), 175
    101-/102-key
      Enhanced, 176-179
    104-key Enhanced, 179
Scandisk, 236
Scandisk.exe, 236
scanners, troubleshoot-
  ing, 166-167
scanning modes,
  167-168
Screen Saver tab, 190
screen size
  recommendations
  (monitors), 189
screen sizes
  CRTs, 189
  LCD panels, 189
screwdrivers
  flat-blade, 229
  Hex-head, 229
  Phillips-head, 229

screws, mounting, 231
SCSI (Small Computer
  Interface), 91
  configuring,
    troubleshooting,
    97-98
  differential, 92
  single-ended, 92
  terminators, 97
  transfer rates, 91
SCSI adapters, 92
SCSI cables
  25-pin, 94
  A, 91
  identifying, 93
  P, 91
SCSI Configure
  AutoMagically
  (SCAM), 96
SCSI connectors
  25-pin, 94
  8-bit Centronics
    50-pin, 93
  80-pin, 94
  identifying, 93
SCSI devices data
  sheet, 98-100
SCSI drives, 76, 95
SCSI ID, 95
  jumper settings, 96
  setting, 96-97
SCSI ribbon cables, 231
SCSI terminators, 97
SCSI-2 high-density
  connector, 93
SCSI-3 68-pin P cable, 94
SDRAM (Synchronous
  DRAM), 194
sectors per track, 75
security (networking),
  213

selected objects
(keyboard
commands), 172
selecting network
protocols, 216
serial cables (null
modem), 233
serial interface, 184
serial ports, 135
   25-pin, 137-138
   9-pin, 136
   9-pin-to-25-pin, 138
   configuring, 141
   conflicts, 142
   pinouts, 136
   troubleshooting
      (loopback tests), 143
   UART chips, 139
SERIAL.VXD (32-bit
serial driver), 142
setting
   parameters
      hard drives, 75
   primary video
      adapter, 201
   SCSI IDs, 96-97
settings
   DMA, 40-41
   IRQ, 40-41
   jumpers, 87
      Alternative Single
      Drive
         configuration, 87
      Normal Single
      Drive
         configuration, 87
   SCSI IDs, 96
   TCP/IP protocol,
      221-223
SGDRAM (Synchronous
DRAM), 194

shared expansion
slots, 54
sharing
   DMA channels, 39
   IRQs, 37
signal keyboard
connectors, 180-181
silicone sprays, 234
Silver satin phone
cable, 233
SIMMs
   30-pin, 29, 32
   72-pin, 29, 32
single-ended SCSI, 92
size recommendations
(monitors), resolution,
189
slave drives, 77
sliders
   Repeat Delay, 175
   Repeat Rate, 175
slot covers, 232
Small Computer
Interface. See SCSI
socket types (processor
speeds), 19
socket types and specifi-
cations (Intel/Intel-
compatible
processors), 18
"soft" problems (hard
drive), 110
software
   cost (networking), 214
   direct cable
      connections, 226-227
software setups
(networks),
troubleshooting,
223-224
software tools, 235

soldering iron, 230
sound cards, 205
  configuring, 207
  connectors, 205
    audio in, 205
    audio out, 205
    internal pin-type,
      206
    joystick, 206
    line in, 205
    line out, 205
    microphone, 206
    MIDI, 206
    mono in, 206
    speaker/headphone,
      205
  troubleshooting,
    208-210
sound, 207
sound file
  resolutions, 207
sources for updating
  BIOS, 59
speaker/headphone
  connector, 205
specifications
  keyboard connectors,
    182
  local-bus, 196
  processors
    Intel, 13-14
    Intel-compatible
      Pentium-class, 13,
      16
speed
  hard drives,
    improving, 88
  modems, 10
  processor (socket
    type), 19
  RAMDAC, 197
SpinRite, 237

stand-off connectors,
  232
standard capacity
  abbreviations, 10
standard keyboards, 173
standard system
  image, 235
standards (modems), 146
start bit 135
status codes, 74
stepper motor (floppy
  drives), 114-115
stop bits, 135
storage drives,
  removable, 121-122
STP Token-Ring
  cable, 218
strippers, 230
stuck keyswitches, 175
Super ESP (Enhanced
  Serial Ports), 141
SuperDisk LS-120
  Cleaning kit, 234
SuperDrive, 55
supplies, cleaning/
  maintaining PCs, 234
support
  IDE drive, 86-87
  large hard disk, 102
  LBA mode, detecting,
    82-83
SVGA (Super VGA), 188
switches
  /C, 109
  /d:, 125
  /E, 109
  /H, 109
  /K, 109
  /R, 109
  /S, 109
  DIP, 68

Synchronous DRAM (SDRAM), 194
Synchronous Graphics DRAM (SGDRAM), 194
System Configuration Template, recording system settings, 45
System Diagnostics (HWINFO.EXE), 236
System icon, 143
System Information, 236
system resource map, 45, 48
system settings, recording, 45
System Summary, 45
systems
    AT, 12
    PC/XT, 12

T

tabs
    Device Manager, 143
    Resources, 143
    Screen Saver, 190
    Windows Setup, 124
tape backup cartridges, 234
tape backups, 130-132
tape cartridges (QIC-EX), 132-133
tape drives, 129
    cleaning kit, 234
    media compatibility, 129
    Travan, 130
tape formats (QIC-Wide), 129-130

TCP/IP
    properties, 220-221
    protocol, settings, 221-223
    troubleshooting, 225
TCP/IP (Transmission Control Protocol/Internet Protocol), 220
TD (transmit data) pin, 226
terminators (SCSI), 97
TestDrive, 237
testing
    monitors, 203-204
    parallel ports, 159
    printers, 162
testing cards
    IRQ/DMA, 232
    POST, 232
testing/diagnostics utilities
    built-in, 235-237
    third-party, 237
Thicknet Ethernet, 218
Thinnet Ethernet, 218
third-party testing/diagnostic utilities, 237
Token Ring (network protocols), 216
tools
    data transfer, 233-234
    hardware, 229-230
    installing
        drives, 230-231
        expansion cards, 231-232
        external devices, 232-233

motherboards,
231-232
network cables,
232-233
software, 235
Network card
software, 235
operating system
files, 235
standard system
image, 235
Windows 98
Emergency
diskette, 235
toothpicks, 230
Trackpoint, 185
transfer rates
PIO modes, 88
SCSI, 91
UDMA, 88-89
translation, 79
**translation methods
(ATA-2), 80**
**Transmission Control
Protocol/Internet
Protocol (TCP/IP), 220**
transmission speeds, 10
**transmit data pin (TD
pin), 226**
Travan tape drives, 130
**Trident video card
chipsets, 201**
troubleshooting
audio, 207
BIOS, 65
bootable CDs, 128-129
CD-R disks, 127-128
CD-RW disks, 127-128
direct cable
connections, 227

drives
CD-ROM, 127-128
DVD, 127-128
hard, 110-111
IDE/ATAPI
CD-ROM, 127-128
floppy drives, 119
I/O ports, 142-143
IDE installation, 90-91
keyboards, 181-183
media drives, 123-124
memory, 34
modems, 149-151
monitors, 204-205
mouse, 183-186
networks, 223
software setup,
223-224
while in use,
224-225
parallel ports, 160
power supplies, 28
printers
applications,
165-166
connections,
164-165
drivers, 165-166
hardware, 162-164
processor problems,
19-20
resource conflicts,
44-45
scanners, 166-167
SCSI configuration,
97-98
serial ports (loopback
tests), 143
sound cards, 208-210
TCP/IP, 225
video capture
devices, 202-203

true color (16.8 million)
memory requirements,
195
Tseng video card
chipsets, 201
tweezers, 229
twisted-pair cabling, 217
Type B connector, 157
Type C connector, 157
typematic repeat
rate, 175

U

UART (Universal
Asynchronous
Receiver/Transmitter)
chips, 139-141
UDMA (Ultra DMA), 88
UDMA modes, 88-89
UDMA/66, 89
Unicore Software Web
site, 59
Universal Asynchronous
Receiver/Transmitter
chip (UART chip), 139
Universal Serial Bus
(USB), 152
updating BIOS, 55-56
motherboards, 59
precautions, 60
sources for, 59
upgrades
BIOS, alternative to, 58
flash, 147-148
upgrading
BIOS, 86-87
modems to
V.90, 146-148
UART chips, 141
video cards, 196-197

USB (Universal Serial
Bus), 152-155
USB cables, 233
USB connector
pinouts, 153
USB hub, 233
USB interfaces, 184
USB keyboards, 181
USB Legacy support, 181
USB ports, 152-153
UTP Token-Ring
cable, 218
UVGA (Ultra VGA), 188

V

/V parameter, 107
V.90, 146-148
values, binary/
decimal, 10
vendor's list, 239-263
versions
BIOS, 65-66
HP PCL, 161
UART chips, 140
vertical scan frequency,
198. *See also* refresh
rates
VESA (DPMS (Display
Power-Management
Signaling)), 190
VESA Local-Bus (VL-
Bus), 52, 196
VGA (Video Graphics
Array), 188
video connector
pinouts, 191
video display
modes, 191-193
VGA plug, 188
video adapters, 188
memory, 193-194
primary, 201

video capture devices,
troubleshooting,
202-203
video cards
chipsets
ATI, 200
Cirrus, 201
S3, 200
Trident, 201
Tseng, 201
comparing, 199
local-bus
specifications, 196
memory, 195-196
Permedia chipset, 200
refresh rates, 198-199
upgrading, 196-197
video connectors (VGA)
pinouts, 191
video display adapters
memory requirements,
194-195
video display modes
(VGA), 191-193
Video Graphics Array.
See VGA
video modes (Chips and
Technologies 65554
Graphics Accelerator
Chipset), 192-193
Video RAM (VRAM), 194
viewing settings, 40
viewing area
(monitors), 187
VL-Bus (VESA Local-
Bus), 52, 196
VL-Bus connector, 52
VRAM (Video RAM), 194

W

Web sites, 264-267
AMI, 67, 237
Award Software
manufacturer
codes, 68
CheckIt, 237
Iomega, 123
Micro Firmware, 59
MSD, 237
QRC, 237
Unicore Software, 59
Wim's BIOS Web
page, 67
Win95rk.hlp (Windows
95 Resource Kit), 236
WinBIOS, 66
Window RAM
(WRAM), 194
Windows
folder/shortcut
controls (keyboard
commands), 172
keyboard
commands, 171
reloading CD-ROM
drives, 124-125
selected objects
(keyboard
commands), 172
Windows 95 Emergency
Diskette, creating, 124
Windows 95 Resource
Kit, 236
Windows 95/98 I/O
ports, troubleshooting,
142-143

Windows 98
  minidrivers, 200
  multiple monitors, 200
Windows 98 Emergency
  diskette, 235
Windows 9x
  data transfer
    (XCOPY32
    command), 109-110
  direct cable
    connection
    software, 227
  drive migration, 109
  peer-to-peer
    networking, 220
  sound file
    resolutions, 207
  UART chip,
    determining
    version, 140
Windows dialog
  box, 171
Windows Explorer, 172
Windows keyboards,
  169-170
Windows NT
  parameters
    (keyboards),
    adjusting, 175
  UART chip,
    determining
    version, 140
Windows Setup tab, 124
Winmodems, 139
WINMSD.EXE (Microsoft
  Diagnostics), 235
wire, 230
wire cutters, 230
wire pairing, 217-218

wiring (loopback
  tests), 144-145
WRAM (Window
  RAM), 194
wrap plug, 144. *See also*
  loopback plug

X-Z

X2 modems, upgrading
  to V.90, 147
XCOPY command, 108
XCOPY32 command,
  109-110
XGA (eXtended Graphics
  Array), 188

Y-cable power
  splitters, 231
Y2K testing BIOS, 56
  power-off BIOS date
    rollover test, 57
  power-off DOS date
    rollover test, 57-58
  power-on BIOS date
    rollover test, 57
  power-on DOS date
    rollover test, 57

Zip drives (Iomega), 123